Exploring Far Away Places

Dreamers And Doers

Part III

ARLENE GALISKY

i

SCRIPTOR HOUSE
THE EPITOME OF GREATNESS

Scriptor House LLC

17434 Bellflower Blvd Ste 200-188 Bellflower, CA 90706

www.scriptorhouse.com

Phone: +1209-554-8271

Paperback: 979-8-88692-396-4

eBook: 979-8-88692-440-4

You are a child of the universe, no less than
the trees and the stars; you have a right to be here.
And whether or not it is clear to you,
no doubt the universe is unfolding as it should.
The Desiderata

CONTENTS

Prologue 3

Chapter 1: Across the Timor Sea to Bali................................ 5

Chapter 2: The Java Sea and Singapore 13

Chapter 3: Straits of Singapore and Malacca........................ 21

Chapter 4: Port Dickson 28

Chapter 5: Car Tripping in Malaysia and Thailand................. 34

Chapter 6: Trekking in Nepal 40

Chapter 7: Companions on the Trail................................... 46

Chapter 8: A Broken Bridge and Long, Stone Staircases 54

Chapter 9: The High Country 62

Chapter 10: Muktinath and the Kali Gandaki....................... 70

Chapter 11: Annapurna Sanctuary..................................... 77

Chapter 12: Royal Chitwan National Park 83

Chapter 13: The Boxing Day Tsunami 90

Chapter 14: Touring in Thailand 96

Chapter 15: Celebrating Songkran 102

Chapter 16: Windy Lady.. 111

Chapter 17: A Hong Kong Education 114

Chapter 18: A Graduate Degree in Istanbul......................... 121

Chapter 19: More Touts and Rug Merchants 129

Chapter 20: Jersey and Cancun.. 137

Chapter 21: Bangkok.. 141

Chapter 22: Athens and Delphi.. 148

Chapter 23: Lisboa and Rio 157

Chapter 24: La Paz, Bolivia.. 166

Chapter 25: Lake Titicaca 177

Chapter 26: Cuzco and Machu Picchu................................ 185

Chapter 27: Arequipa, Peru 192

Chapter 28: My Brother's Chile..197

Chapter 29: Chile on Our Own 207

Chapter 30: China and the Silk Road...216

Chapter 31: Cambodia 230

Chapter 32: Vietnam 244

Chapter 33: Chennai, India 255

Epilogue 263

Glossary...264

PROLOGUE

In July of 2002, Dave and I are living on our sailboat in Darwin, Australia. He is now sixty-three and I'm fifty-six. Physically, we're in the best shape of our lives, thanks to regular workouts at a gym in Townsville, where we waited out the uncertainty after *9-11*.

We should be getting ready to sail across the Indian Ocean and through the Red Sea to the Mediterranean, but the haunting images of the twin towers have left the world unsettled and our plans in disarray. We've decided to seek safe haven in Thailand for a year or two instead, in the hope that threat of war in the Middle East subsides.

Only eight years earlier, we were living in Prince George, BC, 500 miles from the ocean, and had never been on a sailboat. Like everyone else we knew, we'd spent the previous twenty years involved in jobs, families, and community. An unexpected realignment of the stars then made it possible for Dave to retire when he turned fifty-five, and he started to dream. A year later, a month after his birthday, he bought a forty-foot sailboat, and we moved aboard four weeks later.

We spent a year preparing *Windy Lady* for sea, then learned to sail by circumnavigating Vancouver Island. In June of 1996, we sailed out of Victoria harbor, heading for Brisbane, Australia. We were at sea 25 days on the first leg to Hawaii. Our route then took us south across the equator to American Samoa, Tonga, New Zealand, Fiji, Vanuatu, New Caledonia, and Australia. During this seventeen-month-long odyssey, we spent 102 days at sea, sailed 10,300 nautical miles (nm), and our lives were changed forever. (*Crossing the Pacific, Dreamers and Doers, Part I.*)

With *Windy Lady* as a base, we traveled in and around Australia for the next five years. We bought a ten-year-old Ford station wagon, filled it with camping gear, and drove nearly 28,000 km, making one trip around the coastline during the wet, and another through the outback during the dry. We then returned to sea and sailed against prevailing winds to Tonga. We were at sea 40 days on this very challenging round-trip voyage that took us 4,272 nm.

With coups in Fiji and the Solomon Islands the following year, and reports of pirates common from the Philippines to the Red Sea, we decided to continue north on an around-the-world trajectory. We were sailing up the Great Barrier Reef on route to Thailand when 9-11 occurred, so hunkered down in Townsville. We continued on to Darwin the following cruising season. (*Beneath the Southern Cross, Dreamers and Doers, Part II.*)

CHAPTER 1
ACROSS THE TIMOR SEA TO BALI

The heat and humidity in Darwin during July and August are extreme. I only survive because we're tied up in a marina and able to plug into shore power, which allows us to use our large fan. Otherwise, *Windy Lady* has just two small, battery-powered computer fans in the berths that blow air onto our heads at night.

Hoping to improve air circulation inside the boat before we go north, Dave talks to a shipwright about installing two small hatches in the cabin roof. The man agrees to do the work but progress is slow; then, after cutting the holes, he disappears for days on end. We're left chewing our fingernails, wondering what to do with a boat with two holes in the roof.

By late August, cruising season is nearing an end and winds at sea are getting lighter. Dave has replaced porthole screens that have rotted away, serviced the engine, and jerry jugged 380 liters of diesel. I've made courtesy flags for Malaysia and Thailand and mosquito-net covers for the new hatches. I now study charts, looking for hazards on the route north, then study a nautical almanac, trying to understand how the moon's transit affects tidal currents in the straits between Indonesian islands.

According to weather reports, air quality across SE Asia is poor, and smoke in some areas is so bad that masks are being distributed. We hear from friends who sail only 30 out of 100 hours on the crossing to Kupang in East Timor. They are not impressed when they arrive and complain about garbage and filth on the beaches, a stench in the air, and the 0430 call to prayer from the local mosques.

The day finally comes when the hatches are finished, and the boat seaworthy again. We race over to Customs and Immigration to obtain our clearance, then prepare the boat for sea, expecting the 1,000-nm crossing to Bali to take ten days. We're a month behind schedule when we motor out of Darwin harbor just before noon on August 31, 2002.

We now motor for four hours through the heavy layer of heat and humidity that blankets the Timor Sea. There is not a breath of wind, and even the forward movement of the boat barely stirs the air; the water is flat and gurgles around the stern as we pass. A long, low swell then ripples slowly across the water from the west, a few more follow, and by nightfall, there's enough wind to raise the sails. The wind dies four hours later, and we motor for the next four days.

When at sea, one of us is always on watch, and my shifts run from 0800 to noon, 1600 to 2000, and midnight to 0400. That means getting up and going to bed three times a day, and it usually takes three to four days before I start getting enough sleep. With the autopilot doing the steering and no sails to monitor, the duty is now long and tedious. Dave also services the engine daily when it runs this much, and the sweat pours off as he works in sauna-like conditions in the cabin at midday.

During the afternoon of Day 2, two sharks about five feet long circle the boat for an hour, and overnight, the mirrored surface of the water reflects the stars. Next day, we see our first Indonesian trawler, rumbling along slowly and dragging a long net behind. We stay well clear, not wanting to risk snagging the net with our six-foot keel. But we're also concerned about pirates, as yachts have been boarded in this area. The incidents are usually described as crimes of opportunity.

A trawler comes over the horizon while Dave is working on the engine on Day 4 and is only a mile away when he starts it again. He keeps an eye on the vessel while motoring away and sees it alter course and head straight for *Windy Lady*. Perturbed, he turns on the radar and tracks it, and when it closes to within half-a-mile, he increases the boat speed from 4.5 to 6 knots (kt).

I'm resting, but get up when I hear the change in the sound of the engine. Dave is in the cabin, digging out the flare gun, and is visibly disturbed. I follow him up to the cockpit while he tells me what's going on, then scan the empty sea around us with growing apprehension. There is little we can do to protect ourselves. We had talked about bringing a rifle with us, but would have had to turn it in at every port of entry. If we didn't, and authorities stumbled upon it during an inspection, *Windy Lady* would have been confiscated.

For the next four hours, we wait and watch, but the trawler comes no closer. When it turns away, I wonder if maybe we'd just been going in the same direction. Still, this is one occasion when I'm happy to have the diesel engine. Just before noon next day, an Australian Air Force Orion passes overhead. The big four-engine plane flies a pattern over the nearby ocean, then noisily dives on *Windy Lady* as it returns.

We start running into strong currents near Indonesia, where spring tides are now racing through the straits. That evening, when sailing 20 nm off Roti Island, we're swept half a mile off course in thirty minutes. After I adjust the autopilot, *Windy Lady* crabs along with the bow pointing twenty degrees off our direction of travel and her speed drops.

Six hours later, during my midnight watch, lights appear off the starboard stern. They're a long way away, but I study them closely. The vessel appears to be coming from Roti Island, and after satisfying myself that it will pass behind us, I go below to do engine checks. When I next look, the lights are much brighter, with a green navigation light visible on the port side and white lights fore and aft. That tells me it's a freighter on a parallel course, and I'm surprised at how close it is.

I turn on the radar, which takes two minutes to warm up, then set the cursor on the edge of the blip closest to the center, which is our position. My eyes pop out when the blip moves straight toward us, covering close to half a mile in little more than a minute. In a panic, I figure the vessel could be making close to 30 kt and try to think of my options, but there is no time. Grabbing the helm at the inside steering station, I turn the bow ten degrees away from the approaching boat, then another ten, and anxiously glance out one of the large cabin windows.

The huge bulk of the freighter blots out the night sky, and I instinctively pull back on the throttle and continue turning through 360 degrees. This procedure takes a couple of minutes, by which time *Windy Lady* is dead in the water and the vessel has gone past. I feel no bow wave, so it doesn't come that close, but I'm in shock. At that speed, the vessel would have been in sight for maybe fifteen minutes.

A low swell appears as we enter the deeper waters of the Indian Ocean, and by daylight, *Windy Lady* is rolling in five-foot waves. As she rides up on the swells during my morning watch, I catch sight of a small fishing boat with high prow and low cabin at the stern. An hour later, three pods of dolphins appear briefly, their black bodies glistening against the white froth created as they break the surface.

More dolphins visit the following morning, and as I move to the side of the boat to greet them, Dave exclaims, "Oh, look at that fish jump—a triple roll!" We then see that a school of fish are desperately trying to get away. They are long and slender, probably twenty pounders, and their silver sides glisten in the sun as they leap and roll well above the surface. A few minutes later, both species have disappeared and all is quiet.

On our eighth day at sea, the wind rises out of the south, and by noon, we're sailing in 8 kt of breeze. For the next twelve hours, *Windy Lady* takes us on a magic carpet ride, more than making up for the endless hours of motoring. As the sun slides down a cloudless horizon and sinks into the sea during my watch that evening, I feel at peace with the world and am content.

At midnight, we're still 50 nm from Benoa harbor, so Dave starts the engine, as we want to enter with the high tide at 1100. We start off making 7 kt, but adverse currents have our speed down to 3 kt while crossing the wide strait to the east of Bali. At 0800, the harbor is still 12 nm away, and at the next waypoint, we're an hour behind schedule. When we turn into the strait next to the Bali shore, the boat speed drops to 0.2 kt. Dave gets it up to 2 kt by pushing the throttle to maximum cruise rpm.

Sky and water are now a dull grey, and heavy cloud blankets the island beside us. The waves then part, revealing a brightly-colored fishing canoe some 75 feet off the beam. The small boat has a mast, a small, flaked sail on a boom, and two outriggers attached by spider legs. Our speed picks up as the tide turns, then the cloud begins to lift, revealing a grey-brown smog covering the land. When some of it blows away, I see a low headland and a long, low-lying plain with red-roofed villages dotting the shoreline.

It's a little after high tide when we enter the busy, 1.5-nm channel into Benoa Harbor. As Dave is at the helm, I go below to monitor radar and the computer navigation program. I return to the cockpit after we're safely inside and am stunned by the confusion around us. Several tandem seadoos race between the fishing boats and tugs using the channel, as does a power boat towing a long banana carrying five screaming passengers. Numerous small water taxis and fishing dinghies also flit about the edge of the anchorage, along with two power boats towing colorful parasails.

The marina is full, and cruising boats are rafted up four deep beside the dock. The anchorage is almost full, and Dave has to search for a spot big enough to anchor in. Almost as soon as we're finished, wake from a passing vessel hits *Windy Lady*. She instantly spins about and charges off to the end of the chain. When it happens again, she spins off in a different direction, coming uncomfortably close to another boat.

Meanwhile, airplanes take off from a nearby runway every fifteen minutes, and messages on a loudspeaker intermittently drift to our ears. At 1600, two large catamarans and a hydrofoil, their decks crowded with tourists, set off on their Sunday evening sunset cruises. The boats turn back at the harbor entrance, so motor up and down the same stretch of water four times in just over an hour. One vessel then goes by with pop music blaring and disco lights flashing, and another anchors a couple of hundred yards away for an hour.

We're flying our yellow quarantine flag, so are limited to talking to friends on VHF radio. But as soon as Customs and Immigration are open next morning, Dave rows across the harbor and clears in. The flag then comes down, and cruisers stop to visit as they pass in dinghies. Soon, we're arranging to meet friends at the marina restaurant.

With the first anniversary of *9-11* approaching, our American friends are a bit antsy, and not without cause. While we were at sea, two US citizens were killed when a busload of tourists was attacked on Irian Jaya (the Indonesian side of New Guinea). As Aussies frequently mistake us for our American cousins, Dave raises a large Canadian flag, declaring, "I don't want the locals to have any doubts." (A month later, two nightclubs are bombed in the adjacent tourist district, killing 202 people from twenty-one countries.)

A few boats depart later in the week, allowing us to move to a spot that isn't quite so exposed. Before doing so, we motor over to the marina and fill our diesel tanks. Four brawny young men are there to give us a hand, for which I'm thankful, as strong currents push *Windy Lady* onto the cement fuel dock when we arrive and wind holds her on when we leave.

The fuel has a reputation for being dirty, and Dave spends two hours running 500 liters through a Baja filter. He has a steady stream of visitors, so I wander about, talking to people on the dock. We're both told that the water is metered and billed, but not potable, and the low-grade power takes twice the normal time to charge batteries. I find the place to be hot, noisy, smelly, and crowded, and by the time we leave, we've decided to remove our name from the waiting list for a berth. That means we won't be touring the island, as we won't leave the boat unattended in the harbor for more than an hour or two.

After motoring back across the harbor, we set about dropping the anchor, but Dave shuts down the engine before we're finished. I yell out in protest, as *Windy Lady* immediately heads toward a small catamaran. Before disappearing below, Dave hollers back, "The engine water is boiling! The gauge reads 100°C!"

I grab a couple of fenders to jam between the boats, then try to explain our predicament to the German couple onboard the cat. Unfortunately, their English proves no better than my German. The boats drift apart then come back together, at which point they reluctantly accept the lines I offer and we raft up alongside.

Dave quickly inspects the seawater cooling system and finds sea growth plugging the intake thru-hull. But he cracks a hose to the strainer in the process and has to cut a piece off, then needs to move the strainer closer to the thru-hull in order to attach what remains. As the auxiliary bilge pump is in the way, he moves it first. This all takes too long for the captain of the small *cat*, who casts us adrift at sunset, pulls up anchor, and departs. Fortunately, Dave has the engine running ten minutes later, and we get into no more trouble.

One morning, we walk through the heat and humidity to a box store downtown. It takes the better part of an hour, and half the time is spent crossing a long causeway to the marina. Garbage litters the rocky shoreline, and I particularly notice small woven-leaf plates, some with flowers and rice cakes still intact. More garbage is caught in the lower branches of mangroves at the far end, where the stench is intense. When we return by taxi, our driver explains, "See all those people on the edge of the causeway? They're attending a cremation ceremony."

The downtown streets are packed with vehicles and lined with small shops selling baskets, rocks, and furniture. They all have small shrines placed near the entrances. We then pass several cafes, a motel, and a MacDonald's outlet. Aisles at the box store are packed to the roof with consumer goods, but little of what we consider real food. I find the staff unfriendly, as nobody smiles, and I see a coldness, resentment maybe, in the eyes of some.

Tired of living in the middle of a busy harbor, I sit down with my tide tables that afternoon and calculate the influence of the moon on currents in the strait. I figure we should leave at noon in four days' time, and Dave agrees when he hears that it'll be two weeks before conditions are again as good.

Next day, the smell of diesel fouls the air as the sheen of a spill drifts about with the tide, but it doesn't seem to affect the activities of seadoos and powerboats pulling long bananas. When we return from our last trip ashore, we see the outline of a high volcano for the first time. It's just visible through the haze to the north.

We lift anchor at 1000 on a Monday, then motor through the gauntlet created by power boats in the entrance channel. A boat towing a paraglider pulls out in front of us, and afraid the tourist will decorate our mast, Dave turns the bow ninety degrees until it's safely past. When the tow is higher than our mast, the driver re-crosses in front of us. Disgusted, I mutter to Dave, "I sure wouldn't want to trust my life to those clowns!"

CHAPTER 2
THE JAVA SEA AND SINGAPORE

Tidal currents are against us as we start up the 45-nm-long Selat Lombok, and we make only 2 kt for the first hour. Heavy, grey clouds cover the sky and blanket the island, and heat and humidity are oppressive. I see what appears to be driftwood on the shore, but when I look through binoculars, I see a jumble of masts, booms, and outriggers. Dozens of small canoes have been pulled above the high-water line. Two canoes then race out, trying to cross in front of us, but Dave easily avoids them.

With the turning of the tide, *Windy Lady* gradually picks up speed and we're pushed through the narrows at 8.6 kt. The tide turns again before we're through, and during my evening watch, I avoid stronger currents by steering closer to shore. We then round a headland, and with the sun low in the sky, deep shadows hide the shoreline. Suddenly, a small canoe darts out, with a dozen others close behind. They're far more maneuverable than *Windy Lady* and pass in front and behind before I can react. Minutes later, they are gone.

The cloud lifts just before dark, revealing a high, cone-shaped volcano rising behind bleak-looking terraced cliffs that overlook the strait. Minutes later, night sweeps across them, and I see a few dim, scattered lights high on the terraces. Ahead of us is the blackness of the Java Sea. Although day and night are now of equal length, it'll be hours before the temperature noticeably cools.

Winds remain light during the 970-nm crossing to Singapore, but we manage to sail for six of nine days. Three freighters pass within a mile of *Windy Lady* the next afternoon, and at sunset, at least twenty canoes cross in front of us, their small sails etched against the sky. After dark, another ship appears several miles away and a bright glow marks the stern. When it passes, several bright lights are visible across the back, which Dave believes is a security response to the recent uptick in pirate attacks.

Trawlers make regular appearances during the next three days, all geared down and dragging long nets. The vessels are maybe fifty-feet long, with high prow, not much freeboard, and shabby-looking paint. We're close enough to see the stream of water from the prop bubbling to the surface behind one, as well as the two heavy cables supporting the net that stretch out into the sea.

During my midnight watch one night, four such vessels, motoring abreast, cross in front of *Windy Lady*. I track their lights to the horizon on the port side, then see two small lights appear near the third boat. I watch them curiously, and twenty minutes later, in the mid-distance, see a greenish glow followed by a yellow flash. When it is repeated, I belatedly realize that I'm looking at a signal flare. Peering intently at the two lights, I make out the outline of a small boat that is a few hundred feet away and coming toward me. I turn twenty degrees and let it put-put across in front of us.

Day 4 starts off hotter and muggier than usual, and to relieve his boredom, Dave tunes in a cruisers net on VHF radio. The channel is one used by yachtees who follow an invisible trail through Indonesian waters. They anchor most nights and travel in groups of up to six boats for safety. After discussing anchorages and facilities, someone reports that hours were spent pulling a boat off a sandbar in the river on the way to the orangutan sanctuary at Kumai on Borneo. We listen with interest, but have no desire to join them. We dayhopped along the west coast of Canada when we were learning to sail, and now prefer to keep moving, having learned that sailing at night brings its own rewards.

At midday, we're off the south coast of Borneo; the sea is quiet, and heavy cloud cover has brought a reprieve from the heat. When the sky clears at night fall, the shadow of a cross appears on the headsail as a full moon rises behind the mast and spreader. Next morning, a huge chunk of rock with high, sheer cliffs rises up out of the sea in the distance. It doesn't appear on the chart, and with *Windy Lady* rolling in seven-foot seas and haze, we can't make it out with binoculars. The mystery deepens when radar measures it at 9.2 nm; we've never seen a freighter beyond 8 nm.

The haze thickens during the afternoon, and by nightfall, we're off the southwest coast of Borneo and the smell of smoke is strong. The weather forecast reports that forest fires in Indonesia have worsened the brown haze covering SE Asia. Next day, we solve the mystery of the unreported rock when we pass within a few miles of one of the new car carriers. It has the same craggy, notched profile. We also pass several well-marked oilwell platforms.

The sky is more cloudy than hazy on Day 7, and about midday, winds on the stern push up a rough, following sea that swings the bow back and forth through sixty degrees. Otto, our Hydrovane wind-powered self-steering unit, can't cope and we hand steer for twenty hours. Otto then works for twelve hours, at which point the wind dies, leaving *Windy Lady* rolling in rough seas. The v-belt on the waterpump breaks minutes after Dave starts the engine, and he spends an hour replacing it, lying on his belly on the sole of the cabin in 35-degree heat, with his head in the engine compartment and his ribs riding over the floor joists as the boat rolls.

We cross the equator about midnight and next morning is steamy hot. An appalling smog covers the sky, reminding me of the steely-grey look of a short, cold winter's day. The sun only becomes too bright to look at three hours after sunrise. We're now into Day 9 and will transit the 50-nm-long Riau Strait that night, so double check our current calculations and GPS waypoints.

I'm on watch and we're motor sailing when we enter the strait at 1700. A small fishing canoe soon rides up on a wave nearby, then disappears, and others bob about on the waters ahead. Running below, I turn off the autopilot, so I can steer around them using the helm in the cockpit. An hour later, lights appear in the deepening shadows in front of me, so I run down again and turn on the radar.

When I return to the cockpit, a small canoe is drifting down the port side, barely 50 feet away. The boats are getting harder to spot in the fading light, and I need to furl the headsail, which blocks my view, so I turn on the autopilot again. Just as I finish, a bright, glowing light appears right in front of the boat. As I can't steer from the cockpit with the autopilot on, and can't steer from inside as I can't see over the bow, I race below and adjust the autopilot by ten degrees.

When I return outside, a canoe is sliding down the port side, maybe 30 feet away. The fisherman calls and waves, and believing the cockpit to be dark, I wave my hand over my head. He turns on a flashlight, shines the beam fully on me, and yells excitedly. I'm standing on a cockpit bench looking over the dodger roof, and because of the heat, wear only my underwear. Flustered, annoyed with both him and myself, I scurry below and pull on a long tee-shirt.

I've just resumed my post, when two more lights appear in front of the bow. I run below and adjust the autopilot, but this time *Windy Lady* is slow to respond. When the two canoes pass down the starboard rail, their lights are close enough to wake Dave. He pokes his head outside to find out what's going on, then takes the helm. I now keep watch at the bow, and we thread our way through canoes for the next two hours. The fishermen usually wait until we're within spitting distance before showing a light.

I get a couple of hours sleep before starting my midnight watch, and we're then approaching the oil port of Tanjung Uban. Blinding lights soon block the channel ahead, and unable to see what's in front of us, I steer to port, then steer to port again. Tidal currents reduce our speed to 3 kt, then 2.5, so it takes a while to draw abreast of the four large tankers that sit side by side, their stern lights ablaze. Another large mass of lights farther from shore appears to be a loading platform.

The main shipping channel is now to port, and as we skirt its edge, a vessel with three vertical lights appears on our starboard side. When it slips between *Windy Lady* and the brightly lit loading platform, the solid, blocky shapes of a tug and barge are revealed. Minutes later, another mass of lights appears, again with three vertical lights. This time, the tug is towing a barge with a high tower. The larger lights on the tower cause me some confusion, as I initially think they are closer than the smaller lights on the tug. Once I've sorted it out, I turn ten degrees to starboard and watch the vessel motor down our port side.

As our speed picks up to 3 kt, the lights drop away behind, and patches of lights appear miles ahead. They could be small villages on shore but something seems strange about them. Puzzled, I turn on the radar, but there are so many blips from land and buoys that it doesn't help. But I do see a blip close by on the starboard side, and when I check, a large ship is coming up fast behind us.

The patches of lights eventually materialize into cruise ships passing through Singapore Strait at the T-junction it makes with Riau Strait. The ships have strings of lights running from bow to mast to stern and are backlit by lights on the far shore. The radar shows as many as eight ships in the channel at one time. Lightning then flashes across the night sky, but the storm brings little in the way of wind or rain.

We turn into Singapore Strait just before change of watch at 0400, and then opt to stop at Nongsa Point Marina rather than cross the shipping lanes to Singapore. We stand off the entrance until first light, then make our way through the channel and tie up at the end of the dock. Two hours later, the marina office opens, an Indonesian official comes down to check our documents, and we're free to leave.

We wander around for an hour and learn that the marina is part of a resort complex with pool and restaurant. We recognize a couple of boats, but a downpour sends us scurrying for shelter before we can check them out. That night, we join a group of some twenty cruisers for a drink in a quiet upstairs lounge. Many of the couples are Kiwis or Aussies, with kids under ten and plans to cruise for two to five years. Two couples are like us, drifting around the world. Rain drums on the deck during the night and another storm brings four hours of heavy rain next day.

The following day, we catch a shuttle bus into a nearby town. There's a surprising amount of new construction along the road, and I curiously peer out the window at half completed houses crammed onto flat, sterile building sites that appear to be gated communities. I also see small shacks half hidden in tired-looking vegetation, and a block of row housing surrounded by trash, with dead trees standing in a pool of water nearby.

We hope to buy fresh meat and produce at a shopping mall, but the fruit is brought in from Australia, the vegetables are in very small packets, and the meat counter seems to have a lot of chicken heads and feet. The staff seem friendly, as everyone returns my smile, but I'm bothered by the uniform appearance of the women. Their long-sleeved tunic tops and long skirts vary in color but not in style, and carefully pinned headscarves conceal all traces of hair and neck. Faces are often partially shaded by the scarves, so only the fingers are truly exposed. The women look neat but are indistinguishable, anonymous really, and I can only imagine the restrictions imposed by wearing such clothing.

We spend a day in Singapore, taking a high-speed ferry across the busy, ten-nm-wide strait. With the shoreline shrouded in haze, there's not much to see during the thirty-minute trip, but a passing freighter throws up some pretty rough waves in mid channel. We then take a taxi from the terminal, as it's miles into the downtown.

We go first to the Republic of Singapore Yacht Club, and any lingering regrets we may have had about not coming here are quickly dispelled. Boats tied up at the visitors' dock rock wildly in waves that sweep in the entrance channel from the harbor. A club member tells us that the city buys its drinking water from Malaysia, and recently introduced recycled water into the system. He then directs us to an older section of the city for boat supplies. While the streets are busy and people rush about on the sidewalks, we find nothing there that we want.

The main business in Singapore is transshipment, with containers from one freighter being offloaded and redirected to ships going to different destinations. There are also several large oil refineries. The new towers downtown reflect these global interests and could have been anywhere. The older buildings retain their character, however, and provide a focus when we stroll about the city center. After crossing a small river to a park, we find a somber monument dedicated to the city's WW II civilian dead. It was erected in 1962, after mass graves left by the Japanese were found.

I study the streets as we take a taxi back to the ferry terminal, now noticing that trees and grass all look uniform. It appears that trees in any given area are the same age and species. I then recall seeing a plethora of *No* signs downtown and decide that I don't much like the planned, orderly look of the city. I wonder if this is the future, with government controlling all aspects of our lives. If so, it's not a place where I'd want to spend much time.

During the week we stay at Nongsa Point Marina, the heat and humidity are brutal. We're not hooked up to shore power, so can't use our large fan, and the small computer fans in the berth barely stir the air around our heads at night. Dave doesn't seem to notice it as much, but I can't sleep and feel more exhausted with every day that passes. By the time we leave, I'd prefer to be heading for cooler climes.

CHAPTER 3
STRAITS OF SINGAPORE AND MALACCA

Dark clouds are building in the eastern sky the morning we leave Nongsa Point Marina, and a squall blows down on *Windy Lady* as Dave backs her from the berth. When she's blown against the side of the dock, two men from neighboring boats are there to give us a hand. A cold, heavy rain then limits visibility as we transit through the entrance channel. I go below and monitor radar and navigation program for thirty minutes, while Dave stands at the helm and is soaked through.

Tidal currents are strong as we motor west through Singapore Strait, and we start off making 6.5 kt; two hours later, we're making 8 kt. These shipping lanes are amongst the busiest in the world, and not knowing what to expect, we keep each other company for the first eight hours. When a second squall overpowers the autopilot at midday, Dave again takes the helm. This time, a cold rain chills him to the bone. We now cross to the north side of the strait, passing easily in front of two east-bound freighters, but wait mid-channel for a larger vessel to clear the west-bound lane.

The drama comes later, as we pass through the commercial anchorage for Singapore and Johor Bahru, the neighboring Malaysian city. More than 100 large ships sit at anchor, and they tower over *Windy Lady* as we wind our way through. We monitor the radar and skirt around two slow-moving vessels that we think are waiting to pick up pilots. The captain of a third then briefly toots the ship's horn to get our attention.

Storm clouds clear late in the afternoon, and as we head northwest into Malacca Strait, opposing tidal currents are not as strong and don't last as long as expected. Buoyed by this news, we decide not to anchor overnight and are well into the strait by nightfall. A stream of lights now moves through the shipping lane on our port side. I count the lights of eleven ships in the lane at one point, and blips from three or four large ships always appear on the four-mile radar screen. Several local freighters pass to starboard before morning, which isn't a problem as long as I can follow their progress on radar. A ship at anchor, however, confuses me for a while.

After daylight, visibility is poor in smoke and haze, and at 0900, we're searching for a small island where we hope to spend the day. We're within half a mile before seeing the shadowy outline, at which point we decide not to stop. At midday, we're approaching Melaka, a Malaysian port of entry. The heat and humidity are now intense, and we're both very tired, having only napped overnight.

Knowing that ships from China, Arabia, India, and Europe have anchored here for centuries, we opt to stop and clear into the country. While they had been seeking silks, spices, sandalwood, and other exotic goods, we simply want a safe harbor. (During a later visit, we see the beautiful, richly-embroidered garments made of silks and satins that were then worn.)

After we've dropped anchor, Dave calls Harbor Control on VHF radio, but gets no response. We put the dinghy in the water and he rows ashore anyway, only to find the office closed for a two-hour lunch. He has something to eat, and when he returns four hours later, he gets into the booze and falls asleep in the cockpit.

I spend some time cleaning up the boat, then sleep for a bit, but feel awful when I wake up. I ache all over, my head hurts, and watery sweat runs from my pores with the slightest movement. The temperature in the cabin is 38 degrees C. Sitting in a stupor, I force myself to stay up until dark, and when I lie down, my pillow is soon soggy from sweat. An hour later, the propane alarm in the engine compartment goes off. In a fog, I get up and switch off the breaker, shutting off the electrical supply. Then, when Dave moves from cockpit to berth, his fan doesn't work; turns out, it's on the same breaker.

About 0200, the boat starts to rock, waking me up. The air has cooled a bit, waves slap lightly against the hull, and I hear thunder rumbling in the distance. I get up and check the depth gauge, as we anchored in shallow water. When it reads 16 feet, I go forward and let out more chain, increasing the chain-depth ratio from 3:1 to 4:1. That's supposed to increase the anchor's holding power, but we've never anchored in shallow water before and I can only hope it works.

Dave is sitting in the cockpit when I return, and we watch as the storm moves in. Long, brilliant flashes of lightning streak the blackness over the town, and the crash of thunder is so loud that it hurts my ears. Waves grow higher, tossing *Windy Lady* about roughly, then sheets of wind-driven rain envelop the boat. For half an hour, we're unable to see beyond the cockpit, and the boat movements grow more violent. When scattered lights reappear, they're a blur and it's impossible to fix on any object ashore.

Uneasily, I check the depth gauge, which now reads 10 feet. Not trusting it, as it has a long history of false readings when we need it most, I turn it off then on and get nothing. When I check the GPS, the numbers seem close enough. Dave soon tries the depth gauge again, just as we're hit by a long 36-kt gust. We stare in disbelief when readings of 6.5, 6.1, and 5.8 flash up; the keel would be dragging on the bottom at that last depth. A lightning flash then reveals a rock breakwater not far off the port side, and he jumps up and races below, knowing we didn't anchor anywhere near it.

When the engine throbs to life, Dave points the bow away from the lights on shore and heads out into the blackness of the strait. I go forward and pull in the anchor, then remain there in the dark, shivering uncontrollably in a cold rain. My mind is in turmoil: *How come we didn't know the anchor was dragging? Why did it drag?*

I go through our procedures in my mind and am confident that we followed the same routine we'd used to anchor safely hundreds of times before. But I realize that I'd grown complacent. When my instincts warned me that something was wrong, I'd made only perfunctory checks of depth gauge and GPS. Dave had been the one to respond to the danger, though probably still half-pissed.

Ten minutes later, we re-anchor in 8 feet of water, then sit in the cockpit until the wind eases. We now try to sleep, but the boat still rocks uncomfortably in the waves. Two hours later, at first light, we're underway. After anchoring near our original position, we look at the reclaimed land along the shore and realize our error. *We hadn't checked the holding!* Tons of sand had been dumped along the shoreline and currents had moved it about, turning the bottom into something resembling loon shit.

We need a clearance to remain in port, so put the engine on the dinghy and motor a short distance up the river. After wading ashore through the mud, Dave leads the way to the harbor office. We're served by a husky female officer, and I try not to stare, but can't tear my eyes away. She wears a dark, bulky, uniform jacket with large epaulets on the shoulders, and it hangs well down over a long skirt. A beautiful, carefully-draped headscarf covers any sign of her hair or throat, and the ends are pinned to the center of her breast by a large ornate broach.

After leaving the office, we walk through the old part of the city, following narrow lanes that are plugged with vehicles. We end up walking beside a deep, narrow gutter, only inches wide, which runs in front of small shops lining the road. After stopping to send emails at an internet café, we continue on to a large shopping mall.

I again try not to stare, but I'm fascinated by the Muslim women I see. With their tunic tops, long skirts, and headscarves, they seem anonymous. I start to feel uncomfortable, as I've worn only tee shirts and shorts since moving onto the boat. My anxiety eases some when I see Chinese women with bare heads and long pants. A few teenage girls then catch my eyes; they wear tight-fitting blue jeans, long-sleeved, form-fitting tops, and color-coordinated headscarves, not exactly what I expected.

As we leave the air-conditioned mall, we walk into a wall of heat and humidity that is almost tangible. When we reach the dinghy, the tide is out and the air reeks with the sour smell of exposed mud banks. Sand plugs much of the river mouth, and plastic bags and other garbage float about in pools. Taking my seat in the bow, I pick a route downstream through shallow water that slides over thick black ooze.

Another storm is expected that night, so we're to bed early, but I'm up every hour or so, making sure that lights on shore are where they're supposed to be. When thunder starts to roll just before 0200, we get up and close the hatches, then head for the cockpit. With winds gusting up to 30 kt, sheets of rain hide the lights in front of us for thirty minutes, but lights off to one side remain visible and constant. The worst is over within an hour and we then return to our berths. Heavy rain soon drums on the cabin roof, after which the wind shifts, holding *Windy Lady* beam onto the waves, and she rocks violently for two hours.

At daybreak, we tiredly sit in the cockpit and watch the haze lighten as sunrise comes and goes. We're underway soon after, as the tide will turn against us in a couple of hours. Numerous small fishing boats dot the flat water in front of us, and after dodging around several large fishing nets, we steer out into the strait, where we skirt the edge of the shipping lane. As the hours go by, the tide changes direction, clouds form, winds remain light, and a constant stream of freighters passes in both directions.

We start studying the shoreline with binoculars near Tanjung Tuan, looking for a new marina at Port Dickson. A power launch speeding past now turns in a big circle and comes alongside. The driver talks to Dave on VHF radio and gives him the channel used by Admiral Marina. After calling them, we're met by the marina's work boat, guided to the entrance, and instructed to anchor for an hour, as the tide is very low.

I study the shoreline while we wait, admiring the white, sandy beaches that line the bay, where several large hotels are spaced well apart. Small groups of people are out enjoying themselves, and a few seadoos and a banana boat roar up and down along the shore. Although thunder rolls across the sky, I see no sign of a storm.

The work boat meets us as we pass through the rock breakwater into the marina and guides us to a berth, where four men take our lines and secure *Windy Lady*. The docks and pilings are new, as is an attractive three-story building with curved staircases and sprawling terraces. One of the men brings down a power plug and attaches it to our electrical cord, and soon our big fan is at work, removing hot, stale air from inside the boat.

After supper, I go up to the resort building, where a pool, gym, restaurant, meeting rooms, and offices are located. After showering in a clean, spacious change room, I linger in the darkened pool area, admiring two curved footbridges mirrored in the surface of the water; they lead to a balcony overlooking the marina. Next morning, there's a bit of color in the western sky as the sun rises behind heavy cloud cover, and the temperature's a comfortable 29°C. We both slept well, and turning to Dave, I confess, "This last week has been tough, and I've just wanted to get through here as quickly as possible. What a difference a day makes!"

He laughingly responds, "Maybe we should think about staying here, instead of going up to Thailand."

In fact, the location suits us. The marina, ten km south of Port Dickson, is semi-secluded, with a long, winding driveway through the trees to the main road; it's quiet and peaceful. A small Malay restaurant is within walking distance and we enjoy the spicy, local food the first time we try it. But the deciding factor is Kuala Lumpur International Airport (KLIA), which is a sixty-minute drive away. We plan to travel in the region and having good access to the airport makes sense. Before the end of the first week, we extend our stay to a month, and by the end of the month, we've paid for a year.

Chapter 4
Port Dickson

Port Dickson lies two degrees north of the equator, and the weather is hot and humid all year round. The wet season brings more thunderstorms and they tend to be violent, with great, jagged streaks of lightning flashing across the sky and thunder rolling and crashing, practically shaking the ground. Rain then pours down for thirty minutes, leaving the air cool and fresh for a short time (about the only time daytime temperatures drop below 30 degrees C.)

The area was hit hard by the Asian meltdown five years earlier, and countless deserted high-rise buildings stand in various stages of completion along the shoreline. Country roads are lined with rubber tree plantations, and I'm surprised when I first see the trees. They look so ordinary, with slender stems, grey bark, and silvery leaves. Long-legged, skinny cows wander about, and occasionally we pass a herd of small goats, a few sheep, or a water buffalo. Dozens of monkeys hang out in a few places, sitting along the side of a road or watching from perches on telephone lines.

We locate a wet market in town that provides fresh vegetables, fruits, eggs, and even pork (in a discreetly placed stall in a back corner). A small Chinese shop has Australian cheese and frozen meat, and a department store called *The Store* supplies the rest of our needs. On one of our first trips into town, young men with shiny new uniforms and haircuts have taken over the streets; the nearby army base has just had an intake of 2,500 recruits.

During our first weeks at the marina, cruising boats on route to Thailand frequently visit. Most are crewed by couples like ourselves, and a few stay on. We're soon meeting at the pool in the late afternoon, seeking relief from the heat. The pool is the most beautiful I've ever seen, with a thin sheet of water running over one end and palm trees casting reflections/shadows on the water at all times of the day.

We buy two cheap Chinese bicycles, but don't ride them for long. Not only is it very hot, but the narrow road into town is busy. I tolerate the trucks that pass beside me by gluing my front wheel to the edge of the pavement, but the motorcycles get to me. We share the same space, and they tend to brush my elbow on the way by. Within a few months, our exercise regime is limited to the air-conditioned gym at the marina.

After bus trips to Kuala Lumpur (KL) and Singapore, Dave decides to buy a car. We make a second trip into KL, and he hires a cabbie to take us around to used car lots. After settling on a 1992 Proton, the Malaysian national car, we go to an HSBC branch downtown to get the cash we need. Armed guards check our ID at the door and escort us up and down from the upper floor, which makes me a bit nervous when we leave with 17,000 ringgits ($6,800 CA) crammed into my pouch.

The cabbie picks us up and takes us back to the used car lot, and when the paperwork is done, he leads us through the streets to the highway to Port Dickson. We have no map, only a vague notion of the route, and the signage along the road is in Malay, so the ninety-minute drive is a bit tense. Fortunately, Dave became comfortable driving on the left side of the road in Australia, so has only to adjust to the vehicle's standard transmission, which has the gearshift lever on the floor to his left.

By the time we reach the marina, I've decided to learn Malay. I find a tutor, work with her for a month, then start speaking to people. I'm astonished at the response, as everyone exclaims in English, "Why you speak Malay? We need to speak English!" In the end, I have to be satisfied with reading menus and street signs, as we have little contact with ethnic Malays.

When we drive into KL for the first time, we follow the *Pusat Bandar* (city center) signs to the downtown, park the car, and walk. We then try a different route and get completely lost. The city is a busy metropolitan area with four-lane traffic circles, flyovers (elevated roads), and terrible traffic. Eventually, however, we explore most of it, from Batu Caves to the Butterfly Park to Petronas Towers.

We're not really comfortable driving in Malaysia, and both of us keep watch while on the road. Drivers disregard lane markings, pull out onto the road in front of us, and pass at high speed on the left, the right, or even the shoulder. Motorcycles prove to be a law unto themselves. There are also many high-speed exits on the road into KL and missing just one means we're screwed because there is never an easy way back.

We discover Sungai Wang Shopping Mall on our first trip and return there whenever we're in the city. The shops are located on multiple floors around a central atrium that is open to the roof, and we're fascinated by the many computer stores and outlets selling cheap, pirated movies and computer programs. The wide aisles are crowded with shoppers, and I'm amazed when we first walk through as I can see above the crowd. Most people aren't any taller than I am! However, I never do become comfortable with the hole-in-the-floor toilets.

Dave buys a new laptop computer, then spends hours loading the programs he wants and transferring files. As internet access is only available on in-house computers at a few shops, he downloads emails onto a pen drive. The service is unbelievably slow; it's like watching grass grow. He soon acquires a virus, which gets into his new laptop, and he's very unhappy when he has to wipe the hard drive. A year later, another virus in a rental computer sends pornographic pictures to everyone on his mailing list, plugging up their emails. He's then not only unhappy but also unpopular.

Ramadan starts soon after we arrive and initially seems like a festival. Food stalls are set up in every parking lot, and large tents outside the Pasar Raya (a department store) sell artificial flowers, prayer rugs, and clothes. In reality, the Muslim faithful do not eat or drink all day for a lunar month, breaking the fast only at designated times after sunset and before sunrise. In the late afternoon, people visit the stalls and walk away with little pink bags containing their meals. The day after Ramadan ends, the parking lots are deserted, not a food stall in sight.

Muslims then celebrate Hari Raya Aidilfitri, with many returning to their home villages. A series of open houses are held for a month, which this year takes them into the Christmas season and the start of the two-month school holiday. Traffic on the roads is hectic and there are some twenty highway deaths/day for nearly a week in December (in a population of 22 million). The majority of them involve motorcycles.

In early January, Hindus hold a major festival in KL, and a million people jam the streets to watch the 15-km pilgrimage from the downtown to the shrines at Batu Caves. A few pilgrims poke skewers into their chests or faces on which they hang gifts for the Gods (small milk pots are traditional). This is followed by Chinese New Year in early February; it's a two-day holiday celebrated over 15 days. As many of the Chinese-owned shops are closed throughout, the locals stock up on groceries.

Before we become too impressed with the multiculturalism of the country, someone mentions the race riots of the 1960s. Malaysia gained its independence from Britain in 1957, and Singapore joined the country in 1963. Riots the following year resulted in Singapore seceding in 1965. Racial tensions again flared up in 1969.

Apparently, the constitution favor Malays, and they certainly fill all government jobs. Those in favor with the regime also obtain lucrative positions in any foreign company that wants to do business in the country. The 25% of the population who are Chinese seem to run small grocery stores and service outlets, and the 6% who are Indian (Tamil) operate small restaurants or drive taxis. At the marina, the dock supervisor is Malay, the dock boy Tamil, and the woman in the office Chinese.

The country enforces sharia law, and occasionally we hear reports of sharia police sweeping up non-Muslims in their operations, but have no such experience ourselves. Some states are stricter than others, but the state we're in has large minority populations of Chinese and Tamils and imposes it only on Malays. (If you are Malay, you are Muslim.) We're told that wearing headscarves is a recent phenomenon, that Malay women were bare headed twenty to thirty years earlier.

In an effort to comply with local norms, I'm guided by the example of Chinese women. I wear tops that cover my shoulders and upper arms, and buy a long, pleated skirt to pull on over my shorts when we're out and about. I have little contact with Malay women, but usually smile a greeting when we meet on the sidewalk. Sometimes, they smile back. The one exception occurs in a handicraft store in one of the stricter Islamic states. A young Muslim woman shyly comes up to me and asks, "Will you pose in a picture with me and my two friends?"

We have to leave the country every ninety days to renew our visas, so tie that into scheduling flights to Canada, Australia, and SE Asia. Alternatively, we drive across the border into Thailand or Singapore. We're usually ready for a break from the heat by then, and interestingly, the heat gets harder to bear the longer we're in Port Dickson.

We visit Brisbane in February, 2003, and transit through Singapore on our return. The city is then reporting its first cases of SARS (severe respiratory syndrome). The virus appeared in southern China in November, but wasn't reported to the World Health Organization. After showing up in Hong Kong, it spreads to Singapore and Malaysia, and air travelers carry it around the world.

We're booked to fly to Vancouver in April, but Toronto then becomes the focus of world attention with thirteen deaths. When Malaysia restricts air travel from Canada, we delay our trip. We try again in June, transiting through Taipei, but two weeks before the flight, they're reporting fifty new cases a day. The local newspaper reports that China has cases of SARS in 24 of their 36 provinces. The overall death rate averages 10-15%, but is more like 50% for people over age 60. Some of the survivors are said to be in pretty tough shape and may never completely recover.

We make it back to Canada just before my dad's ninetieth birthday in early July, but miss the celebration as we self-quarantine in Vancouver for two weeks.

Chapter 5
Car Tripping in Malaysia and Thailand

Malaysia is a small country, about 800 km long and 320 km wide, that occupies the bottom half of the Malay peninsula. Several mountain ranges run north to south through the interior, as does a toll road that passes through miles of oil palm plantations. The large, long fronds of the palms hang halfway to the ground, and lacy, green plants climb up the heavy, thick trunks. Narrow plains lie along east and west coasts, and the highway on the west side winds between small towns.

Our first road trip takes us 300 km down the west coast to Melaka and Singapore. We do a bit of exploring, but this trip is mostly about becoming familiar with roads, traffic conditions, and available services. We return via the east coast, driving along the South China Sea to KL. This highway isn't as busy, and large isolated resorts dot the coastline between a few large towns.

We learn that Malay communities are easily identified by the tall spires of their mosques, and the decorative staircases leading up to the front doors of older homes. Dragons run across the roof lines of Chinese temples and their homes have small red shrines in the front yards. Indian temples have steeply-sloped roofs that are crowded with strange-looking, brightly colored figures.

Our next trip takes us north into Thailand. We again follow the west coast, and the road deteriorates significantly after we cross the border into the adjacent Malay state. As traffic slows, drivers grow frustrated, then aggressive, and soon every vehicle ahead is just another obstacle to get by. Dave drives no differently than others, but is picked out by a policeman standing at the edge of the road. After waving him over, the officer says accusingly (in quite good English), "You overtook on a double line!"

I'm thinking, *so what, everybody passes on a double line,* but he's insistent and motions for Dave to get out of the car. He escorts him back to a second policeman, who's standing beside a vehicle hidden in a narrow lane. Dave later explains, "They told me this was very serious and they were going to issue a ticket and I'd have to appear in court. This went on and on until I finally asked when and where I'd have to appear." The tenor of the conversation seems to have changed at that point and he ends up with a warning. He doesn't push as hard after that.

In heavy traffic in the next town, a bus is stopped in the middle of an intersection. A crushed motorcycle lies beneath the front wheel, and a woman looking like a rag doll lies on the pavement. The accident has just happened and people are running to her assistance from parked cars. She wears a helmet and I watch as a man lifts her scarf off her face and see blood on her forehead. Then we're past and I'm very afraid for her.

After driving some 300 km, we spend the night in Lumut, which is home to a naval base with 26,000 sailors. Our hotel happens to be on the street to the base, and it's noisy for most of the night. Next morning, we eat steamed rice with a fried egg on top and tiny dried fish called billis. I never do develop a taste for steamed rice for breakfast, or for billis, for that matter.

Another 200 km up the coast, we cross a kilometer-long bridge to George Town on Pulau Penang. We stay at a hotel in Lebuh Chulia (Chinatown), where the narrow streets are being widened in a major redevelopment project. Next day, we explore the waterfront and come upon a rabbit warren of small sheds, some partially built on stilts out over the water. We walk out onto a nearby dock to inspect three small fishing boats and see cooking pots and a bedroll in one of the sheds; people are living there.

We visit a Buddhist temple, climbing up the many stairs and stopping to admire the ornamental gateways, groups of statues, and flowers at the various levels. On the ever-changing roofline, the carved figures of demons are framed against the deep green of steep, jungle-clad hills. We end the day by riding a funicular railway up to the top of Penang Hill for spectacular views of the city and the bridge across the strait.

Next day, we leave our car in a fenced parking area and take a ferry to Langkawi, where we spend two days touring the island in a rental car. We check out several marinas, but see nothing that we like better than Port Dickson.

Crossing the border into Thailand is pretty routine until we're caught in traffic on the far side. We then sit in the heat and dust for twenty minutes, listening to a cacophony of beeping horns from a long line of merging trucks. As best I can figure, the drivers use their horns instead of their brakes.

It's another 500 km to Phuket, and we now follow highway route numbers, as road signs are in Thai script. Road conditions are good, but 60 km from the border, we get hopelessly lost in the city of Hat Yai. I'm not able to read the small English signs in time for Dave to change lanes, and heavy traffic sweeps us through narrow, canyon-like streets that twist and turn. We finally come to an overpass, and from there, route signs guide us back to a divided highway. By then, we've lost all sense of direction and turn the wrong way. We eventually notice that the sun is on the wrong side of the car, but have to drive 20 km before we can reverse course.

We spend the night in a small town, and next morning cross a flat coastal plain dotted with steep-sided limestone outcroppings. These butte-like hills are about 500 feet high and come in various shapes, with whitish-grey sides and stunted vegetation. The countryside becomes drier as we proceed north, and we're soon passing racks of fresh pineapple that line the edge of the road for miles. At noon, we're crossing the bridge to the island of Phuket.

After checking into a hotel in Phuket City, we find that motorcycles have taken over the streets. Their drivers weave in and out of traffic, drive on the wrong side of the road, pass on the wrong side, and take over entire lanes at busy intersections. When we walk, the bikes are parked on the sidewalks.

We spend two days exploring the island, while visiting with cruising friends and inspecting marinas. In the resort town of Patong, hundreds of large umbrellas hide the narrow strip of sand that is the beach. We don't stop, as the streets are plugged with traffic and there's nowhere to park.

From Phuket, we drive across the peninsula to the east coast. Not far down the highway, Dave stops the car near a rubber tree plantation, where white mats are draped over a line. We're curious, as we saw similar lines on the drive north. Walking down a faint track onto the property, we see that the mats are maybe four feet long, half that wide, and have a pattern imprinted on them. They appear to start off white, but discolor as they dry in the sun.

We don't see the tall, thin man watching from the porch of a small shack until he steps down and walks slowly toward us. He waves one hand in the direction of nearby trees, where another shed nestles in the shadows. Waving again, he turns and starts down a track toward it. Following along behind, we pass rows of slender, leafy trees that have small cups attached to the lower trunk to collect the sap that drips from rounded slits in the bark.

At the back of the shed is a roofed, open-walled area with a cement floor. Metal tubs containing a white substance are stacked in a corner, and a woman is in the process of dumping the contents of one onto the floor. She then works the thick mass with a wooden rolling pin. A few feet away, a man rolls a similar pile and water runs out on all sides. Two metal wringers sit on a nearby table. As we don't speak each other's languages, we watch in silence. Dave can't resist sticking a finger into a tub, and although the contents are quite watery, he rubs off a rubber coating.

As best we can figure, the latex collected in the cups is mixed with something (a diluted acid, it turns out) and left to coagulate in the tubs. These cakes of raw rubber are washed to remove the acid, then rolled to remove the water and ran through a wringer, possibly imprinting an ID, before being left to dry. After watching awhile, we smile, wai our thanks, and return to the car. (The wai is a gesture of respect, with hands placed palms together in front of the chest and head bowed.)

On the east coast, we check into a beautiful hotel in the resort city of Songkhla, then sit out in the balmy night air at a nearby restaurant and enjoy excellent Thai food. Next day, we walk the streets for miles, admiring colorful gardens, beautiful flowers, and small golden temples. Leaning into a strong sea breeze blowing off the Gulf of Thailand, we hike down sandy beaches that are devoid of tourists. At the end of the school day, we pass a group of boys and girls and stop to exchange smiles and nods. The younger boys are crouched down on the sidewalk and look like they might have been playing marbles.

Next day, we drive south along the east coast, and soon are passing large ponds dug between highway and sea that contain shrimp farms. We then turn onto a winding road that leads to the Malaysian border. Villages are scarce as we pass through narrow valleys in rugged hill country, but suddenly, we round a corner and find a Friday market sprawled across the road.

As we slowly drive through, a woman draped from head to toe in black walks in front of the car, peering through a slit in front of her eyes. I counted five similarly clad women that morning, but this one is up close and personal and sends a chill down my spine. (The south of Thailand is populated by Muslim fundamentalists, who are constantly at odds with the Buddhist majority.)

Eventually, we come to a large community five km from the Malaysian border. A rubber depot sits on the busy main street, with bales of mats piled out front and more being unloaded from a pickup truck. The town feels different, perhaps it's a sense of being isolated from mainstream Thailand, or maybe it's the frontier air of a border town. In the 1950's, communists hid in nearby caves and crossed the border to attack authorities in Malaysia. Next day, we're back onboard *Windy Lady*.

CHAPTER 6
TREKKING IN NEPAL

Initially, Dave has no interest in going to Nepal, but cruising friends change his mind, and he decides to hike two trails, the Annapurna Circuit and Annapurna Sanctuary. We'll climb up to 17,600 feet (5,416 meters) on the first and walk a total of 350 km, so will be out at least a month.

We leave for Kathmandu in September, 2003, and right from the start things don't go according to plan. The taxi that is supposed to pick us up at 0545 and take us to the airport doesn't show up. We have no phone, and at that hour, marina facilities are locked up tight. I look unhappily at Dave, who suggests, "Well, we can always take the car and leave it in long-term parking." There is really nothing else we can do.

He drops me at the terminal, and I check in while he deals with the car, but he's very quiet when he returns. As we walk down to the gate, he murmurs, "I don't know if we'll have a car when we get back." When I turn and look at him, he continues, "There is no long-term parking, and the day rate at the parkade is 48 ringgits. That would add up to more than $1,000 CA for the two months we're away. Even the guest rate of 30 ringgits at the Pan-Pacific Hotel would cost $675." He then hands me a business card on which the name Raymond and two phone numbers are handwritten and confesses, "The valet at the hotel offered to park the car in the driveway of his home, and I just handed him the keys."

Mulling over the possible consequences of this decision keeps us pretty quiet during the two-hour flight to Bangkok. We then board a connecting flight to Katmandu, and I pick up a newspaper before starting down the aisle. When I open it, a headline jumps out at me, *"Thai Nationals Warned Not to*

Travel to Nepal." The article goes on, "Since the breakdown of the ceasefire with Maoists three weeks ago, dozens of people have been killed. Kathmandu is under curfew and a three-day general strike has been called for later this week." Dave is as stunned as I am when I show him the article. We thought the ceasefire was still in place. We don't even think about the car during the 3.5-hour flight.

When the airplane emerges from the clouds, we're flying low over an emerald green valley that looks like every picture I've seen of Shangri La. Studying the narrow terraces climbing up valley walls, and small temples sitting on promontories, I feel a growing sense of excitement. Minutes later, we're on the ground in Kathmandu and rain pours down so hard that we wait for a bus to take us 200 feet to the terminal.

After struggling through long queues at Immigration and Customs, we exit through the front doors, where two security guards keep a shouting, waving mob of touters at bay on the far side of a single-lane road. We wait beside them while Dave searches the crowd for a sign bearing his name. When he spots it, we run over to join Hit Kaji Gurung, the owner of the Laughing Buddha Hotel, who has come to meet us.

I stare wide eyed out the van window as we drive into the city. Soldiers with rifles surround a checkpoint at the airport entrance, where half the street is blocked by razor wire. The narrow streets beyond are chaotic, crowded with vehicles and booby trapped with deep potholes. Drivers lean on horns constantly as they maneuver from one side of the road to the other, getting around stopped or turning vehicles. Several patrols of armed men walk the sidewalks, and we're stopped at a second checkpoint.

Our room costs $10 US a night, and after checking in, we have tea with Hit and his wife. He tells us, "We opened this business four years ago, after I retired from the British Army. I was in the Gurkha Regiment for fifteen years."

When we press him for information on trail conditions and Maoist rebels, he explains, "All transportation in the country will be shut down during the three-day general strike, so you have two days to get to the trailhead at Besi Sahar."

Dave needs to buy a backpack, so we rush over to the tourist district for a quick look around. The narrow lanes are lined with small shops, and so crowded with pedestrians that only a few trishaws or motorcycles try to find a way through. The garage-style front doors of the shops are wide open, revealing hiking gear, handicrafts, and souvenirs. Goods are set out on the street too, where venders keep an eye on them while trying to lure tourists inside. As we walk, street peddlers fall into step beside us, pitching carved elephants, small embroidered pouches, jewelry, and tiger balm.

We return next morning, after getting directions to a reputable outfitter from a couple at our hotel. The shop is owned by an ex-European mountain climber and his Sherpa wife, and they happily dispense information as we buy the gear we need. We learn that a suspension bridge is out on the Annapurna Circuit, some two or three days from the trailhead, and that all shops in Nepal will shut down during the three-day general strike. With a shrug of his shoulders, the shopkeeper explains, "We run the risk of being firebombed if we open the store. It's just not worth it."

We now scurry around trying to find out more about the bridge, and at a trekking office confirm that one was badly damaged by a rock fall ten days earlier. But the clerk assures us, "No need to worry. Supplies have to be delivered to villages on the other side, so locals will have found a way across by the time you get there."

Not wanting to be trapped in the city during the strike, we continue with our preparations. We pay 4,000 rupees ($100 CA) for trekking permits, and withdraw 50,000 rupees from an ATM to cover costs for guesthouses along the trail. (They're said to average 1,500 rupees/day.) We also have an emergency fund of $650 US, in case we need to fly out.

Hit offers to pick up bus tickets to Besi Sahar, and when Dave asks about the tourist bus, he's told, "There is nothing wrong with the local bus; it goes all the way and is quite safe." Hit then takes us to the bustling terminal next morning, for which I'm grateful, as hundreds of passengers, snack venders, and souvenir sellers roam about between dozens of buses covered in Nepalese script. He sees us safely aboard our bus, with backpacks locked in the back.

We're underway promptly at 0630, with much honking by the driver and whistling and banging on the frame by his assistant, who helps him through several tight spots in the parking lot. The 150-km trip takes eight hours, and ten people and five goats eventually ride between the rails on the roof. I'm actually shocked at the first rest stop, as the men pile off the bus, then stand gazing out into a field while relieving themselves into the ditch. The few women stay in their seats. Although it's hot, I sip sparingly from my water bottle as I'd just as soon not need a toilet until we reach our destination.

The country's main east-west road runs through steep-walled river canyons that run between the high Himalayas and the flat Ganges plain. Countless landslides have blocked them over the years, and the oversized tires of the bus bounce over rocks and holes left by makeshift repairs, then skirt the edges of high cliffs that drop straight down to the river. Long lines of buses and lorries wait at four police checkpoints, where armed guards with rifles stand behind sandbagged walls. Local people are made to leave the bus and carry their belongings through security, then an officer climbs aboard and inspects who and what is left.

Haze cloaks much of the countryside, and cows, goats, and chickens wander about rubbish-strewn streets in ramshackle villages. Men with crowbars pry loose big rocks from a dry riverbed, while lorries wait nearby. As best we can figure, the rocks are dumped farther down the road and smashed with sledgehammers. We then see one or two people squatting near small, cone-shaped piles of gravel in front of homes, breaking up larger pieces of rock with hammers.

The bus comes to a stop on the outskirts of Besi Sahar, and a man bangs on our window, motioning for us to get out. We're told that we have to check in at the park office, and our backpacks are tossed out onto the street. Bewildered, we lug the now dust-coated packs over to the front of the building and go inside, where our details are entered into a large ledger and our permits stamped and initialed.

Shouldering our backpacks, we walk up the street, looking for a hotel. When we pause near a sign that has hotel written on it, with an arrow pointing off to the right, a shopkeeper appears in a doorway across the road, points in that direction, and nods his head. The hotel is a block away and looks rather bleak, but we check in anyway, as we're tired and hungry. We then wait an hour in an empty dining room for a lunch that is barely edible.

We later walk into town and pass a goodly number of hotels and shops along the way. A jeep carrying six soldiers goes by twice, but otherwise we see only a tractor with a long steering column and no muffler that totes a few goods back and forth. The trailhead proves to be a kilometer down the road.

We're greeted excitedly by our host when we return to the hotel, and he informs us, "A group of fifteen Malaysians and their guide will be arriving tonight; they're coming a day early because of the general strike." We had been his only guests. Several young Nepali men now hang around, hoping to find work as porters.

Next morning, we're in the dining room at 0630, watching rain cascade down outside. While I wonder what it will do to trail conditions, the innkeeper glumly tells Dave, "The Malaysians didn't arrive! The army stopped them in a small village about fifty km away; they're stuck there until after the strike." Apparently, Maoist rebels are headed this way and government forces anticipate trouble.

While we wait for breakfast, one of the men we saw the previous night brings us coffee and offers his services as a guide or porter. He turns away with a shrug of his shoulders when Dave responds, "Not interested!" A second man refills our cups and is more persistent, asking about our route and how many days we've allowed. He speaks good English and tells us confidently, "My name is Yadav Gautam. I'm a guide/porter and charge 600 rupees a day, 300 for each service. I've done the circuit thirty times and have taken old people before."

Dave repeatedly explains, "We want to start off on our own. If we need help, we'll hire someone along the way." Yadav responds doggedly, "It's much more expensive to hire a porter after you leave Besi Sahar, better to hire one now."

When we leave the hotel at 0830, carrying our backpacks, Yadav waits outside. Falling into step beside us, he assures Dave, "I'm going to visit my grandfather and his village is two hours down the trail. I'll walk that far with you, no charge, and will stay there if you don't want to hire me."

The rain has now nearly stopped, and as we walk down the street, I feel like I'm in a parade. Everyone calls out to our companion and men come over to shake his hand. Yadav, a small man, beams hugely and smugly admits, "I'm the Singer Man. Everyone knows me on the trail because I entertain hotel staff at night with my songs."

Chapter 7
Companions on the Trail

From Besi Sahar, the Annapurna Circuit trail follows a river valley up into the mountains. The elevation at the trailhead is 2,665 feet, but after leaving the village, we descend down a long, steep hill until we come to a wide, devastated riverbed. We then make our way over rocks, around boulders, and across shallow trickles of water. When we come to a deep channel, we climb up on a large rock and jump across. The next one is much wider, so we remove our boots and wade. As I struggle to find footing in the strong current, water swirls halfway up by thighs.

On the other side, we follow an old road that winds up and down through subtropical forest. It's potted with holes, slashed by washouts, and new trails branch off frequently, avoiding landslides, overflowing creeks, and muddy slopes. Our light cotton shirts are soon soaked through, as we each carry thirty pounds in our backpacks. The monsoon heat and humidity will probably last another week.

When we reach the fork in the trail leading to grandfather's village, my pack has grown heavy, my legs are tired, and I've long since given up trying to choose which trail to take. In fact, I've been considering the route ahead and thinking, *maybe we should hire a guide.* I find myself holding my breath when Yadav stops and repeats his earlier words, "If you don't want to hire me, I will leave you here."

I heave a sigh of relief when Dave responds, "You're hired!"

Yadav now leads us to a suspension bridge that soars high over the Marsyangdi Khola. The river is in flood and milky-grey glacial waters surge and boil around boulders and ledgers, and its boom reverberates across the valley. I'm not really paying attention when I step onto the bridge, so am taken aback when it moves beneath my feet. The deck seems to be higher when I put my foot down than when I picked it up. In fact, the bridge moves with each footfall, and the more people on it, the more it snakes up and down. As there's nothing to hang onto, I focus on keeping my balance.

On the other side, we climb up a 1,000-foot ridge that is stepped with ten-foot-wide rice terraces. A stream has been diverted to flood the plants and excess water runs down the trail, which is steep and muddy. Once on top, we follow the ridge to a village, where small homes set a few feet off the trail are within spitting distance of each other.

Yadav introduces us to his 75-year-old grandfather, who sits on a porch in front of one of the dwellings, and while the men visit, I study the structure. The rock walls are coated with a layer of mud, leaving a smooth, hard surface that looks well maintained. I can't imagine how it would survive a heavy rain, however, and Yadav later tells us that the mud finish has to be redone every few weeks.

Without warning, he now asks for an advance of 3,500 rupees, explaining, "The Hindu festival, Dashain, starts in eight days and my wife needs to buy new clothes and prepare special foods." Sorrowfully, he adds, "Families across the country will gather together to celebrate, but I'll be away for the eighth year in a row."

I've been trying to forget about the cash we carry, and now dig it out of my backpack with the whole village watching. I count out the required amount and hand it to Dave, who gives it to Yadav, who passes it to an auntie, who will take it to his wife in the south of the country. I can only hope that our remaining cash covers our expenses.

We continue along the ridge top after leaving the village and hike into a picture postcard. Mountaintops on either side of the wide valley are wreathed in clouds, the river rages below, and the slopes in between are covered with terraces and forests. By the time Yadav stops at a teahouse for lunch, we're again dripping with sweat, and when we go on, Dave barters with a man beside the trail for two walking sticks.

After hiking for five hours, Yadav leads us to a guesthouse in a small village. Our small, dark room has three narrow cots squeezed into it, and the mattresses are hard, the pillows harder. As I spread out our sleeping bags, I wonder how often the sheets and pillowcases are washed. A small shed at the edge of the property contains a shower and toilet. The shower, in a wooden stall, provides a thin stream of cold water from an overhead trough. The toilet is a hole in the floor with a bucket of water and a dipper beside it. There's also a basket for those of us who bring toilet paper.

We now unhappily wait two hours for dinner, and Yadav responds to our grumbling with a lecture. "You should have ordered when we first arrived! It takes time to prepare a meal because the cook makes everything from scratch and the stove only has three burners. She also prepares meals in the order requested, and the four trekkers who arrived after us ordered before you."

When we walk back to our room, hundreds of large white moths flutter around a bright fluorescent tube that lights up half the yard. They also cover a wall in our room, and when we try to get rid of them, we discover that the roof is open under the eaves. All we can do is tuck in the mosquito netting that hangs over the beds. Dim light then shines between vertical stalks of bamboo that form the wall with the next room, and the sounds of whispers and coughs carry clearly.

After breakfast next morning, Dave starts the day by pumping water through our ceramic filter and filling water bottles. (We've been filtering drinking water ever since arriving in Nepal, as all water here is suspect.) I repack our backpacks, shifting some of the sixty pounds to Yadav, who will carry part of our load.

We shoulder our backpacks at 0830, and as we start down the trail, low grey clouds sit down on the ridge lines and the vegetation ahead is lush and green. A footbridge over a stream near the village has been washed away, and we sidle across on four long, skinny bamboo poles. The trail is then cut by a recent landslide, so we detour down into a riverbed. The river has carried off some of the debris, but a muddy, unstable slope about 100 feet high and twice that wide rises steeply above us.

As we climb back up to the trail, Yadav stops to watch two men and a woman standing at the top of the slide. They're looking for a route down and soon are slipping and sliding down a vertical water course. I sympathize, as they are expending a lot of energy and still have the day's trek in front of them. Yadav stays until he sees that one is a Nepali, then turns away.

Light rain begins to fall as we cross a long suspension bridge and continues as we traverse up the side of a canyon. An hour later, we stop at a teahouse, where the couple from the landslide catch up with us. Looking the worse for wear, the woman explains, "We've been hiking with another trekker and he's set a really fast pace. I've almost been sick trying to keep up. It was his guide who got us into trouble today."

Turning to Yadav, Dave murmurs, "Maybe you should guide them, too."

We talk awhile longer, one thing leads to another, and by the time we leave the teahouse, our small group of three has become five. Bill is English, Sylvia Dutch, and they're in their late twenties. They appear physically fit and enthusiastic, but their packs hang sack-like off their shoulders, so we're not surprised when they admit to not having backpacked before.

The rain is much heavier when we now start off, but the day is warm, so we wrap our ponchos around our backpacks rather than wear them. That keeps our backs dry, and with our wide-brimmed hats, we're reasonably comfortable as we climb upward. The other couple pull on jackets, sweat profusely, and look tired and miserable when we reach the top an hour later.

The rain eases as the trail drops steeply down the side of the canyon, and torrents of water now thunder off the mountain, following deep chasms that have been gouged through solid rock. Several landslides scar the opposite wall, and I have to wonder just how many rice terraces are destroyed each year.

We're late checking into the next guesthouse and eat supper on the balcony in the light of a kerosene lamp. A narrow strip of sky overhead clears as the night grows darker, then fills with brilliant stars. Looking up in amazement, Bill confesses, "I grew up in the city, in London. I've never seen a sky like this." I happily point out the Milky Way and the planet Mars, which is then rising in the east. When Sylvia exclaims at the sight of a falling star, I feel sorry for them both. I'd always assumed the magnificence of the night sky was a birthright that belonged to everyone.

We're away at 0830 next morning, but Bill starts slowly, then slips and falls. I'm concerned that his backpack may have caused him to lose his balance, so we have a short conversation about packing methods. We separate soon after, as we hike at different paces. Yadav starts and stops like a jackrabbit, Bill and Sylvia take regular rest stops at tea houses, and Dave and I stop only when necessary, preferring to finish early in the afternoon.

We now hike through a narrow canyon, where the trail clings to an almost vertical wall. Stinging nettles and marijuana plants grow in scattered patches of soil, while streams of water fall down the sheer rock face opposite. We stop early, two hours away from the broken bridge, as Yadav thinks hotels there could be full. Trekkers who've turned back have told him that it won't be repaired for weeks. When I shower, a thin trickle of blood from my first leech is running down my calf.

Taking advantage of warm sunshine, I set our boots out to dry, then rinse out a few clothes. As I work, I watch a steady line of porters plodding through the village. Some have large, overflowing wicker baskets on their backs, others have four-tiered wire cages containing live chickens or pigs. The entire weight of the load is borne by a tote strap around the forehead. One porter then squats beside his cages, and soon clucking chickens are walking around him and a small pile of grain he's put out.

Late in the day, a man with an injured foot is helped into the village by his mates. A rock landed on his foot at the bridge site, and they're taking him to a doctor farther down the trail. When Yadav asks me if we have medicine for a bad cut, I shake my head. Our first aid supplies are good only for blisters and scrapes. Looking down from our balcony, I see the man sitting on the grass, his injured foot twice its normal size.

We've been asked for medicine by a number of women and children waiting outside of villages, many with pus-filled sores on arms or legs. Making no pretense at having medical knowledge, we can only shake our heads. We respond similarly to children asking for pens, balloons, and candy. Trekkers are asked not to give them anything because such handouts turned previous generations into beggars.

When we wake up to heavy rain next morning, Yadav advises, "Best we stay over, it's not a good day to cross the broken bridge." As coughs and sniffles are spreading in the guesthouse, we spend the morning sipping hot lemon drinks, then have garlic soup for lunch. When the rain stops soon after, Yadav insists on showing us a nearby waterfall.

As we descend down a cliff face on ladder-like stone stairs, I notice the grass has recently been cut and a few rocks reset. We then cross a short suspension bridge that hangs 100 feet above a seething, rumbling river. Men, women, and children work on the trail on the far side, and pass in front of us while we're admiring the waterfall. Many carry bundles of grass on their backs that they're taking home for their animals.

Yadav then takes us to an open-sided shed at the edge of the village where a woman is making rakshi, the local moonshine. She squats on the stone floor, feeding dried corncobs into a small fire under a large kettle. As the mash in the kettle simmers, rising vapors pass through two clay pots and condense on the cone-shaped bottom of a copper pot containing cold water; drops then roll down into a collection pot. Yadav explains that the mash is made with either millet or rice and has fermented up to two months. Dave joins him for a drink after supper and tells me, "It's pretty rough stuff!"

In the late afternoon, a little girl runs past the hotel, anxiously pointing toward a small garden at the edge of the jungle. Several older children and their mothers rush in that direction, and I see branches shaking in the trees, then a number of monkeys on the ground. They've come to raid the garden. We walked by it earlier and saw corn and chili peppers drying on mats in the sun, with ginger and sugarcane plants still in the ground. After a brief standoff, the monkeys move on.

That evening, Yadav introduces us to a new song he's working on. The first verse is a lament about how unlucky he is, having no parents and so very poor. In the next verse, he describes trekking in the mountains and how fate one day brings him a trekking father and mother. Tears roll down his cheeks as he sings the last verse, fantasizing a future life in which they really are his parents.

Yadav has called us "Father" and "Mother" from the beginning, and I assumed this was either Nepalese custom, or just easier than learning our names. But during the past four days, he's frequently been depressed, moaning about being poor and having no father or mother. I've tried to cheer him up, but now wonder: *Are we being set up?*

CHAPTER 8
A BROKEN BRIDGE AND LONG, STONE STAIRCASES

Minutes after leaving the village next morning (Day 5), a wide stream of water gushes down across the trail. A new landslide has taken out more terraces. We now wait for two groups of trekkers to cross the muddy slope above. (They turned back at the broken bridge.) Suddenly, Yadav yells, "Leeches!" Looking down, I see half a dozen on my boots and others galloping across the rocks toward me. They're maybe an inch long, with feet at either end that they bring together. I scrape them off with my walking stick, then move around gingerly until we move on.

By noon, we're at the broken bridge, then Dave stays with our packs at a hotel in the village, while the rest of us rush off to the gorge. When the twisted, broken wreck comes into view, porters are swarming across it, some still carrying tote baskets. The bridge is maybe 300 feet across, and high on the cliff face opposite is the raw scar left by the rock fall that hit it, causing it to heave and twist.

The upper and lower cables on the upstream side now cross each other midway, and some of the metal fencing wire attached between them is still in place. One cable is missing on the downstream side, and the fencing wire attached to the other hangs like a curtain below the bridge. A small crew works beside the boiling waters of the river downstream, but all that spans it is a cable that hauls a basket back and forth.

I now hear Yadav calling, "Mum, Mum, come!", then see him standing at the edge of the cliff near the upstream cables. He disappears as I walk towards him, and when I see him next, he's thirty feet out over the gorge. Gripping the upper cable with his hands, he steps sideways on the lower one, and now calls again and waves me on. I've learned that he can be annoyingly persistent, so heave a sigh and step up onto the cable. I intend to go only a few feet, but when I stop, Sylvia is close behind and there's no turning back. Bill has wisely joined the spectators on the cliff top.

I'm annoyed when I look down at the swirling, grey waters some 50-60 feet below. First with Yadav, as we never discussed crossing the bridge, then with myself, for being trapped into it. Giving myself a mental shake, I concentrate on placing my hands and feet and keep going.

Although I'm not aware of it, the cables are gradually growing closer together vertically, while spreading apart horizontally. I only find out when my weight suddenly shifts from my feet to my hands, leaving me looking straight down at the river. I freeze, conscious of how precarious my position is, then instinctively bend my knees, putting my weight back onto my feet and yell a warning to Sylvia to do the same.

Another twenty feet or so bring us to a section where fencing wire forms a basket-like surface between the cables, and I'm able to hop along with hands on cables and feet on the wire. The cable that was under my feet then becomes the upper cable for the last half of the crossing. The remaining cable on the downstream side is a long step down, and I slide my feet down the fencing wire, feeling blindly for it.

Large boulders fill the riverbed beneath me as I inch sideways, and soon I feel myself stretching upward as the cables separate. I shift my hands to a strip of fencing wire hanging below the cable, praying that it's secure. Finally, I'm scrambling up the ten feet of steel decking that hangs down from cement pillars on the far side.

As Sylvia joins me, I see Yadav watching and tell myself: *Okay, you got us across, so how about bringing over our packs and let's get this show on the road.*

He doesn't say a word, however, just climbs back onto the bridge and waves for us to follow. When we return to the hotel, Yadav babbles about our success and Dave incredulously asks, "Why? Why would you take them across the bridge twice?"

Exceedingly pleased, Yadav responds, "It was a training run, and you and Bill can cross after lunch!"

That pleases neither of them, as Dave thinks it's a waste of time and Bill isn't keen on crossing at all. We all give Bill advice at lunch, then I recall watching him walk a log that morning and fall silent. It had been too high for a walking stick to help and he'd had a real problem with his balance. I wonder at the wisdom of expecting him to cross the bridge not once, but three times.

I'm guessing that Sylvia and I spent maybe ten minutes on the bridge, and Dave crosses almost as quickly as the porters. Bill takes much longer, and Yadav has to point out every hand and foothold; it's agonizing to watch. Having faced my own trial by fire while crossing the Pacific, I feel for him. When he's safely on the far side, I tell Sylvia, "I think we should go get the packs because Bill's not coming back."

He doesn't, and when the other men return, Yadav reports, "Bill's going to spend the night on the far side."

I'm adamant. "No. We can't leave him there with no shelter or water. We'll have to go on to the next village."

Dave's not happy at that suggestion and neither is Yadav, who complains, "It's several hours at least to the next village, and there's no food or shelter along the way."

At that, Sylvia announces, "I'm going over to join Bill."

That ends the discussion and we return to the hotel for our backpacks, which we carry across the bridge. (Actually, Yadav takes mine across.) Bill is embarrassed when I greet him and won't meet my eyes. Trying to be reassuring, I tell him, "Hey, you made a tremendous effort and got across. A lot of trekkers wouldn't even try."

A large marijuana field growing beside the river now squeezes the trail against the base of high cliffs, and as we start up steep, stone stairs, the thunder of the river grows louder. The stairs go on forever, and every step brings magnificent views of high mountains and roaring waterfalls. Dave then points ahead to where he sees light reflecting off water. It's higher than we are and appears to be the river, which is now hundreds of feet below us. As the trail snakes higher, the gradient of the gorge increases rapidly, with giant boulders filling the bottom and turbulent water boiling around them.

At the top of the gorge, we walk through the narrow entrance of a small, hidden valley that was once a mountain lake. A gloomy twilight descends, as high mountains shade it to east and west. I gaze in wonder at the high, vertical walls, the quiet, meandering river, the horses and mules grazing peacefully in flat fields.

We stop and register at a police checkpoint in the village, then cause consternation when we arrive so late at a guesthouse. We wait while our hosts scurry around trying to find food, then wait some more when they need to borrow gas from a neighbor for the kitchen stove. I find that I fed three leeches that day and barking dogs keep me awake for hours overnight.

We're now at 5,500 feet and get up to a leaden sky next morning, with a dusting of fresh snow on a nearby mountain. As we hike through the upper valley, we pass fields of bearded barley, then cross several suspension bridges. About mid-morning, we're following a four-foot-wide path around a cliff face when we hear shouting. Looking up, I see a Nepali man waving us off the trail. He's not satisfied until we've climbed up against the cliff face.

I now see that he's leaning into a rope that runs back over his shoulder, and when the other end comes into view, it's attached to the nose ring of a wild-eyed, wickedly-horned bull. The animal tosses his head imperiously as he lunges down the trail, pulling two men behind him on the end of another long rope. Casting a foul look in our direction, the bull allows himself to be guided past, but the men strain every muscle in their bodies to keep him moving in the right direction.

Near the next village, we pass under a stone arch (kaani) and come to a mani wall. A few stones in the wall bear the Tibetan Buddhist inscription "Om Mani Padme Hum". It also contains prayer wheels about the size and shape of a two-pound coffee can that are filled with sheets of paper bearing prayers. Spinning them sends the words up into the sky, bringing good fortune to a believer. We faithfully spin each one as we walk down the left side of the wall.

We've generally been hiking in a northerly direction, but that afternoon, the river valley forks and we head northwest. A cold rain sets in as we scale another long, stone staircase and continues as we hike up through a forest of blue pine, hemlock, maple, and oak. By the time we near a village at 7,500 feet, I'm cold, wet, and tired. We then pass a field of flowering buckwheat, the bright pink and white heads nodding on tall, slim stocks, and I feel my spirits lighten.

Our guesthouse that night is home to a family, and the wife allows us to huddle beside her wood-burning stove in a dark, smoky kitchen as she prepares our meal. Two children play quietly in a corner of the dining hall while we eat, and an old woman, a grandmother I presume, sits in a corner, fingering prayer beads and whirling a small prayer wheel.

The cold rain continues on Day 7, and Dave and I now wear our ponchos, but drape the backs overtop our packs, allowing air to circulate as we climb. Our companions appear wearing tee-shirt-style tops made of a manmade fabric. When I ask Sylvia if they'll be warm enough, she responds, "We figure we'll be okay as long as we keep moving."

We walk for hours through a pine and spruce forest, with rain dripping off branches as we slog through pools of water and mud. When the rain eases, a detour has us clambering down a steep hillside with deep mud sucking at our boots and rocks rolling underfoot. At the bottom, a new, small wooden bridge crosses a turbulent stream, and the trail then zigzags up a slippery clay slope left by a landslide.

I soon see a man climbing down a rocky section of trail ahead, with another man close behind. When we meet, I step off the trail and wait, as a long line of men now emerges from the misty drizzle. With rain dripping off hats and jackets, the twenty men pass silently in front of me, all carrying rifles. They're looking for Maoist rebels.

We're stopped at two military checkpoints in the next hour and show our papers at each. Yadav later tells me that his pack was inspected. The long, grey day ends at a larger village, and Yadav leads us across a bridge decorated with strings of prayer flags to a guesthouse run by a Tibetan family.

The temperature drops overnight, and we get up to more rain on Day 8. Dave takes Yadav shopping for a poncho, and Bill and Sylvia go along. They return with long-sleeved pullovers that look similar to their tee-shirts. When leaving the village, we walk down a long mani wall with about sixty prayer wheels and spin each one. After passing another field of flowering buckwheat, we come to a stone wall around an apple orchard. At a corner of the wall, the trail leads back into the forest and turns to mud.

The trekkers we see that morning are decked out in various kinds of rain gear. Half a dozen members of one group use large garbage bags that they've slit up one side and hooked over their heads. A few porters are wrapped in sheets of light plastic. The rain doesn't seem to slow them down, and I watch four men go past wearing flipflops. They seem to step in each other's footprints.

We soon come to a narrow gorge, where the walls drop vertically for hundreds of feet down to the unseen Marsyangdi River. Thin, lacy streams plunge down the sheer rock wall across from us, and a few are caught in small basins that overflow and drop again. It's spectacular. We then pick our way across an uneven rock shelf that was blasted out of the cliff face, and through low cloud, I catch tantalizing glimpses of a large sloping rock face. The huge slab of smooth, grey shale looms high above the trail and is several km across; it's magnificent.

A long, steep, zigzagging trail takes us up the next cliff face, and I stop when I hear the tinkle of bells. When a horse and rider come into view, I think maybe I've climbed into a previous century. The rider wears a Mongolian-style hat that fits snuggly around his head and his teeth flash whitely against his dark skin and drab clothing. A brightly colored blanket skirts the saddle of the small, surefooted pony he rides and small bells tinkle against its head. I watch with admiration as the animal delicately places each trim hoof while stepping down steep, stone stairs and maneuvering around large boulders.

We end the day by climbing up through a pine forest to 10,400 feet, and I'm astonished to see familiar plants, including birch and willow, wild roses and kinnikinnick. We're all a bit short tempered when we reach the next guesthouse, and I assume that the high altitude and a third day of cold rain have taken a toll.

I then recall that Dave and I have started eating eggs twice a day and wonder if we're noticing a lack of meat in our diet. That starts me thinking about the chickens running around the villages. *The porters bring cages of live chickens and baskets of eggs up the trail, so why keep chickens?* When I ask Yadav, he looks at me strangely and mutters, "The porters get meat." I have to assume that only the trekkers go without.

Sylvia comes down to dinner on her own and tells us, "Bill doesn't want anything to eat. He's so cold that he's shaking and has gone to bed to try to warm up. He complained about being short of breath today, and I think he could be suffering from Acute Mountain Sickness (AMS)."

Concerned, I respond, "He should have some hot food inside him, at least a bowl of soup. That will warm him up the fastest." Half an hour later, Bill arrives at the table wearing sweater, coat, and wool hat. As I watch him wrap glove-encased fingers around a spoon, a light bulb flashes in my head and I blurt out, "Bill, you've got hypothermia!"

Bill and Sylvia look at me blankly; they've never heard of it. Nor is it mentioned in the hiking guide, which includes every other conceivable ailment a trekker might experience. But anyone who has spent much time outdoors in a cold climate should recognize the symptoms, as hypothermia can cause poor muscle coordination, even disorientation, and kills people. I do my best to explain, "You're shivering, Bill, because your body temperature has dropped, probably due to hiking in this cold rain."

Sylvia protests that she feels fine, and I reply, "Women have an extra layer of fat, which gives us more protection." Neither of them responds, and when Bill is finished eating, he asks for hot water in his drinking bottle and goes back to bed.

Chapter 9
The High Country

Next morning, the sun rises in a brilliant blue sky, and looking out a window, I see what could have been a pre-historic settlement 300 feet up the mountainside. Wreathed by blue smoke from cooking fires, the small, stone-walled buildings have flat, mud roofs edged with large rocks. Terraced gardens climb up the steep slopes on either side.

We now hike through a high mountain valley, where bright sunshine sparkles on the tops of three snow-covered mountains, Pisang, Annapurna II, and Annapurna IV (19,800, 25,800, and 24,500 feet respectively). We then climb up a steep, forested ridge to a bluff that provides a spectacular view of the wide, flat Manang valley, with Yilicho Peak (23,000 feet) at its head and snowy ranges on either side. Another half-hour brings us to the village of Hongde, which sits at 11,220 feet, and is home to the first of two airstrips on the circuit.

This valley is much drier than previous ones, as high mountains to the south block monsoon rains. Fields of ripe barley and buckwheat line the trail, and yaks graze here and there, along with a few goats, cows, and horses. Wild rose bushes grow in one area and the rosehips are twice the size of any I'd seen before. Nearby, a small flock of hoopoes probe the ground with long, curved bills. The birds aren't large but are striking, with an orange crest and a broad, white stripe running across black wings.

Buddhist temples, monuments, and mani walls become more numerous at the upper end of the valley, and a large, covered prayer wheel sitting on a diverted stream sends a constant stream of prayers into the heavens. Then, as we start up the last ridge to Manang, I become aware that my feet are dragging on anything other than a gentle slope. I'm also fiddling with my backpack, which is suddenly uncomfortable. We're at 11,500 feet and I'm feeling the altitude.

We check into a large hotel and take turns using the shower, luxuriating in the plentiful supply of solar-heated hot water. I then wash clothes at a tap near the garden and think about the trail ahead. It's still 6,000 feet to the pass and we'll probably run into snow and cold temperatures. Oxygen levels, which are now only 65% of that at sea level, will drop to 50%. According to my trail guide, AMS symptoms appear six to twelve hours after a person is affected. If they persist, that person needs to make a quick descent.

I now think about the incident at the broken bridge. We didn't discuss crossing it prior to doing so, and it didn't go all that well. It did reveal, however, that the four of us were in this together. So, at supper that night, I start a conversation. "As we climb higher, the weather will get colder and probably snowy, and AMS could be a problem. It seems to me that from here on, we'll sink or swim together because we all rely on Yadav. If any one of us has a problem, he will have to bring that person down, and the rest of us couldn't go on without him."

Perplexed, Sylvia asserts, "But I can bring Bill down if he has a problem."

Shaking my head, I slowly respond, "No, once we leave Manang, Yadav will be responsible for ensuring the safety of all of us, including anyone who has to turn back." Meeting her eyes, I then add, "I'm also concerned that you and Bill don't have the proper clothing."

That ends the discussion until breakfast, when Yadav unexpectedly announces, "I guarantee that Father, Mother, and *Sylvee* will make it over the pass, but I cannot guarantee that Bill will." He then goes on, "It's not possible to hire a porter because the harvest starts tomorrow, and all the villagers will be working in the fields."

Bill and Sylvia go off to mull over this sudden turn of events, then scour the shops for clothing. They return to announce that they are turning back and will fly out next day. She is understandably disappointed, resentful even, while he is dejected. I try to reassure him, pointing out, "Bill, you climbed 9,000 feet in nine days, and you crossed the broken bridge! You've accomplished so much and can try again another year."

He bitterly responds, "I'll never pick up a backpack again."

That afternoon, everyone in town assembles at the helipad to watch two emergency evacuations, one for an American, the other for a Malaysian. Both men suffer from AMS. Another Malaysian is helped back down the trail early next day, and rumor has it that he has pneumonia and is coughing up blood.

We set off again on Day 11, following Yadav through streets that are empty and strangely quiet. At the edge of the village, we enter a long, winding, stone-walled passageway, and I stop to let several men go past. They tote huge bundles of freshly cut green stalks, and one of them climbs a ladder up to a rooftop, where he spreads his load out to dry. Villagers cut stalks of grain with curved knives in an adjacent field. The harvest is underway.

The trail now leads across open slopes of alpine grass and juniper, where small, scattered herds of yaks and horses peacefully graze. The sky is bright and sunny, the air crisp and clear, and every step brings fabulous views of the mountains. After maintaining a slow, steady pace for 90 minutes, we stop briefly at a teahouse. When we go on, we climb up and down across a barren landscape, with a few trekkers or porters always in sight. We climb up 1,600 feet in three hours, well over the 1,000-foot daily maximum recommended in the guidebook.

We spend the night in an isolated guesthouse at the bottom of a steep-sided pass at 13,000 feet. Joining a large group of trekkers and guides in the lee of the building, we soak up the sun until it drops behind a mountain at 1600.

The air cools quickly, and Yadav escorts us into a dimly lit dining hall, seating us at a large table that has blankets draped over the top and wide, padded benches. He disappears briefly and returns with an open-topped, square can that contains live coals, which he places at our feet. We tuck in the blankets around our knees and are soon feeling toasty.

After dinner, twenty or more porters gather at one end of the room and Yadav entertains them. Clapping to the rhythm of his songs, they join in the choruses, all seeming to know the words. He then comes over and wants "Mum" to dance with him. Not wanting to argue, I prance around the dark, smoky room in my hiking gear.

Dave coughs a lot overnight, neither of us sleep well, and I wake in the morning with a raging headache. It eases a bit over breakfast, and at Yadav's urging, I agree to go on. (The first rule in the guidebook: *Never take a headache higher*.)

We leave at 0900, trudging across a barren, rocky landscape under a grey, overcast sky. Right from the start, I can't keep up. I concentrate on picking up each foot, thrusting it forward, pushing my body after it—and fall farther behind. Yadav returns, takes my backpack, and fifteen minutes later we stop at a teahouse for hot drinks. We're 45 minutes into the day's hike and have climbed up 650 feet.

After a brief rest, I pick up my backpack and we set off again. The trail now traverses the side of a valley, and a deep gorge lies between us and high, vertical cliffs opposite. A few ponies graze nearby and small herds of yaks are visible in the distance. Yadav points to two herds of blue sheep on the cliff tops, but I need binoculars to see them. While we watch, the cliffs disappear behind a white haze, and a cold wind soon hits us, bringing dropping temperatures.

Half an hour later, we're again climbing up and down across rolling, barren terrain, and I'm looking at even the slightest decline with despair, knowing

I'll have to climb back up it. Every step is now an act of will. The snow then overtakes us, the fine, dry flakes hiding the landscape but not accumulating on the ground. I keep moving for another thirty minutes, but run out of steam when I start up the last ridge. I just stop, not even able to call for help.

Yadav materializes beside me, takes my backpack, and under his urgent prodding, I take a few steps. I stop frequently, but with two packs, he also needs to rest. Dave trudges on ahead. After climbing up 1,660 feet in three hours and fifteen minutes, we arrive at the next guesthouse.

The buildings are grey and wintery-looking as we approach, with a skiff of snow on rock walls and stones paths. A string of small, shaggy ponies stands at the edge of the terrace, saddled and eating out of nosebags. We're provided with a room in a motel-style unit built of rock and mud and have our own toilet (a hole in the floor). Collapsing on our beds, we sleep for two hours and when I wake, my headache is gone.

We cross to the dining hall, where we eat hot garlic soup and drink tea, and with an electric heater warming the space beneath our table, the room is very pleasant. We stay for several hours, visiting with trekkers who are all much younger. When we talk to two Australian girls, one asks, "Are you the sailors?" Seeing the dumbfounded looks on our faces, she laughingly explains, "We talk to everyone on the trail and heard reports of an old couple, known as *father and mother,* who are making the climb." Yadav, it appears, also talked to everyone.

Next morning, the sky is again grey and overcast, and the trail zigzags back and forth as it climbs up a scree slope. I concentrate on keeping my movements slow and regular, breathing in and out with every two steps. Dave climbs too fast, gets winded, then has to watch as I go by. It's a long, hard slog, and soon after we start, clouds roll in like fog, bringing snow. After climbing for seventy minutes, we gain 1,140 feet and reach High Camp at 15,600 feet.

Sitting in the dining hall, we drink hot tea and watch trekkers materialize out of the gray cloud surrounding the guesthouse. A trace of snow settles on the ground, and the moving cloud then exposes steep, rock-covered slopes behind the building. When the delicious aroma of garlic and tomato waft from the kitchen, we peer in to see the cook stirring a large pot of tomato sauce. We eat spaghetti and fresh bread for dinner and the sauce actually tastes as good as it smells.

By 1700, there are sixty people in the room, most are young, many are women, and few know how to shut a door. Two large groups are from France and Israel, but there's an older German couple, and a Korean brother and sister in their 60's. The guides/porters are Indian, Tibetan, and Chinese. The bathroom is an outhouse with a hole in the ground and a bucket of water that sits in a hollow maybe fifty feet from the windows; it's kept pretty busy.

We're early to bed and I pull on wool cap, long underwear, and socks before climbing into my sleeping bag. When I can't get warm, I pull up a heavy quilt about an inch thick that's on the bed. An hour later I'm seized by a violent coughing/sneezing fit and can't catch my breath. Pushing the quilt down, I wonder about allergies, now remembering that I'd noticed something in the air when we entered the room, maybe mud dust. Loud voices outside and in the next room keep us awake until late, then Dave coughs a lot overnight and I wake up frequently, gasping for air.

Yadav wakes us at 0400 and we set off an hour later, wanting to be through the pass by noon, when strong headwinds will set in. We need a flashlight to follow the trail, as despite its covering of snow, the mountain hides in the darkness. We climb steadily, the snow crunching underfoot, cold air biting at our faces, and brilliant, merciless stars looking down. My hands and feet are soon freezing.

Moving lights mark the progress of two groups ahead, giving us a sense of our direction of travel as we cross in and out of ravines formed by gravel moraines. By 0630, it's light enough to make out stark, black figures against the snow ahead. When the sun climbs over the horizon, it's easy to believe we're on the roof of the world. Despite the desolate, rocky landscape and last night's snowfall, the trail is easy to follow as herdsmen have been bringing sheep and yak over the pass for hundreds of years.

We're climbing well when we come to a teahouse at 16,350 feet, so don't stop. Our pace slows soon after, as the trail rises steeply, taking us up switchbacks over moraines and rocky ridges. It's not as difficult as the previous day, except that my pack feels twice as heavy. A few trekkers eventually overtake us, but they're not moving much faster than we are.

When our pace slows again, Yadav calls out encouragement, "Only twenty minutes to the top." I struggle to keep moving, concentrating on lifting each foot and placing it down, trying to move in rhythm with my breathing, but I feel light-headed and my stomach churns. He then cries out, "Only another five minutes!" I keep pushing forward as the incline becomes more gradual, then look up and see multi-colored prayer flags framed against the white of the snow.

Yadav comes forward to congratulate us as we near the stone cairn and fluttering flags marking the 17,600-foot (5,416 meter) summit of Thorong La. The last 2,300 feet took us two hours and 45 minutes. Entering a small stone hut, we sip hot tea in the darkness, then join dozens of people outside admiring the views. The pass is awash in breathtaking brilliance as the snow reflects the rays of the sun. Around us, three magnificent mountains, all nearly 20,000 feet, are framed against a deep blue sky.

We now hike west through a saddle between the peaks, and thirty minutes in, I hear a distant whooshing sound. Turning toward the south, where deep cornices balance on a high ridgeline, I see an avalanche of snow and ice cascading for hundreds of feet down either side of a long, black rock face.

Near the far end, patches of gravel appear in the snow beneath our feet and we're buffeted by strong winds. We then look over the edge of a precipice, where the ground drops away for 5,000 feet. Yadav points out our destination, and the small green dot looks ridiculously small in the midst of the dry, brown canyon-lands far below. Beyond them, snowcapped mountains stretch across the horizon.

The trail is steep as it zigzags down, and soon grows even steeper. Two hours later, about halfway down, my knees give out. It feels like bones in both knees are chafing against each other. I pull a neoprene brace over one and wrap a triangular bandage tightly around the other, but neither really helps.

Dave takes my pack and gives me his walking stick, and leaning heavily on the two sticks, I painfully make my way down. Yadav has been watching and now informs us, "I'm going to go ahead and get something to eat. I didn't have breakfast because the kitchen staff at High Camp were too busy feeding tourists to feed the Nepalis."

We catch up with him an hour later at a teahouse, where we also rest and eat. The grassy slopes beyond are not as steep, but I'm exhausted and in a world of hurt. It takes another hour and a half that seems like forever before I totter down the wide street into Muktinath.

CHAPTER 10
MUKTINATH AND THE KALI GANDAKI

Our third-floor hotel room in Muktinath seems extraordinarily luxurious, with a shower, sit-down toilet, and warm sunshine streaming in two windows. It turns out that the village is a destination for Hindu and Buddhist pilgrims. Sitting on a sunny balcony off the second-floor dining room, we have an early dinner while admiring the snow-clad slopes of Dhaulagiri (26,500 feet) that rise high in the sky across the valley.

Below us, villagers come and go at the town tap on the far side of a dirt square. The tap spews a constant flow of water into a cement basin that drains away underground. A woman squats there for a while, washing clothes, and lends a basin to a rider who stops to water his horse. Nearer the hotel, another woman sets up a loom and tries to sell colorful scarves to the occasional visitor who strolls past. A few dogs and chickens roam about, as does a cow or two, but a couple of loose horses are viewed as troublemakers and chased away.

A clanging cowbell signals the arrival of a mule train, and a bobbing head appears at the foot of the street, followed by twenty heavily loaded animals. Half the mules carry large bundles of split wood and continue up the street. The others have large, flat rocks in baskets on their sides and turn into a lane opposite, following a lead mule that appears to be unguided and takes them to a building site. Minutes later they return with empty baskets and head toward the southern hills.

I sleep eleven hours that night and intend to spend the next day resting, but Yadav has other plans. There is much we have to see. So, we hike up the side of the valley, then climb up a long, stone staircase to the Temple of Vishnu Mandir. A second staircase leads to a walled courtyard where sacred water pours out of 108 brass cow heads. Pilgrims shower beneath each one in order to be sufficiently cleansed to enter the temple. But the water's very cold and Yadav wets only one hand and dries it on his hair as he works his way round.

We next follow a path across a stony slope to an old Tibetan building that houses Jwala Mai Temple. Here are enshrined the elements that bring the pilgrims: earth, water, and fire. After making a donation, we peer into a darkened crevice and see the flickering of the perpetual flame (a natural gas jet) and hear the gurgling of the sacred spring. Before we leave, Yadav has us wash our hands in a stream of sacred water.

Heavy rain falls overnight, and next morning, a line of snow is visible beneath the grey clouds that sit on the mountains across the valley. Trying not to think about the day's 3,000-foot descent, I stay at the window and watch the rising sun chase the clouds away. A woman opens the door of a small shed and turns out two cows and a calf, then another woman struggles to carry a heavy sack up a ladder to a rooftop, where she spreads grain out on a tarp to dry. Meanwhile, a large herd of cows gathers above the village, then disappears into the southern hills.

The town square is inches deep in mud when we cross it, and gushing streams rush off the mountainside as we start down the trail. On the lower side, terraced gardens of barley, buckwheat, corn, cabbage, and spinach rise up from the valley bottom, and a few yellow leaves cling to the branches of scattered poplar trees. Turning for a last look at the precipice below Thorung La, I make out the grassy slopes around the small lodge where we stopped on our way down.

I lean on two walking sticks, trying to protect my knees, and after descending 2,000 feet, I'm still keeping up with Dave and Yadav. The terrain is now rocky and barren, with only a few scattered shrubs, and passing pilgrims have left many small rock cairns beside the trail. But as we approach the rim of an intersecting canyon, I see the zigzagging path plunging down a 1,300-foot vertical wall and my heart sinks. I slowly start down and painfully totter into the village at the base of the cliff an hour behind the two men. Dave waits to guide me to a dilapidated guesthouse.

Our second-floor room is accessed across a flat rooftop, and the wind whistles eerily through piles of chopped wood stacked around the edges, while bean pods are spread out to dry in one corner. In another corner, the skull of a blue sheep sits on a post, its horns painted black. From this vantage point, we see villagers industriously digging potatoes and cutting stalks of grain in fields at the base of the cliffs.

We're now in the canyon of the Kali Gandaki, which cuts through a valley described as the deepest in the world. The river drops to an elevation of 7,150 feet as it passes between two 26,000-foot mountains that are 38 km apart. The trail alongside it has long been used by traders from Tibet, but we'll hike only in the mornings for the next few days, as strong winds blow upriver in the afternoons.

On Day 17, we join the stream of trekkers, pilgrims, and mule trains flowing up and down the trail. High, vertical canyon walls, similar to the one we descended the day before, are maybe half a kilometer apart, and the braided channels of the river meander over gravel flats between them. While taking a shortcut across a gravel bar, we watch a man on horseback drive two big, black yaks into the water on the far side; he pushes them slowly, giving them time to pick a route. We find a safe place to let them pass as the animals have wicked looking horns. When the canyon narrows, the waters merge into a fast-moving river that plunges down over rocks and ledges.

We meet numerous pilgrims making the trek to Muktinath, and Yadav explains that they fly into Jomsom, our destination that day, and walk from there. Pointing to large letters chalked on the surface of a half-hidden, sheer rock wall, he informs us, "That's the pilgrim's prayer, *Om mani padme hum.*" After hiking for three hours, we check into another decaying guesthouse and spend the afternoon in the dining room, watching the wind whip up the dust outside. Before nightfall, a herd of about twenty yaks meanders down the street out front.

The airport at Jomsom sits at an elevation of 9,000 feet and closes daily at 1100 because of the wind. It's the second and last on the Annapurna Circuit. When we pass near the terminal at 0800 next morning, passengers are loading into three small planes, and they depart while we're walking down the runway.

The first uses the entire 2,500-foot length and gains altitude slowly as the ground falls away down the valley. The second takes off in the opposite direction (into wind), also uses all the runway, then makes a hairy 180-degree turn between the canyon walls. The third is a Canadian-built Twin Otter that takes off down the valley, uses only part of the runway and climbs out nicely.

Mule trains are now more numerous, some with twenty or more animals, and I'm surprised to see that many don't have halters. They carry a wide variety of goods, including propane bottles. Yadav points to a pissing spot in a hollow on the trail and from the smell it seems every mule must use it. As the animals tend to bunch up in narrow sections and have nowhere to go but overtop me, I keep my walking stick braced in front of my body and don't hesitate to use it. The day before, a driver pushed his mules down on top of us and I'd barely had time to throw myself clear of a pack box.

After hiking for two hours, we follow Yadav down a narrow, winding street into a small village. Water gurgles beneath large, flat stones beneath our feet, and I notice that the narrow alleys and covered passageways branching off are sheltered from the wind. Minutes after we check into a guesthouse, Yadav is knocking on our door.

A few days before, on the first day of the Deshain festival, he'd been more depressed than usual and shocked us both by dramatically declaring, "I think I should commit suicide." As a result, we'd ended up agreeing to stand in for his parents on *tika* day, when families across Nepal gathered to exchange blessings for a long life and good fortune in the coming year.

He now enters, carrying a small plate scattered with rice, a smidgen of red powder mixed with water, and two small yellow flowers. Sitting down in front of Dave, he bows his head, places his hands in front of his chest, and turns the palms in. Dave takes a bit of rice between his thumb and fingers and places it on top of Yadav's head, then his forehead, and ends by placing a blossom on his hair. He repeats the ceremony with me, and I do the same with the two of them. Tikas are also exchanged, the small red dot placed between the eyebrows.

We have lunch in the dining room afterward, and although we've seen people eat with their hands before, Yadav is the first we share a meal with. He carefully washes his right hand, then wanders around the room with water dripping on the floor. When his meal is served, he mixes the veggies and rice together with his fingers, picks some up, then turns his hand over and pops it into his mouth.

We later visit a Buddhist gompa, climbing a long, steep flight of stairs up a cliff face at the edge of the village. Ancient books wrapped in cloth are stored on the monastery's shelves, and numerous students wearing yellow robes run about; they're quite boisterous and some are surprisingly young. On the way down, we pause to study the village houses clinging to the side of the cliff. The stone walls and flat roofs edged with stacks of split wood look more like a rabbit warren than a place where people live.

We hike for seven hours on Day 19, and by noon, dust devils swirl in the dry riverbed, blowing sand and grit into our faces. The canyon then makes a large bend, and we're out of the wind. We stay in a very comfortable guesthouse that night, and at dinner, our host places a pail of live coals at our feet. An old woman enters soon after and lies down on the bench across from us. An old man then appears, but won't sit down until I wave him to do so. When we return to our room, a full moon is rising in a clear night sky, and the light glows radiantly off the snowpack of a high mountain that we see from our balcony.

The trail descends 4,100 feet through a steep gorge next day, and I'm dreading it. But soon after we leave, I glance at Yadav and am reminded of something Bill noticed. "Yadav walks differently than us," he'd said, "he walks on his toes." Wondering whether it could make a difference, I try to copy his movements.

Pointing my foot out slightly, I step forward onto the toe of my boot, then lower my heel. I'm soon elated, as there's definitely less stress on my knees. But the movement isn't natural, and when I grow tired or distracted, my knees start hurting again. It also doesn't prevent the jarring when I drop down long steps on steep slopes. But after eight and a half hours of climbing up, down, and around steep, unstable ground, I hobble up to the next guesthouse beside Dave.

I come to admire the mules that day, as they cross the difficult terrain and long suspension bridges with remarkable calm. The lead two or three animals in every train now carry pink plumes made of yak's tail on their heads. In the lower section of the canyon, banana plants, orange trees, and rice crops appear, and water buffalo tied with short ropes stand in yards or sheds, eating freshly cut grass.

We stop to watch a woman squatting beside two round, flat stones in an open-sided shed. She rotates the upper stone with a handle, while trickling corn into a hole in the center, and coarse cornmeal spills off the outer edge of the lower one. In a freshly tilled field, a farmer drives a bullock pulling a wooden plow, and in another field, two men twist hay around a stick. When the swath is about eight feet long, they bend the ends back to the middle, and twist it one more time.

While waiting to clear though a police checkpoint, we hear about a large explosion in Besi Sahar, and about Maoist rebels who are collecting *donations* from trekkers. Twenty minutes later, we pass through a second checkpoint, then see a patrol of twenty armed men in the next village. The guesthouse that night is full and noisy.

I count over 300 heavily loaded mules in the first two hours on the trail next day and see evidence of many landslides. We stop to inspect a small roofed hut sitting over a channel in a devastated stream bed and find a water turbine spinning a large mill stone. After a short day, we check into a guesthouse in Tatopani, which translates as hot water, and are provided with a pleasant room in a quiet back corner of the garden.

The two pools that make up the hot springs are below us, alongside a river, but the original spa structure was washed away in monsoon floods a few years before. As I don't have a bathing suit, I look for something suitable in the village. Shopping along the trail hasn't been particularly enjoyable, as merchants seemed desperate. It's no different now. When I leave without making a purchase, the salesman is almost surly, and when I do buy a long, wrap-around skirt, the vendor is still unhappy.

After making our way down to the river, we enter small wooden cubicles to change clothes. With the skirt tied around my chest, I ease my tired muscles into the hottest pool, luxuriating in the feel of the water. I then alternate between the pool and the icy cold of the river and repeat the treatment the following day.

CHAPTER 11
ANNAPURNA SANCTUARY

On Day 23, we start up the trail to the Annapurna Sanctuary. It takes an hour to clamber up the steep, stone staircase out of the river canyon, and it's hot and humid, so our shirts are soon dripping with sweat. Short sections of trail then level off slightly, allowing us to catch our breath before hitting the steep slopes ahead. In 3.5 hours, we climb up 2,500 feet.

We meet many trekkers on the trail, and the guesthouse that night is overflowing. Rumors about Maoists run rife, and we're told that they don't recognize our government-issued permits and will enter hotels to collect trekking fees. The amount depends on nationality, with Brits and Yanks paying up to 2,000 rupees each.

Lights are out early, but it's a while before I can sleep, as voices carry across the courtyard from the kitchen, and the entire second floor shakes when anyone walks down the balcony to the bathroom. Sometime later, I'm woken by the most gawd-awful racket. Dazed, not sure what I've heard, I'm still awake a half hour later when it happens again. Certain that Dave must be awake, I whisper, "Do you have any idea what's going on?"

He responds, "That crazy Frenchwoman on the other side of the wall was banging furiously on it, and the second time she did it, I hammered back."

After that, there is silence. In the morning, a woman is sleeping out on the veranda, her mattress having been pulled outside. I have no idea what the problem was, as I'd heard only the usual coughing. After eating our normal early breakfast, we're away before most trekkers have stirred.

We climb 3,250 feet that day, mostly on stone staircases, and meet many trekkers coming down. Some groups are quite large, with at least twenty hikers plus their guides and porters. A few people lean heavily on walking sticks, and I sympathize. We catch up to a family of four and the youngest, a small girl, is on a horse. I don't envy her when I see how the animal lunges to get up the high steps.

We check into a guesthouse at 8,940 feet, then have an early supper and early night. In doing so, we miss the Maoists who shake down the guests in the dining hall. They hand out receipts and tell folks, "You won't have to pay again." There's a lot of coughing overnight and early risers start banging around at 0400, preparing to leave for Poon Hill to watch the sunrise. We leave at 0730, and Yadav takes us down a back route to the main trail, thus avoiding the Maoists who accompany the returning mob.

The air is cool and we make good time, and by midmorning are on a grassy ridge at 10,300 feet. Around us is an incredible panorama of snow-capped mountains, including our first look at Machhapuchhare (Fishtail). The trail then leads up through a pine and rhododendron forest, emerges on a steep hillside, and plunges down 2,300 feet to a creek crossing. After climbing up the steep slope on the far side, we follow another ridge into the next village at 8,430 feet.

We meet over 100 trekkers on the trail that day, along with many heavily ladened porters. Conversations float around the larger groups in languages I don't understand, and a dozen Israelis sing a marching song as they descend down a steep, narrow ravine beside a beautiful, clear stream. Not really what I imagined hiking in the Himalayas would be like.

The many hotels in the village fill up quickly, and guests congregate on a grassy slope to soak up the sun and enjoy mountain views. The afternoon quiet is then broken by a staccato burst of gunfire, and looking down the ridge, we see two helicopter gunships circling a kilometer away. Disbelievingly, we sit and watch for two hours, as sporadic gunfire continues to drift our way. Yadav has the latest rumors and tells us, "The Army sent 200 men against the Maoists in that village and they ran off into the jungle." I can only wonder in which direction they fled.

The woman running our hotel admits to paying the Maoists 5,000 rupees, adding stoically, "If you want to stay in business, you pay." (*What else can you do when armed men come out of the jungle and threaten you?*) The helicopters disappear when clouds start to form, and by late afternoon we're surrounded by fog.

The air is surprisingly cold when we set off just after sunrise next morning. The trail now descends 2,600 feet, first zigzagging through shaded forest, then crossing over narrow terraces that have recently been harvested. After crossing a creek at the bottom, we climb up the steep slope on the far side, then stop for the night at a guesthouse perching on the rim of a 1,400-foot canyon wall. We're now at 7,050 feet.

Finding a bench with a view, I soak up the sunshine while admiring the canyon lands below, and for the first time consider the wisdom of going on. The ups and downs of the last two days have been hard on my knees, and the next two days will bring more of the same. But it's the 5,000-foot descent when we return from the Sanctuary that is my main concern; I don't know whether I can do it. On top of that, we both have harsh, nagging coughs and are not resting well at night. But when I talk to Dave, he shrugs his shoulders and responds, "I'm going up to the Sanctuary." It doesn't occur to me to stay behind.

Next day, we climb up and down through more rugged terrain, then enter a narrow canyon with high, vertical walls. Mountain peaks tower overhead, waterfalls plunge off cliffs, and a turbulent river roars noisily below. We descend 1,625 feet, climb up 2,700 feet, and spend the night in a guesthouse at 8,125 feet.

The following day, we hike for hours in cold shadows, scrambling up and down high cliffs and clambering up rock stairs that are like ladders. When the canyon widens, we cross two avalanche tracks and stop at a memorial to pay our respects to four climbers who died there eighteen months earlier. Our pace slows as the air grows thinner, but eventually we arrive at Machhapuchhre Base Camp (MBC) at 12,000 feet. The camp is clustered in a hollow in a high alpine meadow surrounded by knolls of rocks and grass. Around it, six mountains soar upward for thousands of feet, and Machhapuchhre's fishtail top is clearly recognizable.

Next morning at 0600, we set off in a cold, grey twilight to ascend the final 1,400 feet to the Sanctuary. Wearing wool hats, coats, and gloves, we maintain a slow, steady pace up the first ridge. An icy wind blows in our faces, grasses beside the trail are coated with frost, and a thin layer of ice surrounds rocks on the edge of a stream. In front of us, the massive bulk of Annapurna I (26,000-plus feet) blocks out the sky. Fifteen minutes later, the first rays of the rising sun gleam on A-I's high snowy shoulder.

Annapurna Base Camp is still swathed in dim, grey light when we arrive. I search for a spot to watch the sunrise and soon am ensconced on a bench above the camp, looking down the backtrail. Closing my eyes, I feel the first weak rays on my face as the sun rises behind Fishtail, then a growing warmth as it climbs up in the sky.

When I turn around, the full glory of the Sanctuary is revealed, with the sun lighting up the high circle of magnificent peaks surrounding a central bowl. The snow-covered tops sparkle against an incredibly blue sky, and sheer cliffs hundreds of feet high separate the peaks from the valley floor. Three or four glaciers run down their flanks, with huge piles of gravel in a wide ravine below.

We stay for an hour, then return to MBC, have breakfast, and pick up our backpacks. I leaned heavily on my walking sticks during the climb up, trying to protect my knees, but there's nothing I can do as we descend and I'm soon isolated in a fog of pain and misery. Dave shepherds me down the long descent that day, and at the end of the next, we're back at the guesthouse on the canyon rim.

We now take the shortest route out of the mountains, plunging down the 1,360-foot canyon wall on a twisting, stone staircase. We then hike down a river valley for eight hours, descending another 4,000 feet.

On the way, we pass through golden fields where villagers are harvesting rice. I stop to watch a woman, squatting on her haunches, as she grabs a handful of stalks, cuts them off with a curved knife called an ahsee, and carefully lays them down. Once a terrace is finished, all the heads lie neatly on top of other stalks.

Outside a village, we meet at least a dozen men on the road, and more stand on a wide gravel bar at the edge of the river. I'm uneasy, as there's not a woman in sight. Yadav points to a large cairn of rocks beside the swirling waters and explains, "A seventy-year-old woman died and her body is interred there; it will be washed away by next year's monsoon floods." (I gather that men played the primary role in the burial.)

We spend our last night in a large village that straddles the river, and next morning, I study a misty-looking Machhapuchhre for the last time. A short walk takes us to Naya Pul, and half an hour later we're sitting in a bus on the way to Pokhara. After a two-hour drive, we're deposited in the middle of a busy town that is oppressively hot, humid, and noisy. It seems none of the motorcycles, buses, or tractors have mufflers.

We rest here for a couple of days, trying to get our coughs under control, and I put together some statistics about our trek. We were on the trail 32 days and spent 8 nights above 11,400 feet. I then add the descents to the change in elevation and realize we actually climbed up more than 38,000 feet.

Dave settles up with Yadav and pays him 1,000 rupees/day, not the 600 he'd requested. Yadav doesn't acknowledge the bonus and only reluctantly takes the cash. A week earlier, he'd asked for money to buy a plot of land with a house and garden. Every day since, he'd pleaded his case. Even if that had been possible, we didn't believe it would solve his problems for long.

CHAPTER 12
ROYAL CHITWAN NATIONAL PARK

While passing through the canyons on the bus ride back to Kathmandu, we see a crowd of people standing beside the road and notice an inflatable in the river below. A bus went off the cliff and 44 people are missing. Then, as our bus climbs a zigzagging road up the final ridge outside the city, traffic slows to a crawl as vehicles maneuver around buses and lorries that have been abandoned on both sides. A police roadblock at the top, now closed, appears to have been the cause.

It takes an hour to go the last five km into the city, then streets are chaotic, as is the parking lot at the bus terminal. A mob of touts surrounds us when we step off, but Dave can see over their heads and finds a taxi driver to take us to the Laughing Buddha hotel. We spend four days here, hacking and coughing, while trying to shake off the bugs that plague us.

On the first day of Dewali, we feel energetic enough to walk through the tourist area, where shopkeepers are preparing for the festival. They wash dust from roll-down metal doors, then mop up floors, steps, and street frontage. Garlands of yellow flowers are draped across storefronts, steps are washed with red clay, and a six-inch-wide path is painted to a place of worship inside. Tiny dishes of oil will be lit and placed along the path at the end of the day to guide Laxmi, the Goddess of Wealth, into the building that night.

As Dave promised Yadav that we'd visit him in Chitwan, we now board another bus. We start off on the same route as before, but deep in the canyons turn south at the confluence of two rivers. This second road is as rocky and potholed as the first, but now cement bridge decks have no curbs or guardrails, and peering over the edge, I see brown, turbulent water 50 feet or more below.

I also see daylight through a circular hole at the edge of the pavement and am horrified. It's maybe two feet across and turning to Dave, I ask, "Where's the roadbed?"

Before long, we're caught up in a long line of buses, and it takes three hours to drive five km. People walk up and down the verge beside us, a few carrying trays with dried corn and peanuts that they sell to bus passengers. At one point, a group of young people get off and walk. Our driver picks them up again after we've passed through the next bad section of road.

We finally reach the head of the line and learn that heavy rain the previous night has brought down another landslide. In front of us is a mudhole, maybe 150 feet across, with some serious looking ruts at the far end. A broken-down bus has been pushed off to one side, and a group of about twenty men stand nearby.

We all watch as the driver of the truck ahead of us takes a run at the mudhole. When the vehicle bogs down, the men spring into action, wading through mud carrying large rocks that they place under the wheels. When the driver still can't gain traction, they gather around and push. After several attempts, the vehicle starts moving and makes it through.

Rubbing his hands together nervously, our driver now shifts into low gear and steers the bus out onto the road. Tromping on the gas pedal, he heads straight into the hole, fighting the steering wheel when mud drags at the tires. Although the bus slows, he keeps it moving and we emerge with a lurch on the far side, to loud cheers from passengers, onlookers, and workers.

The long day ends in a city on a flat plain in the country's south, by which time, we're hot, tired, hungry, and thirsty. Yadav then magically appears, climbing onto the bus at a street corner. He tells us that we're to stay at a guesthouse near the boundary of Royal Chitwan National Park and should stay on the bus. Half an hour later, we're dropped off on the roadside in the middle of nowhere. Yadav disappears in search of a vehicle to take us the last few miles, and we stand around in the hot sun until he returns thirty minutes later with a jeep and driver.

Our welcome at the guesthouse is rather restrained, and instead of being shown to a room, we're seated in the dining hall. After looking at the menu, we each order a beer, and a few minutes later, a young man pedals away on a bicycle. We're still waiting for the beer when he returns half an hour later, and then magically, two small bottles are placed in front of us.

The truth, which is worthy of an episode of Fawlty Towers, comes out when we try to order a meal. With Yadav translating, the young man in charge confesses that most of the staff are off celebrating Dewali. There is no cook, no food, no beer, and no transportation.

We're eventually provided with a meal from a facility down the road, the same one that supplied the beer, and we spend the night in a dingy-looking room with bare concrete floor. It has a bathroom, but all the fittings leak and I'm sprayed with water when I flush the toilet. The mattresses are thin, the beds hard, and neither of us get much sleep. Come morning, we want to leave but have to wait for the owner, who seems to have the only vehicle.

When he finally appears, we're shown a large, bright room with facilities that don't leak and promised hot water in the room and chicken for dinner. We're now both sick again and not up to arguing, so relent. Dave goes back to bed, and next day is running a temperature and coughing up blood.

Our host badgers us daily to take the excursions included in the price of our room, but we put him off until late afternoon of the fourth day. We're then called out to the courtyard, where a rickety two-wheeled cart waits, with a small, tired-looking, bony horse hitched to the front, and a small, wizened man perched on top. We're introduced to our guide, Ram, who directs us to a bench seat behind the driver. We have no idea where we're going.

After we've climbed up and settled ourselves, I see the driver lean forward until he's practically stretched out across the horse's back. Unable to balance the cart this way, he turns and tells me to go sit in the back with Ram. For the next thirty minutes, I see only the dusty, dirt track emerging from beneath the cart wheels.

The road ends at a riverbank, where it was washed away by monsoon rains some years before. We now walk through fields for a kilometer, and pointing to a nearby tower, Ram explains, "These rice farms are in a buffer zone next to the park. A watch is kept from the towers at night, as rhinoceros occasionally leave the park and trample the crops."

When we again come to the river, a herd of water buffalo are crossing from the far side. A few linger in the water and others, sleek and glistening, climb up a bank nearby. A dozen white egrets fly in from upriver, drop low over the water, then circle overhead and land on the backs of the buffalo. Set against a backdrop of green fields and dark hills, with the white peaks of the Himalayan Mountains etched against a blue sky, the scene is the most idyllic that we see in Nepal.

We're poled across the river in a dugout canoe, then walk across a flat, treed meadow on the far side. Seeing the dark shape of an elephant framed against the green grass ahead, I realize that we're visiting the Elephant Breeding Center. But the animal rocks from front to back in a rhythmic motion that doesn't look natural, and when we draw closer, I spot a low post and short chain running to shackles above its front feet. In fact, some twenty elephants are staked off by themselves, and many rock back and forth.

They're smaller than African elephants, with small ears, and the males carry ivory tusks. According to Ram, "The elephants are ridden into the jungle for five hours every day and allowed to forage for food and water." But I'm thinking, *does that mean they stand here for nineteen hours?*

Two babies that are free to wander make the visit worthwhile. The newest is a month old and weighs 300 pounds. He hasn't learned how to use his trunk and tries again and again to pick up a wisp of hay; when he succeeds, he can't find his mouth. He leans up against a post, rubbing his neck and head, but somehow his feet get in the way and he slides down on his rump. While running about the yard, he stumbles into a hole that's a couple of feet deep; he tries to lie down, but it's a just a bit smaller than he is. He totally captures our hearts.

As we pass through a small village on the way back, I see a man in the process of hooking up an illicit power line. He has a wire with two hooks near the end and he attaches them to two cables on a power line across the street from his house. In a neighboring home, a woman sweeps the packed earth around her small yard with a dried bush, then pushes the debris out the back. All the houses are small, with thatched roofs and walls of upright poles coated with mud.

At noon next day, Ram arrives to take us on a hike in the park. It's unpleasantly hot as we walk across a meadow in the buffer zone, and near a village, we see a rhinoceros walking under the trees. It disappears, and when we see it again, the small, adult male is lying in the shade. We notice that its horn appears to be rotting.

Thirty minutes later, we're hiking down a trail in the park and come across a larger rhinoceros feeding in twelve-foot-high grass. Ram won't go past it and tries to make the animal move by cautiously banging on the ground, rustling grasses, and throwing sticks. Half an hour later, we're still there. I spend the time studying the grasses through my binos and catch glimpses of the huge pre-historic-looking head, which is a dirty black, as if the animal had been rooting in mud.

Yadav has accompanied us and now impatiently throws sticks with a little more effort, which produces results. The quiet is suddenly broken by the loud, violent noise of a heavy body rushing through the bush. Absolute silence follows, which is unnerving until the rhino is spotted about twenty feet down the path. Ram then hears more noise and decides there's a second rhino nearby. He wants to try another trail, but Dave and Yadav have had enough and return to the village.

He and I then hike for an hour and a half through the park. The trail is brushed out to about ten feet, but he seems uncomfortable and sets a fast pace. We see lots of rhino tracks and dung, and he points to areas where wild pigs and sloth bears have dug up the ground. We then come to soft mud and see two-day-old tiger tracks. The deep prints of one set are larger than a saucer and have five distinct pads.

On our last excursion, we join a group of tourists for an elephant ride in the park. Each of the twelve animals carries four passengers, who sit on a wooden platform strapped to its back. When our assigned elephant kneels, Dave and I climb up over its rump, then seat ourselves on the platform looking down the backtrail. We're held in by four corner posts with crossbars.

We're in the middle of the line as we start across a grassy flood plain, and I watch the elephants behind sway gently from side to side as they walk. Most pick up water in their trunks when they ford the river and spray their flanks. Our mount then rears up on its hind legs as it lunges up the steep, muddy bank on the far side, and the unexpected movement has me hanging out over the crossbar.

We start down a meandering trail into the shade of the jungle, and suddenly all hell breaks loose. The mahouts start hooting and hollering, and the elephants abruptly change course, crashing noisily into the bush and winding through the trees. I keep an eye out for overhanging branches and catch sight of a rhinoceros that we seem to be pursuing. Our mahout then savagely beats his animal over the head. I think he'd been attempting to cut off the rhino's escape.

We plunge through a pond, and as the circle of elephants tightens, the rhino breaks free. Continuing at a calmer pace, we come to a muddy pool where a female and her calf lie peacefully. A large male is in the process of settling down beside them. After everyone takes pictures, we return to our departure point, having been out maybe an hour.

Our stay at the guesthouse ends on the same note it began, and we can't get away fast enough. We have no water for the last two days and find a full bucket sitting outside our door each morning. The electrical supply is intermittent one night and fails entirely the next. Without an overhead fan, our room is a sauna and the sheets are dripping by morning.

We fly back to Kathmandu, and a few days later, under intense security, board a plane for Bangkok. We check into a good hotel for a week, and I doubt that anyone was ever more appreciative of the comfortable beds, excellent breakfast buffet, pool, gym, and spa. We begin to recover, but Dave's cough lingers for months.

After we return to KLIA, Dave rushes over to the hotel to check on his car. On seeing a valet, he asks, "Is Raymond here?"

The man responds tersely, "No, he's not." Seeing the look on Dave's face, he adds, "Is that your car he has? He's just finished his shift and gone home; he wasn't expecting you until tomorrow."

A call is placed to Raymond and he arrives with the car an hour later. It doesn't look much different than when we dropped it off, except for an additional 4,000 km on the odometer.

CHAPTER 13
THE BOXING DAY TSUNAMI

Life catches up with us in 2004. My dad dies in February and Dave's wife, Teri, passes in July. It's a difficult time for everyone and we spend months in Canada, reconnecting with grieving family members. We're worn out when we return to *Windy Lady* in September, but before long Dave is making plans to drive to Chiang Mai in northern Thailand.

We leave on Christmas Eve and make the long drive up to Songkhla, where we stay in the same hotel as before. We sit out in the balmy night air at the nearby restaurant, enjoying stir-fried vegetables with cashews, chicken pieces and rice. On Christmas Day, we walk the sunny streets and sandy beaches, and this time find many family groups sitting on the sand in a sheltered corner of a bay.

Next morning, the hotel sways slightly while we're preparing to go down for breakfast, but we don't pay much attention. We're on the road an hour later, driving north on a divided highway through rubber tree and oil palm plantations. There's some cloud cover, so the day doesn't get too hot, and just before noon, the front passenger-side tire goes flat.

Dave pulls over onto the shoulder of the divided highway and starts to remove the tire. Within a few minutes, a young man dashes across the road and points back to a building hidden in the trees. With Dave's incredible luck, it's a tire shop. When he's finished, he rolls the tire across the highway. He has to buy a new one, but after it's mounted on the rim, the young man brings it over and puts it on.

Workers have finished for the day when we drive through a long stretch of road construction late that afternoon. An amber traffic light flashes at an intersection, and as we pass beneath it, we hear a loud crash. When plastic and metal debris start raining down, Dave slows the car and moves over two lanes to the right. The only other vehicle on the road is a slow-moving, fully-loaded flat-deck semi that has just entered the highway on the left. As we go by, I see the box of a pickup truck sticking out the backend, the engine and cab are crushed beneath the deck. We saw or heard nothing to indicate that the driver tried to avoid it.

Shaken, we stop for the night in the next large town, but can't find a hotel as we see no English signs. We chase down a Caucasian couple on a sidewalk, and they point us in the direction of theirs. It's been a long day, as we've driven 500 km, and we're tired. I also ache all over and grow increasingly uncomfortable during dinner, so we return to our room and watch a Thai sports channel on TV.

Next morning, Dave turns on the TV as soon as he wakes up and, glancing at it, I wonder what disaster movie is playing. Moments later, I recognize that the channel is CNN and pictures of tsunami waves crashing onto the coastline in Southeast Asia are real. Stunned, we watch as waves strike Phuket and the Krabi coast, realizing we'd been within fifty km when it hit.

We spend the day listening to news reports about death and destruction across the Indian Ocean. The tremor we'd felt in Songkhla the day before had been caused by an 8.9 earthquake off the northern tip of Sumatra in Indonesia. Recognizing that family members could be worried, Dave locates an internet café and sends messages back to Canada. It's late in the day when reports start to trickle in of damage in Malacca Strait. Now worried about *Windy Lady,* Dave phones Admiral Marina but the office is closed. He tries again next morning and is told that everything is fine, there is no need to return.

So, we continue driving north and stay in another small town that night. We walk about, stretching our legs, then eat dinner in a corner of a large food market. I order crab, which I seldom have, and when we return to the hotel, my entire right shoulder is covered in a rash. I assume it's a food allergy, but spend the night sitting up in bed with shooting pains in my neck.

Next day, we make the short drive to Kanchanaburi, the starting point for the 415-km rail line that the Japanese Army built into Burma during WW II. We visit a museum dedicated to the memory of 64,000 Allied prisoners-of-war who had been forced to work on the project. Mistreated and working in atrocious conditions, 16,000 POWs died. Some 200,000 nationals from Burma, Malaya, and Thailand were also conscripted and half of them are believed to be buried along the right-of-way.

We walk upstream along the River Kwai until we come to a railway bridge. (The original was bombed in 1945). In an adjacent war cemetery, the black gravestones of nearly 7,000 POWs stretch across a well-maintained, grassy site. The day is warm and peaceful, and we wander through, noting names, ages, and nationalities. By the time we leave, tears press against the back of my eyes at the enormity of the loss.

The following day, we drive 80 km northwest, park the car, and climb up a steep, well-maintained trail through a bamboo jungle to Hellfire Pass. It's very hot and the countryside is incredibly dry, with brown hills and yellow grass and leaves. We come out on a ridge overlooking a narrow gap dug out of solid rock by men with only basic tools. The gap is maybe three times wider than the width of the track, the walls are 55-feet high, and it stretches for 350 feet.

Returning down the roadbed, we pause at a viewpoint overlooking a shallow valley. The air is warm, still, and quiet, and haze obscures the far hills. I feel confused, unable to reconcile the peacefulness of the countryside with the barbarity that existed here all those years before.

On January 1, 2005, Dave takes me to the hospital. I'd found the heat the day before intolerable and my rash has blistered. I'm examined by a nurse, then a doctor, who declares, "Herpes Zostra". He explains, "It's caused by stress and could reoccur but is not contagious." He prescribes a topical ointment, antihistamines, and painkillers. When I tell him we're on our way to Chiang Mai, he grimaces and warns, "If it gets infected or becomes too painful, you should check yourself into the closest hospital."

I'm directed to the pharmacy, wait fifteen minutes, then receive an invoice that I take to the cashier. After paying, I take the receipt to a third window where I pick up my prescriptions. The total cost is 200+ baht (less than $10 CA) and we're at the hospital under an hour. The ointment brings almost instant relief from the neck pains, and after taking a couple of pills, I sleep through the afternoon and evening. Dave looks up Herpes Zostra in Encarta on his laptop and learns that it's shingles; the rash will take a minimum of two weeks to clear up.

I spend the following day in bed, so Dave has the car serviced, the brakes fixed, and CD joints replaced. The doctor's warning nags at me, as I know infections can be difficult to clear up in the tropics. We start back to Malaysia next day, and I wear one of Dave's cotton shirts as I can't bear to pull on a tee shirt. After seven hours on the road, I'm feeling pretty wretched by the time we stop for the night.

A woman with a bicycle is checking in when we arrive and later appears at the restaurant where we're having dinner. Dave invites her to join us, and we learn that Helen Coony is a Chief Inspector with the Liverpool Police and has taken a year off to bike around the world. She's now cycling from Singapore to Bangkok and complains that headwinds have cut her speed considerably. In the seven months she's been out, she crossed Europe to Turkey, did Israel, and cycled from Bombay to Delhi.

Next day, we drive down the west coast of the Malay Peninsula, passing through an area hit hard by the tsunami. Heavy equipment works in the broken ruins of seaside resorts and villages, cleaning up debris and still looking for bodies eight days on. Several cars are piled in one location, apparently tumbled over and over by the waves. The road is set back from the beach nearly half a kilometer, and palm trees dot the gentle slope down to the sea. Beneath them, the ground has been scoured, but they stand untouched. The lower floor of shops in a long building on the upper side of the road has been flooded, and a line of garbage left by the waves is piled up behind it.

We drive through a small town that has been designated an Emergency Center, and the workers all wear face masks. As we pass a large, roofed-over area surrounded by a high fence, I glimpse rows of bulletin boards covered with photographs. Later, we learn that 1,800 bodies were stored in refrigeration units here, awaiting identification.

Resorts backing onto high hills on the west coast of the island of Phuket took the full brunt of the waves. The beach road at Patong is full of potholes and piles of debris block the side streets, with more piles in front of empty shops. People mill about in apparent confusion, but register at a control center and are assigned areas of beach to clear, as every high tide deposits more debris.

After returning to Admiral Marina, we learn that people were worried about us. One woman reported us missing to the Canadian Embassy in Bangkok and explains, "I was told that you'd been in touch with family in Canada; that they'd been contacted by your sister Pat." Hearing my sister's name from the mouth of a stranger while standing on a dock in Port Dickson makes me realize just how close we'd been to this tragedy. Pat later tells me that she heard a radio announcement asking anyone with information about travelers in areas hit by the tsunami to contact a phone number, so she did.

We listen to English news reports from BBC and CNN and hear of the efforts being made to find and identify the bodies of missing western tourists. We hear little about the villages that disappeared in Indonesia, where survivors lost families, friends, homes, and livelihoods. Left with nothing, they need to rebuild lives in a devastated landscape, where just clearing up debris could take months.

It's a disaster of unbelievable proportions, with 230,000 people killed in Indonesia, Thailand, Malaysia, India, and Sri Lanka. Countless others were left homeless, with livelihoods destroyed. I grow increasingly unsettled as the full scope of the tragedy sinks in, so many lives lost! Chandran, who works at the marina, tells me that local people have quit eating fish, too many bodies in the sea.

I've long recognized that Canadians are sheltered from many of the tragedies that strike other parts of the world. I wonder how many of us appreciate that fact. This time western tourists did lose their lives, but survivors were able to go home to support systems that were intact. For Dave and me, it's a reminder of how quickly life can change and draws us together.

Exactly two weeks after visiting the doctor, I'm able to pull a tee shirt over my shoulder again. I now puzzle over why I came down with shingles. We'd been back on *Windy Lady* for three months, and I'd had no symptoms when we left Admiral Marina on Christmas Eve. The first symptoms appeared on Boxing Day. Had the tsunami caused a disturbance in the air, silent screams carried on the wind?

CHAPTER 14
TOURING IN THAILAND

Two months later, we pack up the car and set off for Thailand once more. With trees alongside the highway in flower, it's a beautiful time to visit. One variety with cascading yellow flowers is especially eye-catching. Bright clusters of red, orange, white, and yellow bougainvillea also brighten the villages.

We spend the first night in Hat Yai but don't stray far from our hotel, as the previous weekend Muslim fundamentalists had set off a bomb that killed two people and injured fifty. The following day, we drive through plantations of rubber trees, oil palms, coconut palms, and pineapples. The highway is busy, and large trucks carry wood, palm fruit, machinery, mushrooms, fish, and prawns, while pickups are piled high with pineapples.

On Day 3, we come within forty km of Bangkok, and traffic is heavy and slow, with many large trucks headed into the capital. It's not yet noon but very hot, and thick haze hides the sun. The afternoon grows hotter as we drive northwest through rice farms in the flat delta lands of the Chao Phraya River. We detour off the main route, and when we stop for gas, I feel eyes watching. Turning, I see several people looking at me from the back of a pickup truck. I smile and wave and they respond delightedly. In fact, the Thai people that we have contact with are all friendly and curious.

We stop for the night in Tak, a small city of 50,000 in central Thailand, 430 km northwest of Bangkok. Having driven over 2,000 km in three days, we stay over a day and spend hours walking beside the Mae Nam Ping River. It's quite wide, with knee-deep, clear water, and probably controlled. Several trees along it bear the cascading yellow flowers that I admire, which I think are Thailand's national flower, ratchaphruek.

We visit a shrine to King Taksin the Great and are intrigued by the large statues of horses and elephants that stand behind it. I'm even more fascinated by the many, small ornamental figures placed at their feet. We then linger in the shade of the trees, enjoying a cool breeze off the water, and watch the people who visit the shrine. Each person lights a stick of incense, places a tribute on a silver platter, and takes a flower lei inside. Feeling an urge to do the same, I select a lei, make a donation, and remove my shoes before walking up a few stairs. Several people kneel before the alter inside, and not wanting to intrude, I place the lei off to one side amongst many others and leave.

We're the objects of many curious glances when we later stroll through a busy wet market. I nod and smile at the women who meet my eyes and they all smile back. At dinner, our waitress tells us that daytime temperatures of 42-43°C are normal, and that the hot chili sauce we like so much is called *nam plaa pik*.

Next day, we drive west toward the border with Myanmar (formerly Burma). We're soon passing through dry hills where slim, bare tree trunks stand out starkly against brown slopes. As the road climbs higher, the air cools a bit and plantations of pine trees appear. In spite of a few wrong turns, we're in the town of Maesot by noon. Five km farther on is the small river marking the border.

Dave parks the car near the Friendship Bridge and we peer across at Myawadi, Myanmar, but see only tired-looking buildings. A few people trickle across the bridge, clearing with authorities at both ends, but many more wade across the stream. They carry bundles, and we think that they're going to the Thai border market, where Burmese vendors are permitted to set up stalls. At least, the nearby border guards ignore them. The market is housed in a building a few feet from the river, and when we stroll through it, we see jewelry, clothing, blankets, and guitars, as well as handguns, knives, and throwing stars.

After spending the night in Maesot, our route takes us 150 km north along the border. We're not surprised to be stopped at an army checkpoint, as mortar rockets sometimes fall in Thailand during fighting on the other side of the border. Our Malaysian license plates prove to be a novelty, but after questioning, we're waved through. Minutes later, we're stopped at a second roadblock.

The road then enters a narrow valley, and as we round a corner, a primitive village comes into view. The houses have high, thatched roofs, walls of upright poles, and sit almost on top of each other. They're squeezed onto a narrow strip of land sloping up from the road to a steep hill behind. The homes go on and on for nearly two km, with a few strands of barbwire separating them from the road.

I suspect thousands of people live here and can't imagine what they do for food, water, or sanitation. Only after clearing through two army checkpoints on the other side, does it occur on us that the village is a refugee camp. Some 100,000 refugees are said to live along this border, most being members of hill tribes who've fled the violence in Myanmar.

The winding, paved road now leads across dry hillsides that bake in the sun, and occasionally we see a small settlement. In a pleasant river valley, the road turns away from the border and immediately deteriorates. We drive up, down, and around through a mountain range for the next two hours, then follow a shady stream down through a shallow valley on the far side. Vehicles are parked beside it for miles, with kids splashing in the shallows or floating on tubes, and adults lying under thatched roofs on small rafts anchored near shore.

After driving 450 km, we arrive in Chiang Mai, the country's second largest city. This ancient capital of the Lanna Kingdom was founded in 1296, and for 500 years was enriched by caravans that traveled through on their way to and from a seaport on the Indian Ocean. On the outward journey, traders brought silk, opium, tea, dried fruit, lacquer ware, and ponies. On the return trip, they carried gold, copper, cotton, betel nut, tobacco, and ivory. Many artisans from China, northern Burma, and Laos settled here during that time.

We spend the next few days visiting a few of the city's many Buddhist temples. Wat Chiang Man dates back to 1296 also, and our guide explains, "*Man* means strong, and this temple is associated with elephants." At Wat Phra Sing, a large hall built prior to 1400 is the attraction. It has a high ceiling supported by wooden columns, with brightly painted murals on the walls, and is airy and cool.

Wat Chedi Luang impresses me most, as behind the golden spires of a newer temple can be seen the earthen dome of a chedi (stupa) built in 1441. Halfway up the tall, 600-year-old brick and stucco structure, a line of badly eroded elephants is in the process of being replaced, and five cement animals now join the one original.

Wat Chaimongkon sits on the bank of the Mae Ping River and has three distinct temples, Thai, Burmese, and Chinese. In a corner of the compound, small cages hold tiny birds and several buckets contain writhing eels. We watch as a woman hands money to a monk, then takes a bucket containing an eel down to the nearby dock. She reads a prayer aloud from a piece of paper provided before releasing the eel.

At Wat Kate, we pause near an open-sided building where many people are gathered. A man approaches Dave and invites us inside, then points toward a corner where piles of flowers rest on a coffin and tells us that his brother has died. An older woman brings over two plastic chairs and cold drinks, and two young monks, 10-12 years old, keep us company.

The mourners tie a soft cotton rope to the coffin, and a monk holds the free end as he leads a procession to a pickup truck, where the coffin is placed in the back. The rope is arranged on top the cab, and flowers and a photograph of the deceased are placed around the coffin. Monks riding on top throw firecrackers in front and on both sides as the vehicle leaves, while smoke from a pot of incense wafts upwards. They are going to a crematorium, and several cars filled with mourners follow behind.

On a very hot and humid afternoon, we hire a car and driver to take us to the Gem Factory, but resist the efforts made to sell us gems. We do spend money at the Carpet Store, where Indians from Kashmir tell us, "We left our country because tourists don't come." Along the way, we visit the Three Kings Monument, which honors the three northern Thai-Lao Kings most associated with early Chiang Mai history.

Only a few traces of the old city wall remain, but sections of moat are still intact and we drive by the east moat on the way back to our hotel. To our astonishment, a long line of men and women stand beside it, throwing buckets of water on passing vehicles. We then see that people in the backs of pickup trucks are throwing water back. Everyone is dripping wet and the pavement glistens. On other streets, people with buckets, pans, hoses, and tubs are grouped around taps, and I count up to six people in the backs of pickups scooping water out of barrels.

They are celebrating Songkran, which officially starts next day, on April 13. Traditionally, the celebration ran for three days; the last day of the old year, a day of transition, and New Year's Day. People visited temples, listened to sermons (merit-making), sprinkled lustral water on sacred Buddha images, and poured it over the hands of monks in a gesture of reverence. Now, celebrations in Chiang Mai seem to extend over two weekends and everyone is a target.

Chapter 15
Celebrating Songkran

We set out warily next morning, first visiting the Flower Market, where shops are overflowing with bundles of flowers and leis. The small, white, fragrant flowers in the leis are sampaquita (a variety of jasmine) and appear similar to those used by Hindus in Malaysia. We then walk down the dry side of the moat, where a few revelers respectfully sprinkle handfuls of water on our arms, or pour bowlfuls over our shoulders. Soon, however, it's an occasional bucket down the back of the neck, some of it icy cold. By the time we return to the hotel, water runs from our clothing, and the passports and money I carry in a concealed pouch are soaked.

Activities along the moat seem to start about 1000 and continue until dark (1900), with all ages participating. Gangs armed with squirt guns roam the streets, a few on foot, but many in the backs of pickups or tuk-tuks. Water streams over tailgates and pools in every depression on the road, and motorcyclists and tourists seem to be high value targets.

Water throwing continues along the highway and in villages when we drive north to Chiang Rai next day. Our hotel there directs throbbing rock music out onto the street, and attracts an endless parade of pickups and their hooting, hollering passengers. By dinner time, water barrels are empty and pickup boxes now bounce up and down as young people dance. Quiet comes with night fall.

We escape the revelers for a few hours next morning, when we drive sixty km northwest into the border country between Thailand, Myanmar, and Laos, an area once known as the Golden Triangle. The road leads through narrow valleys in rugged hill country, then climbs up steep slopes and winds along narrow ridge tops. On hillsides below, tea plants grow where opium poppies once thrived. We're stopped at an army checkpoint and a photo taken of our car. A mortar has hit a refugee camp in Myanmar and 1,800 women and children are expected to cross the border.

We stop in the village of Doi Mae Salong, a ramshackle cluster of buildings that stretches beside the road on a wide ridge top. The village was established by refugees who fled to Burma after the 1949 Chinese Revolution; they were then expelled by the Burmese government in 1961. Cut off from the rest of the world in their mountain villages, they and their pony caravans became involved in the opium trade.

Wandering down the street, we look in shops, then enter a tearoom. When a Chinese man behind the counter offers us tea, I enthusiastically accept. It's served in small porcelain cups in which a longer, slender cup has been inverted. Intrigued, I lift the inner one and aromatic tea runs out into the second. The man explains that the snifter retains a film of aroma in its bottom, identifying the variety and quality of the tea.

A dozen people sit on the floor behind us, stuffing tea leaves into bags, and an older woman stands at a large scale, carefully weighing each one. More leaves are drying on woven-mat trays on trolleys in a back room, where there is also a drying oven. A rather scruffy-looking European man sits beside us, his long hair tied at the nape of his neck, and a small suitcase and backpack placed nearby. After telling us that he's a Czech and has bought 85 kilos of tea, he explains, "It's my order being packaged. I placed it two days ago and the pickers finished harvesting about 1100 yesterday. The leaves were then dried for 24 hours and finished off in the kiln."

By midday, we're in Mai Sai on the northern border with Myanmar. I now see up to fifteen young people riding in the backs of pickups. We have difficulty locating a hotel in the rabbit warren of lanes leading off the highway, and when we do, the parking lot is bedlam. Vehicles are parked two and three deep, and Dave is told to leave the car out of gear, so it can be pushed around if necessary.

Our hotel is only half a block from a small river marking the border, and we soon join the throng of visitors crossing the bridge. We stay dry until we're halfway across, then Customs officials pour buckets of water down the backs of our necks. The first pail is icy cold. In a small building at the far end, we exchange our passports and $10 US each for visitor permits, which come carefully wrapped in a plastic bag.

Rejoining the stream of tourists, we're carried into a mob of touts and tuk-tuk drivers milling about on the street in Tachileik, Myanmar. Some hold up pictures of long-necked women and temples, and while I'm looking around, Dave disappears behind a flow of tourists turning down into a Chinese market. When I see him a few minutes later, he's following a slim, rather shabby, dirty fellow up the street.

I catch up to them at the entrance to a deserted wet market, where the man leads us through narrow, rubbish-strewn aisles. In an open space where several aisles meet, we stumble onto a group of young men dancing to rock music and pouring water on each other. We meekly stand when they rush over with their buckets of water, then leave a trail of water behind when we walk on.

Exiting at the back of the market, we climb up a low hill to a large, gold-painted pagoda that overlooks the town (a replica of a gold-plated temple in Rangoon). As we wander about, admiring the views and studying a line of statues, a few street vendors try to sell us postcards and small birds. No one else is in sight. Our guide now informs Dave that a village of long-necked women is a fifteen-minute walk away. I don't like the looks of the fellow, so am not interested, but minutes later we're following him down a deserted highway into the countryside.

Before long, we hear a boom box and see a group of young men dancing. They've taken over half the road, so we cross to the other side to avoid them. We do the same for the next group, but a third is much larger and spreads across the entire road. When we attempt to walk by, eight young men rush over to confront us.

They're led by a tall transvestite wearing a bra under a t-shirt, a long skirt, and heavy boots. Offering the surprised Dave a hand across a mud puddle, he leads him back to the dancing on the far side of the road. I'm ignored, so tag along behind, then watch as he's drawn into the center of a mob of yelling, foot-stomping young men waving fists over their heads. (I feel sure their high spirits are not entirely natural.)

I'm now pushed toward him, and as our eyes meet, he shrugs, clasps his hands over his head, and shuffles his feet to the beat of the music. I do the same. When the music stops, we're not allowed to leave; we must stay for one more dance. It's not really a choice. After another repetition of the Burmese Stomp, the young men bow and repeatedly say, "Thank you, thank you," and we're free to go.

When we arrive at the village gate, a guide escorts us up a low hill to an open-sided shelter, where two long-necked women work on small looms in the shadows. The women are Padong, a branch of the Karen, one of the hill tribes. Traditionally, the hill people were farmers and grew rice, corn, and opium; their beliefs included animism and ancestor worship. They are often described as fourth-world people, having fled from cultural oppression in China, Tibet, Myanmar, and Laos.

Our guide points to the closest woman, who sits about six feet away, and explains, "She is 59 years old and has twenty gold rings around her neck."

I immediately feel a sense of kinship, as we're much the same age, but am struck dumb when I study her. The neck rings push her shoulders down and chin up, and her body is so thin, her head so small, that I feel like an elephant by comparison. I'm overwhelmed when I think of how different our life experiences have been, then feel intrusive, as if staring at someone with burn scars. Unable to ask even one question of our guide, all I can do is buy one of her scarves.

We meet two girls, ages twelve and thirteen, who wear nine and ten neck rings. The first ones were put on when they were seven years old, and three rings were added five years later. We're told the practice is dying out. Several Akha women and girls now join us, posing in elaborate headdresses with beads, feathers and dangling silver ornaments. I see no signs of daily life, no cooking pots or small children, so assume this area is for tourists.

As it's now getting late, we walk to a nearby resort hotel, hoping to find a ride back to the border. Although it's practically deserted, our guide manages to track down two motorcycle taxis. Dave climbs on one, while our guide climbs on behind me on the other. The drivers slow almost to a stop as we approach the revelers, who show no mercy, dumping buckets of water over our heads. The first one is icy cold.

The gauntlet grows more intense as we enter the town and continues to the bridge. Dave then has to deal firmly with our guide, who suddenly gets greedy. When we reach the hotel, water runs from my shoes, drips from my clothes, and my document pouch and camera case are both soaked through.

Next day, we drive in a south-easterly direction through scenic countryside along the border. The water wars continue, with tubs of water stationed at the ends of driveways. By noon, we're in Sop Ruak, where food stalls, souvenir shops, and tour buses line the bank of the Mekong River. Dave parks the car near a large plaza, where we join a crowd of tourists admiring giant statues of elephants and a towering Buddha.

We buy tickets for a river tour at a kiosk, then are provided with life jackets and escorted down long, steep stairs to a narrow dock. Taking seats in a long-tailed boat, we're soon cruising upstream, with a pleasant breeze offsetting the midday heat. A few minutes later, we come to a bend in the river and our guide explains, "China is 200 km to the north, that's Myanmar on the left, and Laos on the right." Looking around, I recall reading that the Mekong River flows through six different nations and provides livelihoods for sixty million people. (It's said to account for up to 25% of global fishing.)

After crossing the river, our guide turns the boat downstream and opens up the engine. Ten minutes later we come alongside a dock on an island, where a sign reads "Welcome to Don Sao, Laos". Once ashore, we're directed to a booth where we buy permits that read "I am here!" Along with the usual tourist fodder, small shops sell liter bottles that have snakes curled up inside with the end of the tail stuck between the jaws.

Before leaving Sop Ruak, we tour through a museum called the House of Opium. Only a few years before, the Golden Triangle accounted for over 70% of opium sold globally. Thailand has now practically eliminated the cultivation of poppies, while Laos and Myanmar have drastically reduced it. We're curious as to how that came about.

We learn that the Thais built a road into their sector late in the 1980s and implemented a crop-substitution program. An intense effort was also made to educate the public to the serious consequences of using narcotics, not only to their physical and mental well-being, but also to society and the national economy. The program's success is largely credited to support from the Royal Family, whom Thais revered.

Stark exhibits portray the human cost of drug addiction, and one section covers the devastating results of the Opium Wars in the mid-19th century, when Britain and France forced the trade on China. Because the trade generates such huge profits, it's described as an unresolved problem. Even governments are involved, and at one time, opium sales provided 25% of tax revenues for the government of Siam. The government of India is said to still control opium harvesting and sales in that country.

We now drive through a nine-km-long battle zone to Chiang Saen, where townspeople join in the fray. We're stopped at an intersection by a parade and have front row seats as a large image of the Buddha drifts past on a float. Two huge elephants follow, then more floats with banners and images of the Buddha. Columns of people walk behind, with different sections dressed in different colors and costumes, including hats and umbrellas for protection against the water thrown by spectators.

Next morning, we drive south through hills covered by scrub forest. The stands of teak that once grew there are long gone, and logging is now banned. The water wars then engulf the highway for a fifth day, and when we arrive in the large town of Phrae at midday, traffic is backed up all over the place. After taking a circuitous route through the streets, we find a hotel where we hide for the afternoon.

Traffic noticeably eases about 1600, so we venture out for a look-see. Big mistake! All the pickup trucks are parked in front of food and drink stalls in the next block. After another block, we're trapped in a solid line of traffic that carries us into the old city. We end up in the middle of a parade and are directed out of it at a traffic circle. I now see two young men wrestling on the sidewalk, and an older man grips the top of a whiskey bottle threateningly as he exchanges words with a fellow with a tattooed back.

Traffic comes to a stop near the old city moat, and when the line creeps forward again, we're surrounded by groups of partying young men. Everyone openly drinks beer and hard liquor, and up to twenty people sit in the backs of pickups. We draw constant attention and people pour water on the car and wave. It's a bit overwhelming.

We follow one pickup long enough to establish a relationship with a woman sitting in the back. She drinks whiskey with three men, while four kids dip out the dregs of water in a barrel. All are soaking wet. The woman waves at us, offers her glass, then climbs down and walks back to Dave's window and offers him a drink. He refuses, explaining that he's driving, although that doesn't seem to be a problem for anyone else.

A few blocks from our hotel, traffic at a main intersection is gridlocked. A policeman tries to sort it out, but blows his whistle ineffectively. He stops and watches as a man approaches with a bucket of water, then stands passively as it's poured down his back. But he turns and walks away when two other men seem to offer advice.

They start jockeying vehicles about in the middle of the intersection and manage to clear a lane for through traffic. The policeman reappears, incoming traffic from the left starts to move, and within minutes, we're through the intersection. Two minutes later, we're back at the hotel, having driven maybe five km in two hours.

Next day we head south, taking nine hours to drive 770 km through holiday traffic to the resort city of Hua Hin. We stay here for two days and spend hours sitting under a beach umbrella, with a strong breeze off the Gulf of Thailand offsetting the heat and humidity. We attend a Thai boxing competition one night, an amateur event held in a small local hall, and participants in one bout start by doing set exercises to music.

Truck traffic is heavy as we return down the Malay Peninsula, and dozens of pickups carry up to twenty people in the back, mostly men sitting on luggage. I assume they're seasonal workers going down to the fields of southern Thailand. After one more night on the road, we're back in Port Dickson.

CHAPTER 16
WINDY LADY

During our years offshore, we are often asked, "Of all the places you've been, which did you most enjoy?" Our answer was always the same, "Wherever we happen to be at the time." That was true I think because *Windy Lady* was our home. From the very first day, living aboard suited us, and wherever she was, that's where we were happiest.

That's not to say that living on a boat in the tropics doesn't have its challenges. Not having air conditioning is a big one. We've soon acquired two large fans that follow us from berth to salon to galley 24 hours/day. When power to the dock goes off for several hours, which happens a few times, I practically melt into a puddle. Mossies are not a problem, as men in protective gear occasionally fog around the resort, but I keep companionway and hatches covered with mosquito netting to keep out the black flies. We still haul the boat each year as the marina has a hardstand, then clean the hull, apply new bottom paint, and do repairs.

As live-a-boards, we use the showers and toilets in the resort's pool facility, which isn't air conditioned and has no cold water. It gets pretty steamy inside when humidity is high, and we then shower beside the boat using a garden hose. I wait until dark and scrub down under an old bathing suit, and sometimes the water is pretty hot.

Cruising boats passing in the strait frequently stop, so we're able to keep up with old friends and make new ones. Stories about piracy in local waters are soon replaced by those about the increasing threat of kidnapping on the Red Sea route. I have to quit reading local newspapers after the US invades Iraq, as large pictures of injured and grief-stricken women fill several pages every day. They are horrific, and I'm not surprised that local sentiment is against the war.

A pair of sun birds build a nest in the cockpit when we're away one spring. Eggs are in the nest when we return, so we live with the tiny birds until the babies can fly. The nest hangs from a line above the seat where Dave usually sits, and the male bird won't come near if he is there. Instead, it cheeps monotonously from a safe distance, which doesn't bother Dave but drives me mad, and I have to intervene. When the babies fly, we quickly remove the nest, as the parents have several broods each year.

When the heat causes me to give up my daily walks, I take up Tai Chi again. I find books and CDs in a bookstore in KL, then practice beside the pool where the water mirrors the shadows and reflections of date palms and frangipani. When the pool area grows busy, I go out at dawn and do Tai Chi on a section of dock near *Windy Lady.* When the dock moves too much, I find a secluded corner on the clubhouse veranda.

One morning, I've just started working when a dozen people come around the corner. I turn away, following the form, and when I turn back, they are all lined up in front of me, following my lead. After completing that form, I move onto a second and two of them continue to follow. When we finish, they all put their hands together in front of their chests and bow. Utterly humbled, I bow back. Without having said a word, we then go our separate ways. (I believe they were part of a tour group from Singapore.)

Over time, the staff at the marina become friends and we learn a bit about their lives. Chandran, who is Tamil, complains that he is constantly harassed in the frequent police roadblocks. (We are just waved through.) We also hear of people caught up in new housing estates that are never finished; they end up having to make mortgage payments while still paying rent.

The Chinese woman in the office explains that she pays for tutors for her two young boys. A Chinese man later tells us that the public school system switched from teaching in English to Bahasa Malaysu a few years earlier. He then confides, "While that held my kids back for a year or two, they worked hard and are now back on top."

Living in Port Dickson is cheaper than anywhere else we've been, so we occasionally treat ourselves to a comfortable hotel and shopping in KL, especially over Christmas. We go in once for Chinese New Year, and I am fascinated by the lion dancers and follow them from shop to shop.

When we've driven as far from Port Dickson as we reasonably can, we take to the air. It's an easy transition, as we've flown back to Canada many times to see family. Two trips from Australia actually took us around the world, not something we particularly wanted to do, but as often happened, that was just how things worked out...

CHAPTER 17
A HONG KONG EDUCATION

The Y2K phenomenon is a hot topic when we're booking our flight from Brisbane to Vancouver in November of 1999. For months, pundits have been reporting that all the world's computers would crash at midnight on December 31, and that airplanes would fall out of the sky. Of course, come the end of the year, computers don't fail and planes take off and land as scheduled.

In any case, we reschedule our booking when Dave receives word that his daughter is getting married in Cancun, Mexico, in April. Trying to find flights to Cancun from Brisbane has our travel agent pulling out his hair, and he finally asks, "Would you consider an around-the-world route, maybe stopping over in a couple of cities on the way?" After poring through travel magazines and studying costs, we select a couple of cities where we'd like to spend a week or so.

We fly out of Brisbane in late February and land in Hong Kong 8.5 hours later. After making our way to the lower-level train station, we run into our first problem. We don't have the correct change to buy tickets from the vending machines and can't read the instructions. We wander around, looking for someplace to get change, and might be there still if a middle-aged Chinese man hadn't noticed our lost looks. Taking the time to stop and ask, he points us toward a bank of machines where one does make change.

We have no problem getting off at Kowloon station, then lug our bags down to a taxi rank, where the concierge waves up a cab and asks, "Where are you staying?" We tell him the name of our hotel, and he instructs the driver in Cantonese. We're then whisked away through drab, narrow streets lined with three-to-four-story buildings. Every block looks the same, with Chinese characters on signs in lower-floor shop windows and long banners stretching across overhead. We have absolutely no idea where we're going.

After a twenty-minute ride, our driver stops in front of a hotel. As the meter reads $32.60, I give him a $50 bill. He hands me back three coins, and expecting at least one bill, I continue to hold out my hand. Giving me a disgusted look, he adds another forty cents. I am more than a little embarrassed when I examine the coins, as one of them is worth $10. *I wasn't aware that any country had a $10 coin.*

With the change in time, we're awake early next morning and leave the hotel at 0700. As we start walking, the narrow street is dark and dreary, with heavy, black clouds hanging low overhead and puddles from overnight rain dotting the sidewalk. There are few pedestrians and no vehicles, presumably because it's Sunday, and I find myself thinking, *I've entered tunnels that looked more inviting.*

My sense of direction then abandons me for the first time ever, and when we can't find English signs at intersections, we stay on the same street as our hotel. We eventually cross Nathan Road, the main thoroughfare in Kowloon, and after walking several more blocks start to see a few pedestrians.

We now round a corner and find ourselves in a wet market. Stalls are piled high with many varieties of vegetables, and there are cages of live birds and tubs with eels and fish. Around the next corner, stacks of crates contain live chickens. We stop to watch a man hack the shell off a turtle; he then cuts the meat in half and cleans it. When the market becomes busier, I realize we're the only Caucasians in sight and start to feel uncomfortable.

We look for a restaurant on the walk back, but nothing is open. Our hotel has a breakfast buffet that closes ten minutes after we return, so we scrape up what's left of the fresh fruit, sausages, and scrambled eggs, while waiters clear away around us. After hurriedly eating, I put the bill on my credit card. When

Dave later sees the receipt for $193 HK (roughly $40 CA), he is outraged and vows never to return.

We walk in a different direction that afternoon and now find small street signs in English at intersections, which makes me feel more comfortable. The sky is also brighter and my sense of direction returns. We're soon walking down a block where every shop sells shoes. In the next block, it's luggage. White wedding gowns appear in window after window in the third, which doesn't seem very Chinese to me.

In spite of the cool temperature (11 degrees C), large arrays of cut flowers spill out of open shop fronts on Flower Market Road. The vivid colors are in sharp contrast to the grey sky and dark clothing worn by everyone on the street. A few blocks farther on is the Bird Park, where cages with solitary birds hang on the bare branches of small trees. The men who brought them stand nearby and visit (walking a bird is a pastime for men). We return via the Ladies Market, where portable stalls sit in front of storefront shops. Dave tries to barter for a leather belt, but prices are fixed.

After dark, we go out again, looking for somewhere to have supper. All the stores appear to be open, and sidewalks are crowded with young people, most on cell phones. I soon feel trapped, as I can't see past the people walking next to me, and they breath down my neck and sneeze in my face. Being taller, Dave is oblivious to my discomfort and seems prepared to walk all night.

We study menus taped to restaurant windows, but none are in English, and other than a MacDonald's, we see no food that looks familiar. In fact, some odors drifting down the street are downright objectionable. When I can't take anymore, we return to the hotel where I make supper out of some almonds and a tasty Californian orange bought from a street vendor. Dave doesn't eat.

Next morning, I go down to breakfast on my own, as Dave scornfully declares, "I'd rather fast than put up with another meal like the one we had yesterday!" And he does—for another thirty hours! Hunger then gets the better of him and he disappears for two hours. He returns with two small loaves of sweetbread and confesses to buying a sausage from a street vendor.

The following day, we look for a noodle restaurant that we passed on the first day, and I'm now sufficiently comfortable in the city to walk directly to it. We stand outside the window and watch as a young cook kneads a ball of dough. Stretching it out, he grasps the ends and tosses the middle upwards, stretching it out farther. He doubles it, then repeats the process countless times, and ends up with dozens of long, thin noodles stretched between the ends. Cutting the noodles off, he throws them into a pot, but looks exhausted as he cleans up. We return to the café for supper that night and enjoy it immensely; it's our first real meal in four days.

The next night, we spot a simple English menu taped to the window of a Vietnamese café. We enter and order a meal that we enjoy, although neither of us is adept with chopsticks. Half way through, the waitress brings Dave a fork. We conclude that there is only one on the premises. We now notice that customers don't linger over their meals and decide we're probably taking too long. In the days that follow, we learn that all restaurants can produce a bilingual menu, if asked. For breakfast, we drink coffee in our room, while eating oranges and small, flat loaves of sweetbread.

In spite of frequent rain, we walk down to the Star ferry terminal at the end of Nathan Street on three different occasions. High buildings line both sides of the street and with heavy traffic that includes many double-decker buses, exhaust fumes are almost overwhelming on occasion. The ferry ride across the channel to Hong Kong is then rough, as a constant stream of tugs and freighters stir up a three-foot chop.

During our first crossing, heavy clouds hide the mountain behind the city and wreathe the tops of taller skyscrapers along the waterfront. We find permanent stalls selling charms and chops in the shadow of a downtown tower and buy chops, which have Chinese characters that are supposed to represent our names. We climb up the steep streets behind until we come to a covered escalator, which we ride up until clouds obscure the view. The only way down is via a steep staircase that never seems to end.

We take the train back to Mongkok Station and on the street outside see a pair of dirty, bare feet sticking out of a pile of trash. Farther on, someone wrapped in a blanket lies on the ground. The streets are again dark and drab, and small shrines beside shop entrances provide the only bright spots. Colored in red and gold, they include a small bowl of oranges and a few sticks of incense.

When we exit the ferry ramp on our second visit to Hong Kong, we're approached by a middle-aged Chinese man, who exclaims, "Excuse me, I overheard you speaking on the boat. Are you Canadians? I have a brother in Vancouver!" After chatting for a few minutes, he queries, "Where are you off to today?"

Dave responds, "We're going to take the bus to Stanley. Do you know where we can get change?"

Shaking his head, the man starts digging in his backpack and declares, "You can't get change anywhere. The shopkeepers line up at the banks in the morning and take all the cash." Pulling a plastic jar from his pack and searching through his pockets, he comes up with $20 in coins, which he wants to give us. Dave thanks him but swaps them for a $20 bill. Before going on his way, the man shows us where to catch the bus.

Hundreds of high-rise apartment buildings line the winding road through the mountains, and the town of Aberdeen seems to consist only of tall buildings. I see no single-family dwellings anywhere. On the far side of the island, we're dropped off near a tourist market in Stanley, then walk through a maze of narrow lanes and small shops clustered around the edge of the bay. Prices are double what we paid for similar items in Hong Kong, and customers are mostly Caucasian. We find a spot to sit near the beach and study a small junk rocking gently at anchor nearby. Across the bay, on the horizon, a number of ships can be seen at anchor.

We finally have a sunny day for our third crossing. This time, I notice a middle-aged Chinese couple sitting in front of us on the ferry, as the woman holds a camera that is taped together. To our surprise, they approach us on the far side and the man asks, "Are you familiar with Hong Kong?" Hesitatingly, Dave replies, "Well, we've been here a week and have learned a bit about the place."

The man continues, "We'd like to take the bus to Stanley, do you know where the bus stop is?" Dave happily shares knowledge acquired just days before, and after chatting briefly, the man heaves a heavy sigh and describes their strange predicament, "We're from San Diego and speak no Chinese, although people here think we should."

We now make our way to the tram that goes up Victoria Peak. The tracks run at a 45-degree angle to the high towers in front of them and climb 800 feet in eight minutes. At the top, we admire the sparkling view of city and harbor and are astonished by the sheer number of very tall buildings. We descend via the Old Peak Road, which is very long and steep. Sidewalks are crowded as we walk back to the hotel, and I notice that it no longer bothers me when someone jostles my arm.

One day, we take a train from Mongkong Station to Sheung Shui in the New Territories, which is a mile from the Chinese border and as close as we can get without visas. We mostly see high rise buildings and low, grey clouds on route. Rain falls steadily while we're there, and we walk through puddles on narrow streets that look much like those in Kowloon. But I'm uncomfortable, as people stare openly at my blue eyes and blond hair. We stay only an hour, then catch a train back.

On our last day, we walk for half an hour through pouring rain to the jade market, which is set up in a vacant lot. Tarps spread above the stalls keep us dry as we wander through, but venders stand silently until Dave asks, "How much?" They then quickly punch numbers into small handheld calculators, which they thrust in his face. The price is in Hong Kong dollars. If he shakes his head, he's handed the calculator with gestures indicating that he should enter an amount.

At one stall, he selects a pendant, bracelet, and two good luck charms, then turns away laughing when the woman punches in $80. She quickly drops the price to $20; he pays $10. When he shows an interest in a blocky jade Buddha, she tells him, "Worth $600. For you, I give special price $400." I then watch, fascinated, as a rapport develops between them. Dave enjoys the process immensely and pays $250.

We're there two hours, and after bartering with several people, he sees the same Buddha at another stall and asks, "How much?" This woman also starts at $600 but sells it to him for $150, at which point he realizes he has much to learn. I notice that they all try to persuade him to make a counter offer, and if he does, a deal is usually made, as they'll come down to that price rather than lose the sale.

Chapter 18
A Graduate Degree in Istanbul

The next morning, we're off to the airport for a twelve-hour flight to Istanbul. Our route takes us around Vietnamese air space, passes high over Calcutta and Delhi, then comes surprisingly close to Mt Everest as it skirts the Tibetan tablelands. Cabin service is excellent and the flight smooth, with headwinds averaging 200 km/hr. But I'm very uncomfortable, as the air is dry and irritates my nasal passages, lips, and even eyes.

We land at 2130 local time (0230 our time) and go directly to the designated counter to obtain visitor visas. Dave provides a credit card to pay, but the officer in charge shakes his head and demands $90 US in cash. We're stunned, as we have only one ten-dollar bill. When Dave explains that we'll need to get cash from an ATM, not one of the six men sitting there seems to understand. So, we repeat the word *bank* as loudly and often as possible, and eventually, somebody figures it out.

After a lengthy discussion, we're waved toward the far end of the long room and told to see a policeman at the next checkpoint. After explaining what we want to the six officers there, they hold Dave and our luggage hostage and send me off on my own. A young man escorts me through the doors and around a corner, points to sliding doors at the end of another long room and waves off to the right. I nod my head but check with the next guard before going through the doors, ensuring he'll let me back in.

I'm now so tired that the mob waiting in the huge arrivals hall is just a blur as I go by, and by the time I see a bank logo, I've started to worry that I've missed the ATM. To my relief, the machine accepts my card, and I'm impressed when my name flashes up on the screen. But I stare in disbelief at the withdrawal choices, which range from 500,000 to 50,000,000 liras. I have no idea what the exchange rate is! Having little choice, I press the button beside the largest amount, hoping our bank balance will cover it, and receive ten 5,000,000-lira notes.

I retrace my steps to where Dave waits and we return to the visa counter. I lay down a few bills in front of the officer, and when I look up, he shakes his head. I keep watching as I lay down additional bills, and he's still shaking his head after I've put down the last one. It turns out that $90 US equals 54,000,000 liras. Dave hands over his $10 bill and receives $3 in change.

We withdraw another 50,000,000 liras from the ATM as we go by, then take a taxi to our hotel in the Old City. During the twenty-minute ride, we pass a gas station with a posted price of 556,000 lira/liter. The meter reads 5,600,000 when we reach the hotel, so I pass the driver two of the bills. When he seems to have a problem, I helplessly spread out the remaining bills in the dim light. Muttering to himself, he digs around in his pockets and comes up with 4.4 million in change. I never become comfortable with the currency; there are just too many zeros. I can't image how people deal with such inflation.

Our hotel is old, and the small, bare room has an old-fashioned bathroom with a leaky tap. The call to prayer comes at 0530, two of them actually, one over top of the other. The unfamiliar chanting, amplified by a PA system, echoes off rooftops and down dark, empty streets. Soon after, gulls start squawking and grey light filters through the window. At 0700, we take a small elevator down to the breakfast buffet, which offers boiled eggs, cheese, tomatoes, cucumbers, French bread, jam, yogurt, and coffee.

When we leave the hotel at 0900, bare tree branches are etched against a grey, wintery-looking sky across the narrow street. We turn and walk toward the dome of a mosque about a block away, but are sidetracked as we pass through Sultanahmet Square. The site was once home to the ancient Hippodrome, a u-shaped track built by the Romans when they conquered the city in 203 AD. It seated 30,000 spectators and featured sporting events, bazaars, public entertainment, and even riots.

With images of the past running through my head, I follow Dave to one side of the square, where two ancient artifacts still stand. The first is a 3,500-year-old obelisk that is covered with hieroglyphics; it came from the Luxor region of Egypt in 390 BC. The second is a 2,500-year-old serpentine column made of bronze that came from the Apollo Temple in Delphi, Greece, in 326 AD.

As soon as we stop to study them, the waiting hucksters pounce. A young girl, maybe ten years old, is the first; she's selling postcards. A young man gives her about five minutes, then interrupts and shoos her away. She indignantly stands her ground for another five minutes, then slinks off. He badgers us into buying a packet of cards, which is a mistake, as it only encourages the others. They are as annoying as black flies, and we finally leave the square in disgust.

The dome we saw earlier belongs to one of the city's main attractions, the Blue Mosque. Next to it is the Sophia Mosque, which is the reason for the double-barreled call to prayer that we hear five times a day. As we enter the courtyard of the first, a security guard holding a rifle in his hands looks us over closely. When we stop to look around, an older man approaches, and ignoring our suspicious glances, explains, "This courtyard holds 2,000 worshippers, and in the time of the Sultans, both this area and the area inside the mosque would have been full. Now, religion is only for the old; the young are too busy trying to earn a living."

Having secured our interest, he leads us across the paving stones to wide, marble steps at the side of the mosque. Waving his hand toward a shelf of plastic bags, he instructs, "You have to remove your shoes before entering, but you ma'am, don't have to cover your head. I'll wait for you at the exit on the other side."

With Dave carrying our shoes in a bag, we enter a vast chamber and stop to look admiringly at the great space beneath the high, domed ceiling. The dome is supported by huge marble columns, and a dim, bluish light comes through stained glass windows covering the east-facing wall. The other walls are tiled, and large wheels of lights hang low over the carpeted floor. Another man now waves us closer to the middle of the room, where a low barrier fences off the front half of the chamber. Several people kneel on the carpet on the other side.

He quietly explains, "The mosque is a religious building and the faithful are free to come and say prayers at any time; only Muslims are allowed beyond the barrier." He then points out the pulpit where the Imam stands, the balcony that the Sultan would have occupied, and the segregated area at the back where women are required to stay.

Our first guide is waiting patiently at the exit door when we leave and falls into step beside us as we cross the courtyard. He gently guides us down past an ancient Roman horse stable, and a few doors beyond is a carpet shop owned by his brother. Escorting us inside, he declares, "Business always waits on courtesy, and we will have coffee or tea." The brother is sent for and we drink Turkish coffee until he arrives.

The merchant shows us dozens of rugs and talks about single-knot Persian and double-knot Turkish and Kurdish designs. When nothing particularly appeals to Dave, he's asked to pick out the rug he likes most. After selecting one, he's told the price is $1,600 US. Laughing delightedly, Dave responds, "You're going to have to sharpen your pencil if you expect to make a sale!"

After some thought, the merchant lowers his price to $1,350, but Dave isn't interested. Changing tactics, the Turk cajoles him into admitting that he might pay $1,000 for such a carpet. He drops his price to $1,250, then $1,175, and as we prepare to walk out the door, he comes over and shakes Dave's hand, saying, "I accept $1,000. The rug is yours!"

After carrying the folded, wrapped rug back to the hotel, we walk through the narrow streets of the old city to the high, thick earthen wall surrounding Topkapi Palace. For 400 years, the palace was the center of the Ottoman Empire, which ruled over much of the land around the Mediterranean, as well as north into Hungary and far to the east. We enter through a massive double gate and join hundreds of visitors enjoying the warm, sunny afternoon in the palace gardens.

We leave via a back gate and follow a meandering road through parkland, passing cages and pens holding deer, goats, chickens, and a dromedary. Street vendors sell cotton candy and sunflower seeds, a woman cooks pita bread over a charcoal fire, and another shakes a basket-style popcorn maker. A number of people stand in front of a small table, and we watch a man pick up a pellet gun. Aiming at a board twenty feet away that is covered with rows of inflated balloons, he fires and pops one on his third shot.

We return to Topkapi Palace next day and again enter through the massive gate. This time, we tour through empty administration buildings that line the courtyard. Beyond is a second gate and another courtyard, where ruling committee meetings and ceremonies were held. The private living quarters of the sultan lie beyond a third gate, and here we join a tour of the harem.

Cold radiates from marble floors and tiled walls as we walk down the long, narrow hallways, and I'm soon wrapping my arms around my torso, trying to keep warm. We peer into small rooms that are furnished with low settees; most have fireplaces, and our guide tells us, "The floors were heated from below, and rooms were serviced with both hot and cold water." (I think that's what she said, but her accent was very thick for someone leading a tour in English.)

Favorites of the Sultan were housed in small rooms facing out onto a large outdoor bathing pool in a spacious, high-walled courtyard. Concubines serving the family slept in dormitories that we do not see. But the palace was a prison for the women who lived there, as their lives were controlled by the Queen Mother. The one exception was the mother of the Sultan's eldest son, who had some influence as long as he was alive.

We next tour through crowded rooms that are filled with period clothing, dishes, religious relics, armor, and swords. The most ostentatious is a dessert serving set that has diamonds embedded in spoon handles and in small plates that form the bottom of the bowls. The most mesmerizing is the Spoonmakers Diamond, which is displayed against a black background in a dark room, with the jewel reflecting the only light.

To our surprise, we get up one morning and find large, fluffy snowflakes falling outside our window. The street below is white. It's still snowing at noon, so we scurry down a few blocks through the wind and cold to a small shop serving lunch. We point out what we want, and the attendant shaves meat off a chicken roasting on a vertical rotisserie, then prepares a plate of tomatoes, peppers, and pickles, a basket of bread, and black tea. It's tasty but at six million liras seems expensive.

It's stopped snowing by the time we're finished, so we walk another block to an Internet Café. The computer keyboard is a problem as several characters, including the letter *i,* are placed in unfamiliar positions. While Dave struggles to type an email, I stand beside him, studying the eight young men peering at screens in the small dark room. Most are smoking. I'm struck by the seeming conflict between the modern technology in this room and the ancient city outside.

More snow falls overnight, but the sky has cleared by the time we leave the hotel at 1000. The sun has a bit of warmth for a while, but soon a bitter wind is blowing about our ears. When we come to the entrance to Yerebatan Cistern, I happily pay out five million liras, just for shelter. The wide marble steps are a bit slippery as we start down, then I hear faint classical music. The sound swells when we step out onto a landing overlooking the cistern and I stop, dumbfounded at the sight in front of me.

Dozens of massive marble columns rise out of a pool of water in the bottom of the cistern. Soaring upwards, they support a high, domed ceiling, and thanks to incredible acoustics, the taped music soars with them. The unexpectedness, the sheer elegance, takes my breath away. We slowly descend the remaining steps, then stroll down floating walkways between the columns. Carefully placed flood lights shimmer on the water, and hearing a slow dripping, I look upward to see water drops falling from the ceiling. I also notice metal straps encircling a few pillars, probably required after one of the earthquakes they'd survived. When we leave, we walk around the block, scanning buildings and roadways, but find no hint of the structure below.

Having picked up a few brochures, we find a sheltered bench in the sunshine and sit and study them. The city's history dates back to the 8th century BC, when Byzantium was founded by Greek settlers. In the centuries since, the colony had been controlled by Persians, Athenians, Spartans, Macedonians, and Romans, who changed the name to Constantinople in 330 AD. The existing city walls were built early in the fifth century, but didn't stop the Turks of the Ottoman Empire who conquered the city in 1453 and renamed it Istanbul.

The cistern we just visited was built by a Byzantine Emperor in a few months in 532 AD and is the largest of several built to provide water for the city when it was under siege. It is 455 feet long, half that wide, 26 feet deep, and holds 80,000 cubic meters of water. The 336 Roman columns supporting the ceiling are placed thirteen feet apart and came from three different sites.

The centuries of human conflict that created this city are so far removed from my own experience that I need time to take it in. Leaving Dave sitting on the bench, I wander over to nearby Sultanahmet Square, but when my steps slow, the hucksters close in. I turn and flee, as they're really getting to me. They just won't leave us alone!

Our steps now take us to the Grand Bazaar, and at the entrance, a policeman sweeps packages and bags with a metal detector. Unruffled by this strange custom, people just stop and hold out their bags. Hordes of people then push down the narrow, cobblestoned streets inside, which are roofed over and extend for blocks. The small shops sell all kinds of goods, from exotic spices to gold jewelry and leather products.

The exit we take from the market leads to the crowded grounds of Yeni Cami Mosque. Behind it, in a narrow lane, a street market goes on for blocks, with long tables on both sides piled high with goods. Hordes of people push their way through the middle, so I stay close behind Dave. A surging crush of people then cuts between us, and although I push back, he disappears in a sea of dark, drab colors. Anxiously, I push back, am almost overwhelmed, then emerge on the far side. He waits for me at the end of the next block.

I'm so cold by the time we return to the hotel that I huddle beneath blankets until supper time. We eat hot soup and stew at a nearby small café, then have an early night, hoping to be ready for the 0530 call to prayer. Next morning, feeling more like myself, I start thinking about the street venders. *If I can't stop and look at things, I might as well stay in the room!* So, when the next one approaches me, I have a plan. Looking the man in the eyes, I smile and give a short shake of my head. He turns away. It works every time.

When we leave the hotel that morning, we're intercepted by three well-dressed men looking for the Blue Mosque. One of them is a lawyer, and he and his client have an hour to kill before appearing at the nearby main courthouse. After chatting briefly, he remarks, "Istanbul would be perfect, if it weren't for the rug sellers, shoe shiners, and postcard hawkers!"

CHAPTER 19
MORE TOUTS AND RUG MERCHANTS

While walking about the old city, we occasionally catch glimpses of the blue waters of the Bosphorus, the strait joining Istanbul to the Black Sea. We also see hundreds of passengers streaming to and from the ferry terminals on the Golden Horn. One bright, sunny morning, we decide to join them, but near the terminal, we're surrounded by a horde of touts selling private boat tours.

Ignoring them, Dave grandly walks on, and then a voice rings out. "We follow the same route as the ferry and take only three hours, not six, because there's no waiting around." Seeing him hesitate, the man who spoke pushes closer and continues, "You see much more from our boat than a ferry, as we come within 30 feet of shore. We follow the European side on the way up, the Asian on the way down, and have a cabin, so you're not sitting out in the cold. We stop for an hour at the narrows leading into the Black Sea, giving plenty of time to visit the fortress."

Dave looks closely at the younger man, who's about half his size, and asks, "How much?"

"Ten million lira each," is the confident response.

Shaking his head, Dave states bluntly, "We don't carry that much money."

The tout assures him, "I'll take another currency, or a credit card!"

The two men continue to spar while Dave makes up his mind. He then finds a sunny, sheltered spot in which to wait, and I'm sent off with the young Turk, Hasheem, to find an ATM. After paying half the fare up front, we're escorted aboard a small sightseeing boat, which might have held thirty people inside, with room on top for more. We share the space with two other couples and the helmsman.

The wind is behind us on the outward journey, and sea and sky sparkle in brilliant sunshine, so we sit outside. Hasheem points out several mosques, the Clock Tower, and a large palace stretching along the European shore. We pass under Ataturk Bridge, which joins Europe to Asia, and traffic on the 1.5-km long suspension bridge is bumper to bumper. As we proceed up the Bosporus, the wind develops a bite, causing Dave to hunch his shoulders. Hasheem notices and pulls off his own woolen toque and tugs it down over the bigger man's ears, then persistently grabs his arm or shoulder as he jokes around.

When the strait narrows to half a km, a second bridge spans the channel, and soon the boat pulls into a dock on the European side, near the 550-year-old Rumeli Fortress. I'm eager for a closer look at the thick walls and squat towers of the fortress, but Hasheem has other plans. Pulling Dave aside, he murmurs, "There's really nothing more to see than what you've already seen, and I know a good spot to have lunch."

I have to admit the food is good, with hot lentil soup and tasty garlic kabobs consisting of bite-sized pieces of ground meat wrapped in bread dough, served with a flat bread shaped like a thick pita. When it becomes obvious that I can't eat all of the large serving, Hasheem reaches across and takes my plate, scrapes part of what's left onto Dave's plate and eats the rest himself.

While we're walking back to the boat, Hasheem stops at a roadside kiosk and buys a small bottle of raki and two similar sized bottles of water. We then sit in the cabin and watch as he splashes small amounts of the licorice-flavored alcohol into plastic cups and adds water. I feel a nice glow in my stomach after a few sips, and a Belgian couple agree that it tastes like ouzo. As we have our drinks and visit, we barely notice how rough the return passage is, with the boat plowing into large waves pushed up by the wind and spray flying high over the cabin roof.

We don't see much of the Asian side until we come to Leandros Tower, which sits on rocks 500 feet from shore. A small defensive castle built here in the fourth century has had several reincarnations, and now is used to control shipping between the Black Sea and the Sea of Marmara. After circling around it, we return to the European side, where the dome and minarets of the Mosque of Suleyman, the Magnificent, are framed against the sky. On the waterfront, a stream of small, dark figures flows to and from the underground street crossing near the Yeni Cami Mosque.

When we settle up with Hasheem, he's not ready to call it a day. Finding out that we're going to the Grand Market, he volunteers to come along, then guides us to a shop run by "a man from my village." While the men visit, I buy almonds and figs, a box each of Turkish Delight and apple tea, and a good luck charm. The blue and white eye is supposed to protect the home.

After we leave the market, Hasheem takes us down narrow lanes to a restaurant located two blocks from the Blue Mosque. Climbing steep stairs up to a bar, we sit at a small round table and drink raki. He pours the drinks and explains, "The liquor is too strong for the stomach, so each sip needs to be washed down with a swallow of water."

For the next hour, Hasheem waxes lyrical about himself. "I am Kurdish," he tells us. "My village is located 500 km east of Ankara; it's near some hot springs, but not in the mountains. Mt Ararat and Noah's Ark are farther east. People there have been leaving the land and moving to the cities, trying to improve their fortunes."

He then goes on, "I learned English on my own, as my schooling was all in Turkish. I served eighteen months compulsory service in the army, and we did some training with the Russians near Leningrad. I've been married nearly two years and my wife and I are expecting our first child in the summer." He then offers a final piece of advice, "Next time you come to Turkey, you should go to the South Coast; it's much nicer than Istanbul. Like California!"

Dave now calls for the bill and I pay it, as when traveling, he carries the credit cards and I carry the cash. But this doesn't set well with Hasheem. Shaking his head, he scolds, "In Turkey, men control the money, not the women. You really shouldn't let your wife handle your cash."

Dave laughingly protests, "She just carries the money; I tell her what to pay."

"Ah," is the admiring response, "you Pasha!"

When we part, Hasheem wants to meet again the following afternoon. We turn up at the appointed time, but he doesn't appear. We wait a while, then find our way to a restaurant that Dave found earlier in the week. Sitting next to a small fireplace with a brisk fire, I have a bowl of chicken soup and feel warm for the first time in days.

Our dinner of lamb and vegetables is cooked in a clay pot and carried to the table on a tray with flames leaping inches up into the air. Our waiter pours off the liquid, reseals the top with tinfoil, then breaks the bottom of the pot, dumping the contents into a serving bowl. The meal is one of our most successful dining experiences anywhere, very unique and enjoyable, and costs 18.3 million liras.

On our last full day in Istanbul, when we've spent all the money we intend to spend, we go looking for a young man we'd been kibitzing with for several days. He'd been very pleasant and Dave promised that we'd come by for coffee. But when he leads us up a flight of stairs to an elegant, second-floor showroom, Dave feels compelled to warn, "We've just come for coffee. We've already bought a rug and won't be buying another."

We sit down and relax for half an hour, drinking apple tea and casually looking at rugs thrown down in front of us. The rug merchant then arrives and everything changes. He's knowledgeable, experienced, and very entertaining. Within minutes, I sense a relationship building between the two men, and as they test one another, it seems the rugs are all but forgotten.

Methodically weeding out the ones that we don't like, the merchant tells us, "I travel into the far reaches of the country to obtain my rugs. They're all handmade using lamb's wool, which is why the color changes depending on the direction in which they're viewed. Rugs made fifteen to twenty years ago are more valuable because they have *soul;* they were made for family, for future generations. Rugs made today are for commercial sale and don't have the same quality or workmanship."

When all the rugs have been discarded save one, he explains the meaning of the design. "First, it's a prayer rug and the seven tulips represent the seven days of the week it will be used. The five circular symbols represent the five tasks required of a Muslim, which are to believe in only one God and that Muhammad is the messenger of God, to pray daily, to give alms to the poor, to fast during Ramadan, and to visit Mecca once in a lifetime."

"The double-walled border is meant to keep evil away, the red color is special to Muslims, the green rarely seen, and the technique used is double-knotted wool on wool." He finishes by noting, "The central design symbolizes the woman's deep love for a man with whom she hopes to have three children. Women are not allowed to speak of such things to men."

Dazzled by his performance, we are well and truly hooked. He now assures Dave that the rug would sell for $2,100 in the US or retail for $1,200 in Istanbul, then smoothly proposes "a special price for you of $755." Dave has repeatedly said that we're only there for coffee, but can't resist and counters with an offer of $550. After much hand wringing, the merchant drops his price to $750, then $700.

Now involved and enjoying himself, Dave increases his offer to $600; his top price, he states emphatically. The merchant eventually comes down to $601, then neither man will budge. I'm so caught up by this performance that I surprise even myself when I suddenly blurt out, "I'll pay the dollar!" I guess that I didn't want either man to lose face. After turning to look at me, they both laugh, then shake hands.

While the rug is packaged up and our credit card processed, we're served more apple tea, and two assistants begin shaking out smaller silk rugs, scattering them across the floor in front of us. There must be twenty rugs laid out when the merchant smoothly picks up his patter. "The silk used in these rugs comes from silkworms raised in an area south of Istanbul. It was bought by nomads, who take an entire year to make just one rug. Only young girls from twelve to eighteen, or maybe twenty, work on them; after that, their eyesight is too poor or their fingers too large."

Discarding rugs that we don't like until only one remains, he explains, "This design shows the tree of life, and the six birds represent the woman's children for whom she hopes happy lives; the ram symbol is meant to keep evil away." He continues, "In the summer season, I would ask $4,000-$4,500 US for this rug, but for you, my good customers, the price is $2,400."

We're not interested at any price, as we have no place to hang it and don't want it as an investment. But our new friend cajoles Dave into admitting that he might pay $1,500 for such a rug. After a little more conversation, the price drops to $2,000, but Dave shakes his head firmly. After having more apple tea pressed on us, we rise to our feet, pull on our jackets, and Dave repeats, "We can't offer any more."

The merchant now walks over and shakes his hand, leaving us speechless. In response to the shocked look on our faces, he says simply, "Business is slow; I need the money." The two men then wail that each has been taken by the other, and I snap a picture of them standing together, Dave with his empty pockets turned inside out.

We're in the showroom three hours and later agree that spending money was never more enjoyable. While the merchant looked 40, he was 54 years old and had been in business for ten years. The rugs came from villages in central Turkey, and when Dave suggested that we might rent a car and buy a rug directly, he soberly warned, "I've spent years establishing relationships with the Kurds and can travel safely in the area, but the villagers are suspicious of strangers. Long-standing feuds exist between villages, and every boy over the age of ten carries a Kalashnikov AK47." He then added earnestly, "If you want to drive, go to the south coast, not the interior."

After dropping off our purchases at the hotel, we walk through the Grand Bazaar one last time, and the guard at the entrance reminds me of the many uniformed police and soldiers we'd seen about the city. We then take an exit that leads to a large square at the university, and I stop dead in my tracks when I see columns of police lined up at the far end, with numerous vans and a riot vehicle parked along one side. Turning to Dave, I nervously suggest making a detour, but no, he wants a closer look.

As we draw closer, I see that the men wear helmets and body armor and stand behind four-foot-high shields. Unsure whether or not to take a picture, I cautiously raise my camera. Just as I take it, two officers walk into my viewfinder, and one looks directly at me. I freeze, as do they, holding the pose until I lower the camera. Hundreds more policemen are lined up in rows in a narrow lane off the square, and many more police vehicles are parked behind them.

After returning to the hotel, we learn that a rally being held that afternoon is in memory of students killed in a demonstration twenty years earlier. We never hear whether trouble develops, as we leave Istanbul early next morning.

Our final stop in the city is the breathtaking structure that is Sulleyman Mosque, where 5,000 devotees can attend prayers. I feel uneasy, sensing that the magnificence of the building reflects the power of men, not the glory of God. I'd actually felt that same uneasiness years before in the great churches of Europe.

Next morning, the call to prayer is louder than usual due to low cloud, and it's still dark when the hotel car takes us through deserted streets to the airport. My last memories of the city are of a mosque, its flood-lit minarets standing eerily against the night sky, and the land wall, the massive fortification that protected the ancient city.

Chapter 20
Jersey and Cancun

When planning our trip, we had a few spare days between Istanbul and Cancun and decided to spend them in Jersey, in the Channel Islands. So, after a four-hour flight to Heathrow, England, we have a connecting flight across the English Channel. But the flight is delayed by fog, then cancelled, and we spend hours in queues, claiming our luggage and rebooking seats.

When we finally get in the air, views of the channel are limited in haze, and when I see Jersey, the island appears to be dotted with many small ponds. My seatmates assure me that they're actually plastic-covered seed plots containing Jersey Gold potatoes. They go on to explain that the country recognizes the present English Queen as Duchess of Normandy and has a Lieutenant Governor, but is independent of Britain. Although only 19 km off the coast of France, the English language began replacing French about 100 years ago.

Our hotel in St Helier is very pleasant, and next morning we wander through the narrow, cobble-stoned streets of the town, admiring the brightly-painted, village-style buildings and office blocks that house the island's banking industry. We spend the afternoon with a host of other people walking, biking, and rollerblading down the wide promenade alongside a sea wall that curves around a large bay. It's sunny and warm, and I take off my sweater for the first time in two weeks.

An old fort sits out on a rocky point on one side of the bay, while two defensive towers built in the 1700s are lost in new construction along the promenade. Although the forty-foot spring tide is ebbing, the causeway to Elizabeth Castle in the middle of the bay is still underwater. At low tide, long lines of jagged rocks are exposed on the far side, perhaps explaining why no defensive structures are visible over there.

We search out a small, pleasant dining room off a pub that night. With only three of six tables occupied, the proprietress has time to chat and tells us, "The island has been a holiday destination for a long time. People want to move here, but under current regulations, only people who've lived on the island for twenty years can buy real estate. It's very difficult for young people to get started, and my daughter is in rental housing, which is very expensive." (We've already noticed that we're paying in pounds what we usually pay in dollars, so for us, prices have nearly doubled.)

The next day, we tour the island and stop off at the Occupation Museum. The Nazis occupied the island for nearly five years during WW II, and local citizens were forced to provide slave labor to build the Underground Hospital. Food was scarce by the end of the war, and starving German soldiers had been reduced to eating dogs, cats, and rats, while local citizens were better able to live off land and sea.

We return to the same pub that night and are greeted by an English couple who remember us from the previous evening. We chat with them throughout the meal and when they leave, a young woman at a third table eagerly introduces herself, "Hi, I'm Mary. I heard you say you were Canadians and just had to tell you that I work for the Royal Bank of Canada."

Mary is Irish, with long, flaming-red hair, and her partner Steven is Jersey born and bred. They're drinking coffee and liqueurs, and for the next hour, we share a bond with this young couple that is magical. Mary explains that there is no work in Ireland and carries on about the Royal Bank, money laundering, nursing, and mediums. Some of it doesn't make a lot of sense, but maybe isn't supposed to, and we are all in stitches as she blithely carries on. She is quite envious of our sailing adventures and pleads, "Couldn't you adopt me and take me with you?" We're finally politely asked to leave so the proprietress can close for the night.

We now fly back to Heathrow and board a trans-Atlantic flight to Cancun. After meeting up with family members, we celebrate the wedding, then stay over a day after the others leave. The resort city has been taken over by young people on spring break and is a zoo, but we want to take a bus tour to Chi Chen Itza on the Yucatan Peninsula.

Chi Chen Itza translates as Mouth of the Wells of Itza, and Mayans are thought to have occupied the site for almost a thousand years. The people worshipped agricultural gods initially and provided tributes of goods and labor to a ruling class of elites. Over time, they came to believe that gods controlled daily events and could be influenced by offerings. Personal acts of mutilation were made, as were human sacrifices. The goriest ones took place at the temple of Kukulcan, on top the pyramid of El Castillo.

When first seen by Europeans, the pyramid was a bush-covered mound. The site had been vacant for 300 years, and local people had removed stones to build their homes and fences. After thoughtful, careful restoration work, the pyramid now brings in hordes of visitors on the equinox. On that day, shadows cast by the first rays of the sun cause a serpent to glide down the ninety-one narrow, steep steps of the main staircase and connect to a carved snake's head at the base.

We climb the steep steps up the front of the pyramid and see stone structures rising above scrub bush in all directions. We then enter a low, narrow passageway at the base of the pyramid that takes us to a stone staircase going up through the middle. We don't go far, as it's hot, humid, and claustrophobic.

We're amazed as we then wander about the site. The ball court has two walls that are 30 feet thick, 274 feet long, and 120 feet apart. Stone hoops built into the walls are 25 feet above the ground, and relief carvings show players in a game where the losing team forfeited their lives. The observatory is believed to date back to 1050, and at certain times of the year, windows and doors line up with the sun, moon and stars, particularly Venus. The stone steps and columns of the market are best described by its name, *Group of 1,000 Columns.*

I'm consumed by the mystery of these abandoned structures and ask many questions of our guide. Perhaps too many! When I ask, "What happened to the Mayan people? Why did they disappear?" He glares back at me indignantly and snaps, "They didn't disappear! I'm Mayan!"

We stop in Las Vegas for a few days on our way from Mexico to Canada. Our flight to Vancouver leaves at midnight, and the terminal is deserted when we check in. After examining our passports, the airline clerk informs us that our bags have to be inspected. While extra inspections become commonplace after September, 2001, they are done in secure areas with tables, never on the floor of the passenger terminal, which is what now happens.

We first wait twenty minutes for an agent to appear and he has us carry our bags over to a nearby wall. Every item that I've carefully packed is then shaken out, painstakingly examined, and set aside. Our rugs are unwrapped, the jade Buddhas are removed from their protective padding, even the papers in Dave's briefcase are rifled through. The agent then walks away, leaving our belongings piled in high stacks in open suitcases.

I've been sitting on the terminal floor with my back to the wall, seething. *Why would they do this? We're leaving the country, not entering!* I repack as quickly as I can and need Dave's help to close the zippers. When we return to the airline counter, I bitterly complain, "We've just traveled through Asia and Europe, and nowhere have we been treated so badly."

The woman mumbles back, "It's an FAA requirement."

CHAPTER 21
BANGKOK

Yachts are already leaving for the southern cruising season when we return to Brisbane in early May of 2000. We end up spending the season in port, and when the weather warms up in November are again talking about a trip to Canada. Then out of the blue, Dave asks, "What would you say to visiting your brother in Chile?"

Not knowing whether he's serious, I respond, "Sure, when do you want to leave?"

We're soon planning an overland trip through Bolivia, Peru, and Chile. When our travel agent can't get us from Australia to South America, we again agree to go around the world. We apply for the necessary visas and start studying Spanish. After reading that many tourists have their luggage stolen, we opt to take only carryon bags.

At the end of January, 2001, we board a plane for the nine-hour flight to Bangkok, Thailand. It's late when we arrive (2300 local time/0200 our time), and we're arguing as we walk through the nearly empty terminal. Dave wants to take a bus downtown, but given the hour, I want to take a taxi. More precisely, I want to buy a voucher at one of the kiosks we're passing, as information provided with our tickets warned against hiring a taxi outside the terminal.

Dave doesn't stop until he reaches the curb outside, and I have little choice but to trail along behind. The street in front of the terminal is poorly lit, and there's not a bus stop or taxi stand in sight. In fact, it's also empty of vehicles and pedestrians. Turning, we walk down the shadowy sidewalk for a long block without seeing a soul, then pause beneath a dim streetlight.

Before I can say anything, the small, dark figure of a man emerges from the shadows and asks, "You want taxi downtown? I get you one for 600 baht." At least, that's what we think he says, and he writes the numbers on his hand for clarification.

Dave looks at me impatiently, and I angrily glance around the empty street, wanting no part of this. Shrugging my shoulders, I respond bitterly, "Well, what choice do we have? Let's do it!"

Pulling out a cell phone, the man makes a call, then assures us, "Just a few minutes." We seem to wait a long time, but probably it's just long enough for our foolishness to sink in. The man then beckons us to follow and leads us down another block. As we arrive at the intersection, a van pulls into the curb in front of us. I just have time to see that there's no name on the door or taxi sign on top, then the sliding door opens, our bags are thrown inside, and we're ushered into the back seat.

I notice two men sitting up front as the door closes and then we're driving away. Looking for some kind of reassurance, I peer out the window but see no road signs, street names, or even buildings. I anxiously keep looking, and although traffic is steady, the road is dark with only a few lights well off to the side. Before long, I'm filled with dread, convinced that we're going to be robbed and thrown out on some deserted back road.

When the van turns off the road and stops in a dimly lit yard thirty minutes later, I'm prepared for almost anything, except what happens. The side door of the van opens and we're told that this is our hotel. I only believe it when we're greeted by a clerk at the front desk in the lobby. When we later discuss our apparently lucky escape, Dave admits that he too was worried. We decide that the van was probably unlicensed, so couldn't pick up at the terminal, and the driver then followed back roads into town to avoid paying road tolls.

Our hotel proves to be very comfortable; the room is large and pleasant, the breakfast buffet incredible. The fresh fruit alone is worth the price of the meal (papaya, watermelon, and deliciously sweet pineapple). Although daytime temperatures are a muggy 35 degrees C, we walk for hours every day. We're actually lost for a couple of hours the first day, as my miniature map shows only major streets.

Bangkok sprawls around the serpentine curves of the Chao Phraya River and has a population of six million people. Ninety-five percent of Thais are Buddhists and roadside shrines, temples, and saffron-robed monks seem to be everywhere. Traditionally, young men served as monks for two years. The people are extremely loyal to the royal family, and large pictures of the King and Queen decorate the major thoroughfares.

Networks of canals extend off both sides of the river, and the first day, we follow a broad canal downstream. Amongst the trees are the glittering roofs of ornate temples, and we pass a giant golden Buddha standing beside a high tower. Later in the day, we see long, slim boats taxiing passengers up and down a narrower waterway.

The next day, we find our way to the Grand Palace compound, one of the city's main attractions. It was once home to the royal family, and mysterious-looking temple roofs and spires rise behind a high perimeter wall. But the street in front is chockablock with tour buses, tourists, and street vendors, and we have to push our way through. When we see the long queue waiting to enter, we just keep walking.

We follow the popping sounds of firecrackers into a rabbit warren of narrow aisles and kiosks that lead down to the ferry docks on the river. We're soon surrounded by touts selling long-tail-boat rides for 700 baht, then are distracted by the sounds of gongs and drums coming from the entrance. Retracing our steps, we stop and watch a troupe of dancers wearing traditional costumes and heavy, ornate headdresses. They move with the slow, deliberate steps that I believe to be Thai classical dance.

After walking for another hour, we stop and rest on a bench beside a canal near Pak Khlong market. Tuk-tuks filled with fresh produce are constantly leaving the market, some piled so high that there's barely room for the customer. Across the street, we watch as a team of ten men load a large truck with bags and baskets of vegetables. A tall, slim, young man tosses a heavy sack of onions up to a chain of hands that pile it high on the load. More bags follow, and when they're finished, the load is covered with heavy black plastic and the truck guided out onto the street.

We return to the ferry docks another day, when fewer people are about. The price of a long-tail-boat tour is now 500 baht, and unable to resist the chance to barter, Dave offers 400. Next thing I know, we're being escorted down to the river. We're seated in a long, slim boat that has a large, noisy engine high on the stern, with a long propeller shaft angled out behind. Soon, we're racing up the broad surface of the river.

We pass the glittering prang (tower) of the 17th-century Wat Arun, the Temple of the Dawn, and turn into a wide canal on the far side. Minutes later, we come alongside a dock at the Royal Barge Shed. After informing us that he's not allowed to tie up, our boatman instructs, "You have only ten minutes, so you must be quick." We pay 30 baht each to enter, and I'm charged an additional 100 baht to take pictures, which I think outrageous. I'm even more annoyed when I see only eight boats inside; I'd read there would be fifty.

But my irritation evaporates when I see the King's personal barge, which is decorated with gold and is incredibly elegant and beautiful. Filled with admiration, I study the bow where the long, graceful neck of a swan lifts its head up to the sky. I stay so long that I have time for only a quick glance at the remaining craft, the largest of which is 150 feet long and requires fifty rowers.

Our tour continues through the network of canals on the west side of the river; some are wide and busy, others narrow and quiet. We pass canal-side restaurants, a floating market, old houses on stilts, and new modern homes. A woman washes clothes on one dock, teenage boys jump off another, and every backyard seems to lead to a temple.

Our walking tours of the city take us into neighborhoods that are only accessible by motorcycles, where families appear to live and work in sheds about the size of a single car garage. We also walk down wide boulevards around large blocks of land occupied by the royal palace compound and the parliament buildings.

We hire the ubiquitous three-wheeled tuk-tuks when we start traveling farther afield. They are cheap and it doesn't take long to figure out why. The first driver takes us to a jewelry store and sends us inside, saying, "Just for five minutes while I get gas." In fact, he actually receives a gas coupon for every tourist he brings to the store.

We spend half a day at the National Museum, where we study stone tablets engraved with early Thai script, as well as relics from archeological sites. One large room is filled with military equipment, including a full-sized replica of an elephant with long tusks and battle gear; another room features teak manuscript cupboards and storage boxes inlaid with mother-of-pearl.

An early 19th century house once used by members of the royal family stands in a corner of the grounds. Built of teak, with heavy plank floors, thick walls, and high ceilings, the small two-bedroom building is cool inside and simply furnished. Nearby, a beautiful wooden chapel has walls that are three feet thick and a spacious, high ceiling. A golden image of the Buddha sits on a throne in the center of the room, and the interior walls are covered with beautifully painted murals of his life.

We visit Chinatown one very hot afternoon, scanning goods piled high on tables on the sidewalk as we squeeze past. Streets are chock-a-block with traffic, and when vehicles stop for a red light, motorcycles maneuver to the front of the line. They all leap forward when the light turns green, engines screaming and blue smoke rising. Occasionally, the fumes sting my eyes, but it doesn't seem to bother workers in one block, who sit at long, narrow tables next to the curb assembling electronic components.

As we step onto the curb after crossing an intersection, a man calls out to Dave, "Would you be interested in looking at gold chains selling for really good prices?" Of course, he would. We're loaded into a tuk-tuk, driven to an unfamiliar area, and dropped off in front of a warehouse. Inside is a retail jewelry outlet, and for the next two hours, Dave haggles over gold chains and ultimately buys one.

For a change of pace, we take a bus tour to *The Rose Garden,* a cultural center about 35 km from the city. A murky haze covers the sky as we stroll through the grounds, and a small river along one side appears to be in flood, with small islets of vegetation drifting by in the current. Colorful orchids are grafted onto the trunks of cedar trees near the parking lot, and a brilliant mass of flamingoes stands sleeping in the shade beside a pond. When Dave stops to admire a parrot, taking it up on his outstretched hand, it nips him on the knuckle, causing him to gasp in surprise.

We join 2,000 other tourists in a covered grandstand for an exhibition of Thai dancing. One troupe step in and out of bamboo poles that are slowly clapped together, another parade with six-inch-long finger nails and lots of finger movements. They are followed by a choreographed bout of Thai boxing. We then watch a demonstration of working elephants, of which there are fewer than 5,000 in Thailand. Most perform circus tricks, such as blowing water from their trunks, or rearing up and dancing.

Before leaving Bangkok, we take the hotel shuttle bus to a well-known night market, where tables and stalls piled high with a vast array of goods run down the center of a long, narrow lane. We walk up one side and down the other, and only then see the sleazy nightclubs for which the area is famous. While I continue shopping, Dave enjoys the attention of shills who try to lure him inside with promises of all kinds of delights bearing graphic names.

When the novelty wears off, he leads the way to a line of taxis. The first cabbie wants 300 baht for a ride back to the hotel, so we walk down the line until he finds a driver who'll take us there on the meter. Twenty minutes later, for 60 baht, we're back in our room.

The next night, we have dinner at the hotel and are seated beside two American men who we chatted with briefly on the bus the night before. We now enjoy one of those special evenings when complete strangers seem like old friends. The men are from New York and about our age; Gene is a broker and Abe a lecturer. They've just toured Australia and New Guinea, and with that as our starting point, we engage in a wide-ranging conversation that goes on for two hours.

Before leaving Bangkok, Dave visits the Seventh Day Adventist Mission hospital, as wax has built up in his ears. After waiting a remarkably short time, he's examined and treated by an ear-nose-throat specialist and the cost is minimal. In fact, that's the story of all our health issues outside of Canada.

CHAPTER 22
ATHENS AND DELPHI

The Bangkok terminal is unbelievably busy when we check in for our midnight departure, with long queues everywhere and few places to sit. The plane is then uncomfortably hot and stuffy during the eleven-hour flight. We land in Athens just before dawn, and as we wait outside for a taxi, the air is wonderfully crisp and clear. The sky grows lighter on the ride downtown, and I find myself peering curiously at the quiet streets, strangely eager to see this land of ancient philosophers and early democracy.

At 0800, we're checking into a hotel in the old city, *the Plaka,* then climb a narrow staircase up to our fourth-floor room. Construction dust stirs as we pass through the second floor-landing, where renovations continue throughout our stay. The room is much more expensive than the one in Bangkok and about a third the size. The shower stall, which takes up half the floor space in the bathroom, proves to be so small that Dave can't turn around in it.

As the room is hot and stuffy, he immediately crosses to the window to let in some fresh air. But after pulling back the drapes, he stops and calls softly, "Lene, come look!" The window's only three feet wide and inset, so there's no peripheral view, but straight ahead, bathed in the early morning sunlight, are the rugged cliffs of the *Acropolis* and the white columns of both the *Parthenon* and *Erechtheion.*

Our weariness forgotten, we're soon walking down a narrow street where the air is still cool, as it's shaded from the sun. After passing a few stone columns and a rock wall, we come to a sunny, green meadow scattered with white stones that was once the ancient agora, or marketplace. A well-beaten path leads to the entrance to the *Acropolis,* where we pay an entry fee of 2,000 drachmas each.

The path grows steeper as we climb, and soon we're looking down on an ancient theater, the *Odeon of Herodes Atticus.* Glistening, white stone benches that have recently been renovated curve around the steep slope of the hill. In front of them, a three-storied, windowed stone wall looms behind a small stage.

As we climb higher, the view over the city expands until the waters of the Saronic Gulf glitter off to the south. We sit awhile on a stone bench, looking out over vertical rock walls and buttressed slopes at the city below. But my eyes keep returning to the graceful white columns of the temples, now framed against the deep blue of the sky. These incredible structures, built between 447 and 406 BC, somehow complement the rugged strength of this huge rock outcropping, and I am filled with admiration for the society that created them.

Work to restore and preserve them is ongoing, and we're allowed into the entrance structure only, *the Propylaia,* where a wooden walkway protects the stone floor. One end of *the Parthenon* is draped with scaffolding, but that doesn't prevent us from admiring the seventeen Doric columns running down each side, with eight across the ends. At the *Temple of Athena Nike,* we study the frieze over the entrance, which depicts a battle between Greeks and Persians. At the *Erechtheion,* we focus on the *Porch of the Caryatids*, where the statues of six *Korai* (youthful female figures) form the columns.

But my sense of awe turns to bewilderment when we tour the site museum. Almost all the exhibits are damaged, some extensively. The torso of one statue is a plaster cast made from the original, which resides in London; the leg of another is a plexiglass column. Other exhibits are mostly plaster with a few original pieces attached, and some are drawings on which shards of marble have been placed.

When we return outside, I look around with new eyes, now aware that this site overlooking the Attica plain has been home to Athenians for 5,000 years. It was a place of sanctuary, closer to their Gods, and the existing 2,500-year-old temples were built on the sites of even older temples. The people sought refuge here when enemies attacked, and their city had been left vandalized or in ruins many times. Temples that survived were converted to Christian churches during the Byzantine period and mosques under the Ottoman Empire.

In recent history, Greeks fought a war of independence against Turkey, the twelve-year conflict ending in 1833. During WW II, Nazi officers stood where we now stand, and Greeks then fought a civil war, throwing out the Communists.

In the days that follow, we climb Lycabettus Hill, the city's highest point, where a small, white chapel and bell tower are etched against a blue sky. We visit Athens Cathedral, and in its shadow, the Church of Panagia Gorgoepikoos, a small Byzantine chapel built in the 12th century. After walking through Constitution Square, we take pictures of the Parliament Buildings and relax in the National Garden, an oasis of quiet and serenity in the busy downtown area.

We seek out the Panathenaic Stadium, where the first Olympic Games of the modern age were held in 1896. It was built on the same site, using the same plans, as a stadium constructed 2,000 years earlier. While reflecting on the Olympic ideals of honor and sportsmanship, I notice life-sized statues of Olympians placed on six-foot-high pedestals in a plaza across the street. Reminded of the fame and fortune that come with Olympic gold, I think about reports of cheating that are now so frequent. Winning at any cost seems to be what's important and I wonder, *was it always so?*

We continue on to the ruins of the Temple of the Olympian Zeus, where the fifteen tall, magnificent Corinthian columns blow me away. The marble columns, 56 feet high, stand in an open field in splendid isolation from the rest of the city. The temple originally had 104 such columns and took centuries to build. Even more than the ruins on the Acropolis, they speak of the enduring grandeur of the society that created them.

On a grey, cloudy morning, we visit the Ancient Agora, which was once the heart of Athenian political, social, and religious life. As we stroll past the foundation stones of ancient buildings, I picture the busy market that existed here 3,000 years ago, with men sitting in the shade discussing philosophy, or perhaps the work of their councils. Ideas at the core of our own democratic beliefs were first discussed here, as was the new Christian religion. Absorbed in the past, I wander through stone-strewn fields, and Dave finds a bench-height rock to wait for me. He's chased off by an indignant attendant, who warns, "That's an artifact!"

The site museum contains relics that predate the market and were found beneath it. We marvel at the gold rings, bracelets, paper-thin bits of pottery, and burial urns. We then come to a section holding small medicine bottles that came from the ruins of a prison, the same prison where the philosopher, Socrates, was held. When handed a similar vial filled with hemlock, he chose to take it rather than give in to his accusers.

We spend a full day on a bus tour to Delphi, which is a two-hour drive away. In the 6th century BC, Delphi was considered the center of the Greek world. It was home to the most important Greek temple to Apollo, and prophecies by the resident sibyl were believed to be inspired by the god. Consulted by private citizens and public officials for centuries, the sibyl influenced Greek religion, politics, and the economy.

Our guide is a short, buxom, fortyish woman, who speaks good English and is a born storyteller. As the bus is only half full, we're able to spread out in relative comfort as we listen. She starts by explaining a fact of modern life, "Traffic is so heavy in the downtown area that private vehicles are restricted to certain days of the week, depending on the last digit of their license plate number."

Then a bit of history, "We have a royal family, as a Bavarian King was forced on us by Britain, France, and Russia after the War of Independence in 1833. He was never accepted by the Greek people and the current King lives in exile in Britain. If he returned, it would probably cause a great deal of political unrest."

"During WW II, Greece fought with the Allies, then was consumed by a civil war lasting from 1944-49. In the end, the Communists were defeated because Tito, the dictator in Yugoslavia, grew annoyed with the Russian government and closed the border to Greece." She adds tersely, "This country is frequently at odds with Turkey. Cypress is Greek and the Turks are interlopers, wanting to control the Aegean Sea."

Outside the city, she points in the direction of a small manmade lake near the town of Marathon and relates, "In ancient times, the Greek city-states stopped feuding with each other long enough to join forces to fight a battle there. After they defeated the barbarian Persians, a runner was sent to deliver the news to Athens, 42 km away. When he arrived, the man gasped the word *NIKE,* meaning victory. Of course, that was long before marathon running became a sport."

While driving through cotton fields and orchards of pistachio nut and olive trees near Thebes, we hear this tale. "The King of Thebes was told by the Oracle of Delphi that it would be his fate to be killed by his own son, Oedipus." As the familiar story unfolds, we leave the orchards behind and start across a mountainside. Pointing to a crossroads in a valley far below, she confidently assures us, "That is where the battle between father and son took place."

"Unaware that he had killed his father, the young man married the widowed Queen of Thebes. She bore him four children before the fateful day arrived when they discovered they were mother and son. The queen killed herself and Oedipus tore out his eyes. He spent the rest of his life wandering the countryside with his daughter/sister as companion." Somehow, the view of isolated mountain tops and lonely valleys that make up this part of Greece adds poignancy to the words.

We drive past a mountain said to be home to the *Nine Muses*, who were credited with inspiring artists. A higher mountain with snow-capped peak is identified as the home of Apollo. Crossing a summit, we come to a small village clinging to the steep side of the pass. The road narrows to a single lane as we enter, and roofs on either side are not much higher than the bus. When we meet a second bus, the drivers stop and jockey past each other with only inches between them and the buildings.

The road now drops down a broad, steep mountainside, turns a corner, and there before us are the few remaining columns of the Temple of Apollo. The ruins sit on an isolated bench midway up the rugged slope of Mount Parnassus, ten km inland from the Gulf of Corinth. With bright blue sky, sunshine, and a high rocky cliff soaring up behind, the setting is breathtaking.

The complex at Delphi was built on three levels; a gymnasium at the lower site, the Temple of Apollo and a theater midway, and a stadium higher up. All were considered necessary to work the mind and body and create a productive citizen. Visitors are believed to have stayed at the lower site for several days, preparing themselves to climb the mountain and hear the words of the oracle.

We only glimpse the ruins at the lower site, as our tour starts in the ancient agora, or business center, on the upper side of the road. Breathing in clear, cold mountain air, we start up a wide path paved with large stones known as *the Sacred Way*. Rows of smaller foundation stones on either side are all that remains of the small storerooms that once held the many expensive tributes presented to the oracle.

We soon come to a wall containing large, octagonal-shaped stones inscribed with Greek characters, and just beyond is the large, rough rock on which the sibyl perched. Bathed in smoke from laurel leaves, she prophesied in a frenzied trance and her message was translated by a priest. The prophecies were often ambiguous and one king was told, "If you go to war, a great kingdom will be destroyed." He went to war and lost his own kingdom. (It's believed that priests at the lower site gathered information so messages could be appropriately tailored.)

The broad path circles on up the hillside to the Temple of Apollo, the columns now silhouetted against the soft haze of the wide valley. Nearby, rows of seats in an amphitheater hug the curve of the steep slope. Higher yet, at the third site, stone seats line one side of a 650-foot playing field. When we start back down, the high cliff face looms overhead, and before us, the full sweep of the mountainside provides mesmerizing views.

All too soon, we're back on the bus and headed to the site museum. Other tour buses converge on the building at the same time, and the noise inside is unbelievably loud. The floor rumbles as people walk across it, so they speak loudly, and guides shout over top of them. Dave and I wander off on our own and stop to admire a hollow, bronze statue known as *the Charioteer*. It appears almost unmarred and I marvel that it managed to survive the centuries. I then read the sign beside it and learn that the six large horses and two slaves that were part of the exhibit are entirely missing.

Before returning to Athens, we stop for a late lunch at a restaurant in the new town of Delphi, enjoying both the food and the view down the valley to an inlet in the Gulf of Corinth. The day is such a success that we book a tour to the Greek islands a few days later. It's a disaster. The boat is packed to capacity with 700 passengers, rain pours down all day, and we stop only long enough in the islands to visit tourist stalls selling the same production curios we saw in Athens.

A visit to the Port of Piraeus is a must, given our sailing background, so after the rush is over one morning, we catch the train. The station platform is still crowded, so I stick close to Dave as he steps aboard, but a young man cuts between us, roughly pushing me aside. Not wanting to be left behind, I instinctively push back and make it into the car, but a second man forces me farther away. Grabbing onto a pole, I turn and see Dave standing eight feet away. The two men, wearing black leather jackets, stand behind him. I don't like the crowded car or the fact that we've been separated and keep my eyes on Dave as the train starts to move.

Nothing happens until the train slows at the next station, then one of the men attacks him, a quick punch over the kidneys and two more jabs. I'm horrified, unable to believe my eyes, then totally confused because no one else seems to notice! Not even Dave! The doors then open and the two men dash off, followed by shouting and running footsteps on the platform. I anxiously rush over and Dave assures me that he's fine. According to him, "Those fellows were pushing at each other, and I felt something brush my pocket, so I stuck my hand in, thinking they were pickpockets. I did feel a light jab against my lower back, but it was like being jostled in a crowd."

We have no idea what was going on and can't ask anyone, as we don't speak the language. But we'd been deliberately separated and it happened quickly and easily. *Had we been targeted?* Feeling unsettled, I don't enjoy our visit to the port city.

My composure only returns after we return to Athens and are strolling through the ruins of the Roman Agora. Despite the noise of the city, there's a silence, a peacefulness, beneath the columns. This market was in use during the time of Julius Caesar, 2,000 years before. Wide, low stone steps cover over one end, and parts of rock walls, archways, and columns extend down one side. Bits and pieces are also strewn across a large, open courtyard. The adjacent Tower of the Wind has personifications of wind directions carved in relief below the roofline.

Next morning we're off to the airport, and as we drive through busy streets, I realize that my enthusiasm for ancient Greece did not extend to the present. The shopkeepers and site attendants had been morose, with many acting like they thought they were owed a living. I find myself wondering, *could that have anything to do with long-term tourism?*

CHAPTER 23
LISBOA AND RIO

From Athens, it's a 2.5-hour flight to Munich, Germany, then a 3-hour flight to Lisbon, Portugal. We check into a very comfortable downtown hotel, which proves to be a block off the main thoroughfare, Avenida Liberdade. Next morning, fortified by an excellent buffet breakfast, we walk south down the avenue toward the Tagus River.

The air is cool, the sky grey and overcast, but the broad promenade bordering the avenue is really very pleasant, with designs in paving stones, rows of shade trees, and flags flying in front of embassies housed in large office buildings. There aren't many people about, and after walking a few long blocks, we turn onto a narrow, crooked street that takes us into an old part of the city. Soon, we enter a large square filled with black faces, a reminder that Morocco and NW Africa are not far away.

On a low hill nearby is the centuries-old Castelo de Sao Jorge. Two young women greet us as we approach the gate and hand us each a Valentine's Day gift. The small parcels contain chocolates, a foil-wrapped condom, and a card promoting safe sex. (Dave stows the condom in a pocket of his carryon bag and brightens the face of many a customs agent for years to come.)

We stroll through the castle's cobblestone courtyards, admiring the high stone walls and archways, then climb up onto the ramparts. Following them around, we stop to look down on a maze of red-tiled roofs and crooked lanes that lead to the river. Low cloud and haze obscure the view beyond, and it's easy to conjure up images of ancient ships that once visited from Phoenicia, Greece, Rome, and Arabia. After making our way down to the river, we walk along the waterfront, then stumble onto a pedestrian mall that takes us most of the way back to our hotel.

We've been walking for five hours and are tired and hungry, but know that people here eat late, so wait a while before going out for a meal. About 1700, hunger gets the better of us, and we set off to look for a restaurant. After walking only a few blocks, we stumble across one that is open, then sit down at a table and order our food and a bottle of wine. The bottle is empty when the chef strolls in an hour later. Our meal is served an hour and a half after that, so we order another bottle of wine, making for an expensive meal. Many restaurants still aren't open when we return to the hotel.

I now read in my travel guide that we're within walking distance of the Port of Belem. Many of the mariners who first explored the world's oceans left from this port, and I'd thought of them often during our voyage across the Pacific. We had detailed charts, modern navigation instruments, and high-frequency radio to keep us safe, while they had sailed into the unknown. I'd been awed when I thought of their courage.

Next morning, we set off on a sort of pilgrimage of our own. We first walk through shaded, canyon-like streets where the air has a bite, then cross through a rabbit warren of narrow lanes and crowded homes that go up a hill and down the other side. After walking south and west for two hours, we come to the banks of the Tagus River and the Port of Belem. Within a few minutes, we're studying a memorial called *the Discoveries,* which is dedicated to those early mariners.

We spend two hours immersed in history at the nearby Maritime Museum. We learn that Portuguese ships left on the first of their voyages of discovery in 1420, and subsequent expeditions continued for decades as they expanded their body of knowledge. Their efforts resulted in two incredible passages.

In 1498, Vasco da Gama found his route to India around the Cape of Good Hope, and in 1509, Magellan went around the world via Cape Horn.

We study full-sized replicas of the small ships into which sailors were crammed when they went to sea, as well as the old charts and simple navigation instruments that were used. I view the handwritten pilots with something akin to reverence. When I see a chart on the wall showing da Gama's route from India to Portugal, I am inspired. *This could be our route when we leave Australia!*

Marveling at what we've seen, we return to the waterfront and start down to the Tower of Belem, which we can see at the river mouth. But a cold wind blows in from the sea, so we turn and walk upriver. We're soon passing the elaborate façade of the huge Monastery dos Jeronimos, which is decorated with ships and sea forms, (anchors, ropes, fish, etc.) in the Manueline style. The structure was built in the 16th century to commemorate the opening up of a sea route to India.

Taking a bus back to our hotel, we shop for dinner at a small store across the alley and relax in our room with meat pies and two liters of wine.

Next day, with the sky clear and sunny, we walk west and north for another five hours. We eventually come out at the top of a long, gentle slope, with the formal gardens of Edward VII Park directly in front of us. Below the park looms the monument at Praca Marques de Pombal, which leads to Avenida da Liberdade, with the sparkling waters of the river far beyond. The view is spectacular and manmade, as Lisbon was destroyed by an earthquake in 1755. The King's chief minister, the Marquis do Pombal, oversaw much of the re-building using new, wider streets and rectilinear lines.

Our last day is also sunny, with temperatures warmer than we've seen since Brisbane. We walk down to the river and return via the pedestrian mall, which is crowded with shoppers moving in and out of small boutiques. Street venders are scarce, but a few musicians entertain onlookers and waiters set up white-clothed tables on paving stones in front of restaurants. Watching people move freely across this large, open space is a noticeable contrast to other cities we've visited.

Next day, we board a plane for the ten-hour flight across the Atlantic Ocean to Brazil. The lights of Rio de Janeiro glitter in the darkness as we approach, and when we deplane, the temperature is 32 degrees C. The heat hits us like a blast furnace as we're wearing long pants and boots in order to ease the burden on our carryon bags.

As in Bangkok, our travel information recommends buying a taxi voucher inside the terminal, strongly hinting that to hire a cab outside is to risk murder and mayhem. Having learned our lesson, we intend to do just that and look for an ATM. (We're limiting our use of credit cards, as when traveling the previous year, charges were denied and holds put on our cards, which had been pretty inconvenient.)

We can't find an ATM and are told, "Oh, they're only in the domestic terminal." That means lugging our bags over a series of moving sidewalks through half-a-kilometer of corridors. Given our clothing and the heat, we're soon uncomfortably sweaty and tired. When we finally track down an ATM and get some cash, we can't find a taxi kiosk. Now we're told, "Oh, they're only in the international terminal."

That's too much for Dave, who comes to a stop in front of an exit. Looking at me belligerently, he declares, "There's no bloody way I'm packing these bags all the way back to the other terminal!"

But I'm adamant, "I'm not going through those doors without a voucher!"

As we stand in the corridor, glaring at each other, a man wearing a uniform of sorts tries to help. "Taxis are just out through that door," he assures us. When we don't move, he continues to stand there, fingering his security badge.

Taking a closer look at him, Dave asks, "How much?"

"Forty reals."

Picking up our bags, Dave follows the man through the doors. I unhappily trail along behind, sure that we're pushing our luck. Gazing stoically out the car window, I recognize the looming shape of Sugarloaf as we pass, then see only a long, lonely stretch of darkness beside the ocean. Twenty minutes later, the taxi turns onto a dimly-lit street and drops us in front of our hotel.

Our original timeline had us in Rio at the start of Carnival, when all the hotels were charging a minimum of $1,500 for a block of five nights. After shortening our stay by two nights, we still tried three hotels before finding one with a vacancy. So, I'm relieved to find that the one we're in is very pleasant and only two blocks off Copacabana Beach.

Next morning, we stroll down a wide, tiled promenade beside the beach, and waves sparkle in bright sunshine as a gentle surf rolls up on the broad, white sands beside us. On the land side, steep-faced mountains soar over the roofs of hotels and apartment buildings that occupy a strip maybe five blocks wide. Beneath our feet, the small black and white tiles remind me of Lisbon, but the parade of tanned bodies jiggling up and down beside us, mostly young, has to be uniquely Rio.

The day is already hot and sunbathers are out in force, but the beach is in no way crowded as it stretches for 4.5 km. At the far end, we rest awhile in the shade of a small hill behind Sugarloaf, and a light breeze stirs the warm air as we start back. With hardly anyone in the water, we walk on the hard sand at the water's edge, and sometimes wade in the surf. We then stop and eat at one of the large street-side restaurants on the boulevard near our hotel.

We walk in the opposite direction next day, following Ipanema Beach down to Leblon. This area is more up market, with the same spectacular mountain views, but the temperature reaches 38 degrees C and humidity is high. A few fishing boats work the waters off a nearby island, and the guns at Copacabana Fort appear to be pointing toward the beach. Amongst the rocks, we see a scattering of plastic bags, Styrofoam cups, and who knows what else.

Behind the hotels, clinging to the steep sides of the mountains, are the *favelos*, the shanty towns of the poor and the jobless. Tourists are warned not to enter these areas on their own, but that doesn't mean the resort area is safe from crime. One day about noon, as we turn onto the street leading to our hotel, a figure hugging a body board flashes by. Hearing yells, we step back just as half a dozen uniformed figures fly past. We follow them back to the corner and see a large group of men surrounding a prone figure on the ground; presumably, he took something that wasn't his.

We join a bus tour that takes us through the downtown, then drops us off at the tram going up Corcovado Mountain. Our guide points to breadfruit, avocado, papaya, and coffee bean plants growing alongside the track. At the top, we study the 100-foot-high statue of *Christ the Redeemer,* then turn to the panoramic view of the city.

To the left is Guanabara Bay, with the port on the far side and high-rise apartments and hotels scattered along the shore on this side. In front of us, Sugarloaf Mountain soars over boats at anchor near the Rio Yacht Club. To the right is the Ipanema-Leblon resort area, with a race track and large saltwater lagoon behind it.

Our guide explains, "Much of the land in the resort area was part of the lagoon or planted to sugarcane not that long ago. During the reclamation process, the boulevard was widened and the beach area moved out to sea. Two million people packed it for New Year's celebrations in 2001."

As we return through the city, traffic slows to a crawl on the expressway, where policemen carrying rifles direct traffic. We now have a better view of the small shacks piled on top of one another that make up the city's slums. The contrast between the hidden menace of these narrow alleyways and the sunshine and beaches of the resort area is so marked that I wonder how this city of 9 million people survives. Our guide tells us, "Two million residents of Rio are homeless, and twelve million of the country's children have been abandoned."

Streets are noticeably busier on our last day, as Carnival starts the next. Hotels are full, prices are rising, and there's a tension in the air. When we leave the hotel at 0530 next morning, our cab driver takes a long, roundabout route through empty streets to the airport. I can't help but be suspicious, but Dave figures he's avoiding downtown street closures. The day goes downhill from there.

At the terminal, we find a long queue waiting to clear airport security, then our flight number to Sao Paulo isn't posted at the designated departure gate. A nearby flight monitor still shows that gate, so we find a spot to sit and listen for English announcements on the PA system. We notice a mob of passengers besieging a nearby airline counter, but are none the wiser as they speak Portuguese.

When our departure time comes and goes and we've heard nothing, Dave joins the crowd at the counter, as we have a connecting flight to catch. He's made to wait for someone who speaks English and then told, "Your flight has already boarded. You're going to have to run to catch it."

Grabbing our bags, we race down the ramp to the airplane door but are shooed away by a frustrated flight attendant. "Wait 'til you're called," she scolds. I show her our boarding passes and she nods her head and confirms, "Yes, this is the right plane." After waiting for another hour, the boarding announcement finally comes.

The sky is bright and sunny as we fly west along the coastline. but thirty minutes into the flight, the pilot starts doing steep turns out over the Atlantic Ocean. Fifteen minutes later, he turns the plane inland and we see low cloud and haze blanketing the shallow valleys ahead. He then flies low over the streets of Sao Paulo for miles, basically making a long, flat, straight-in approach to the runway, and drops the airplane onto the tarmac so hard that my teeth rattle. It's the worst landing I ever experience and I'm truly thankful that we change planes. I really didn't want to get back on that one.

Waiting customer service staff hurry us along to our connecting flight, and we race madly down endless corridors lugging our bags. Our flight number again isn't posted at the gate, but a flight monitor now shows a different gate. Rushing off, we pass another twelve gates, then follow signs down to a bus loading platform at ground level. As there's no one here, we sit and wait. A bus driver appears fifteen minutes later, and we're loaded onto a bus and taken out to a plane. Heaving sighs of relief as we climb aboard, we stow our bags, then wait another two hours for passengers from other delayed flights.

We later learn that two flights into Rio were delayed by fog, so three departing flights were combined. But not speaking the language made for a very frustrating day. Racing up and down, I'd felt isolated from everyone around us, like we were in some kind of bubble. I certainly gained a new appreciation for the kind souls who'd helped us in the past.

A few years later, we're in the departure lounge at Vancouver airport when a Polish man, who doesn't speak English, is trapped for nine hours in the Arrivals Hall. When he becomes unruly, RCMP are called and he is tasered five times. I am sickened when we hear about his death. I can't believe that not one of my countrymen came to his aid, or his mother's, for that matter; she was in a lounge outside the secure area.

For years, I also have a jaundiced view of cab drivers, thanks to the warnings we'd received at Bangkok and Rio airports. That only changes after a few years in Malaysia, as we frequently use taxis to travel back and forth to KLIA. There are never any problems! Then, after returning from an overseas trip, we find that a taxi voucher system has been introduced. We can no longer hire taxis outside the terminal, and the vouchers cost significantly more. Soon, local cabbies won't take us to the airport, as they can't pick up fares there.

I start to wonder if there was a connection between the warnings we'd received and the licensing of cabs that could pick up at airports. The drama in Bangkok had involved an unlicensed cab. In Rio, it had been okay to hire a cab outside the domestic terminal, just not the international. I tell myself, *don't be so cynical. Nobody would make up stories to scare people into buying vouchers. Would they?*

CHAPTER 24
LA PAZ, BOLIVIA

From Sao Paulo, we fly northwest across Brazil to Santa Cruz, Bolivia. Our route takes us near the border with Paraguay, but all I see out the window is low cloud. I occupy myself by studying the women who constantly walk up and down the aisle, digging into overhead bins. They chatter long and loud in Spanish, spitting out words like machine gun bullets. I've never heard people talk so fast.

After a brief stop in Santa Cruz, we depart for La Paz, high in the Andes Mountains. During the hour-long flight, my eyes are glued out the window, as we gain over 11,000 feet in elevation (from 419 to 3,900 meters). Just after takeoff, we cross a broad plain, where deeply-gouged river channels are stained a rusty red and several roads have been cut. We then follow a narrow valley into the mountains, and as we gain altitude, the slopes around us grow higher and steeper.

Heavy cloud makes it difficult to get a sense of the terrain, but before long a large river glistens in a deep valley far below. I then see a few buildings clinging to a mountainside, and a few more sit on a level area high atop a ridge, with a road zigzagging down into an abyss. We first see Lake Titicaca while circling the airport at La Paz, then more flood-ravaged land appears near the end of the runway.

The plane comes to a stop on the tarmac near the terminal, and as I step through the door, I'm reminded of flying into Prince George years before in the early spring. The day is dark and dreary, a cold rain falls, and there's a sense of arriving on a frontier. The feeling is reinforced inside the terminal, where an oxygen station is provided for anyone who needs it. We book a hotel through a travel agent ($36 US), who warns us not to pay more than $8 for a taxi downtown.

The road into the city brings us out on the rim of a bowl that is 1,300 feet deep and nearly 5 km across. The entire city sits in it and the sight is unforgettable. Commercial buildings, churches, and hotels line a ravine created by the Rio Choqueyapu (now mostly underground), and residential housing climbs to the top of the basin walls.

According to my travel guide, La Paz was founded in 1548 when gold was found in the Rio Choqueyapu, but its future was assured because of its location on the main silver route between Potosi, 500 miles to the south, and the Pacific Ocean. The vast silver deposits there created the largest and wealthiest city on the continent, and underwrote the Spanish economy for more than two centuries.

But a dark chapter in man's history accompanied these events, as thousands of Indian and African laborers were forced to work in the mines. Conditions were atrocious and, according to one report, up to eight million workers may have died over a period of 300 years. The coca plant is believed to have played a role.

The plant was widely used by native people when the Spanish arrived in the early 1500s. Leaves were either chewed or brewed to make tea and said to alleviate hunger and strengthen the feeble. If chewed with the ashes of certain other plants, it provided a high degree of insensitivity to hunger, cold, fatigue, and pain.

When cocaine, the highly processed derivative of the plant, became popular as a recreational drug, the increasing demand for leaves brought widespread corruption and growing social problems to the country, as well as foreign interference in its governance. In the 167 years after Bolivia gained independence from Spain in 1825, the government was replaced 188 times.

Now, as we drive down into the bowl, I study the narrow, unfamiliar streets with a growing sense of unease. When our driver stops in front of an ordinary-looking building and says that it is our hotel, I look out suspiciously. We enter a tiny lobby, where a few kitchen-style chairs sit beside the front door, while stairs to the upper floors are close by the front desk.

We're now more or less accustomed to showing our passports when we check in, but are surprised to be handed small cups of coca leaf tea. The clerk tells us, "It will lessen symptoms of altitude sickness." He then warns, "Don't carry any valuables, ever, especially your passports. If you're stopped by police, don't give them your passports and never get in a vehicle. Tell them you'll meet them at the police station."

The hotel appears to be new, but our room on the second floor is small and dark. A twelve-inch TV sits high on one wall and a narrow window overlooks the tavern entrance below. There's a security safe in a closet, where I deposit our passports, airline tickets, and most of our money. We'll now carry only day money and copies of ID papers, even limit camera use. (When we travel, I carry our valuables in a pouch hanging around my neck, under my clothes, and we have copies of our IDs in our carryon bags, in case we're robbed.)

At this elevation, every breath provides about two-thirds the amount of oxygen obtained at sea level. Visitors are advised to rest for 24 hours and give their bodies time to adapt, as fluid can collect in the lungs, causing shortness of breath, or in the brain, resulting in headaches. But we immediately set off into the grey twilight, as Dave wants to find a money changer. My chest starts to burn within minutes of starting up the narrow, cobblestone street and I have to slow down. Soon, I have a slight headache, but he is not affected.

We walk for blocks without seeing a soul, then enter a square called Plaza Murillo, which is filled with people. Some sit on benches, others stroll about, and all are warmly dressed. After the bare flesh of Rio, it's the first thing I notice. Sprinkled amongst them are Cholas, city dwelling Quecha or Aymara women, with bowler hats perched on their heads, shawls around their shoulders, and long, tiered skirts that make them look an axe-handle wide. Some carry items in an Andes backpack, a colorful, folded blanket draped across the back and tied around the shoulders.

The streets on the other side of the square are busy, and it's only now that we realize Bolivians also celebrate Carnival. Young people, maybe 14 to 18 years of age, dart through the traffic throwing water-filled balloons or spraying snow from aerosol cans. Police wearing military-fatigue-style uniforms are an obvious presence; most carry rifles or side arms and a few have truncheons.

We're approached by a few disabled beggars as we turn down a short, steep lane to a lower street. I then see a young woman half lying on a ragged blanket in the shadows between the sidewalk and a building. She's small, slim, and dark, and to my horror, her breasts are bare, the nipples erect, and a tiny baby lies on her lap.

After walking a few more blocks, we find the money changer and Dave swaps our reals for bolivianos. We start back on the lower street, but soon see a crowd of maybe 100 people in a large square ahead. Warily drawing closer, we make out two groups of young people facing off across a narrow lane. As they appear to be well supplied with water-filled balloons, we climb up a steep lane to avoid them. That causes my headache to worsen and it's stabbing at the back of my eyes when we reach the hotel. I take two aspirin and am out for the night, but the headache is still there when I wake up.

The hotel provides a buffet breakfast of fresh fruit, juice, scrambled eggs, bread, and arrowroot biscuits in a large, pleasant, second-floor dining room. The coffee, unfortunately, is no more palatable than in Rio. Every morning, we're joined by a few young men in blue warm up suits. The sports stadium is only a block away and they're members of a visiting soccer team.

Hotel staff tell us that carnival is celebrated for four days in La Paz, with parades every day, but no one can tell us where or when. We walk downtown to the visitors' center to inquire, but it's closed for the holidays. On the way, we pass through the square where we saw the young people the night before, Iglesia San Francisco Plaza. Local entrepreneurs are busy setting up stalls, so it appears to be central to events.

We find our way back to Plaza Murillo, where we sit on a bench and bask in warm sunshine while watching the ebb and flow of people. The square is the formal center of the city and is surrounded by imposing government buildings and a cathedral built in 1835. With patches of fenced, emerald-green grass, green leafy trees, and a few statues and monuments, it's really very pleasant. Before long, I'm feeling relaxed and comfortable, and my headache starts to ease. I don't want to move and we stay for two hours.

Next day, we get up to heavy rain. As my headache lingers, I try arrowroot biscuits and tea for breakfast and it's gone by the time we're finished. The rain eases two hours later, and we set off in the opposite direction from the day before. We have no idea where we'll end up because streets are not well marked. We think primary streets run between plazas and climb as they traverse the sides of the bowl; the cross streets seem to run from the bottom street straight up the sides.

Within five minutes, a man is running toward us, urgently calling, "Senor! Senor!" As the street is pretty much deserted, we nervously keep walking. When the man comes closer and tugs at Dave's sleeve, we warily stop and turn toward him. That's when I see the dark brown liquid dripping off the back of Dave's yellow jacket. A second man rushes over, pulling a few napkins from his pocket, and with them I'm able to stop the drips. A third man now joins us, speaking in Spanish and pointing at my back. Turns out, I'm also covered with whatever it is.

After thanking the men profusely, we return to the hotel and clean up. I'm able to put Dave's shell into the sink, then sponge off our pants and my jacket. The stuff is sticky but doesn't smell, and looks like it came from a spray gun.

Setting off once more, we come to Av Bolivar, where streams of people are walking in both directions. Turning onto it, we see police setting up positions, so figure this has to be a parade route. We find a spot to stand under a building overhang that protects our backs, then watch as gangs of youths roam up and down, targeting each other with water-filled balloons, water pistols, and backpack units that shoot 50-75 feet. Street vendors have fresh supplies of both water and balloons. Strings of firecrackers now begin to pop, some thrown off rooftops. After a while, the cold drizzle that is falling grows heavier, and we return to the hotel.

We've barely removed our jackets when the boom-booming of a drum comes from the direction of the plaza near the stadium. We rush over in time to see a brass band followed by youths dressed in clown costumes making their last circuit through a large crowd. Trails of water are left by the clowns, who've obviously been targeted by marauding gangs of young people. We wander about for maybe thirty minutes before another band appears with a smaller group of demons. After watching them circle the square, we return to the hotel, where we hear other bands arrive.

When we go down to the dining room for dinner, we choose a table beside a window overlooking the square and watch the crowd that mills about below. As the sun drops down to the horizon, the sky clears to the west and reveals the beautiful, rounded top of a snowcapped mountain. Perfectly framed by blue sky, *Illimani* is almost 21,000 feet high and rises ethereally above a layer of gray cloud.

Next day, we join a bus tour to an ancient ceremonial center near the south shore of Lake Titikaka. (The travel agent from the airport told us about it when he tracked us down to discuss our onward travel arrangements.) We're picked up at 0830, and as the bus climbs upward, heavy grey clouds hang over the rim of the bowl. Pointing to deep gullies washed out near the road, then to the destruction left by a recent landslide, our guide explains, "The ground is very unstable and slum dwellings all around the bowl are at risk."

One million people live in La Paz and another 500,000 live in El Alta, on the plain to the west. Small homes here have four-foot-high adobe walls surrounding their yards. According to our guide, "The walls provide protection from the wind, which never stops blowing on the altiplano." The altiplano is an immense inland plateau at an elevation of 12,350 feet, with 20,000-foot mountain ranges to east and west.

The land looks very bleak as we drive across it, with pools of water in deeply eroded stream beds and just a hint of green in the vegetation. However, our guide insists, "You're lucky to see it now because the fields and hills are yellow in winter, when there is no rain."

After a ninety-minute drive, we stop at the site museum, where we learn that Tiwanaku culture had flourished here for 1,500 years. It ended in 1200 AD, when the Inca Empire seized control of the area. Exhibits include bits and pieces of pottery, a few stone carvings, and a mummy bound in a woven grass sack in a fetal position. There are also human skulls, some of which are long and narrow. Babies of the high born had had blocks of wood bound to their heads, reshaping them to distinguish them from peasants.

A sand model provides an overview of the three temples located on the site. The Temple of the Sky is a terraced pyramid, which had a large pool of water on top that reflected the stars. The Temple of the Earth is a large, flat platform, while the Temple of the Underground is a pit. Astrologically aligned, they are believed to have been used to define planting cycles.

When we're dropped off at the center, the sun is shining brightly, and the morning is remarkably pleasant. Wild flowers bloom near the parking lot, and our guide points out a soft grass that provides animal feed and is used in making rope. Another hard, sharp-edged grass is used for thatching roofs and covering the tops of mud walls.

One corner of the pyramid mound has been excavated, revealing the sculptured blocks of basalt used to edge the three lower tiers. Rocks from the upper two tiers are missing, having been used by local people to build homes. The basalt came from mountains west of the lake, where the blocks were cut and shaped.

As we climb the mound, I feel the altitude and pause frequently to rest and gaze around. To the west, toward Lake Titikaka, the level floor of the plateau is dotted with the thatched-roofed, mud-walled homes of small farms. To the south, the snow line is just visible beneath clouds sitting down on a mountain range.

North of the mound is an enormous, flat, earthen platform, and six giant steps, not meant for humans, lead up to it. A statue covered in symbols stands at the top of the steps, and the sun gate stands in the NW corner, as archeologists aren't sure where it belongs. Giant steps also lead down six feet into the pit-temple, and its walls are lined with sculptured stone faces representing the tribes.

Some reconstruction work has been done using cement and cement blocks, but according to our guide, "Money for the work is not easy to find." There are no marked paths and no obvious effort has been made to protect the site. We actually stumble over a shallow drainage ditch leading to the platform that contains a makeshift pipe made of sculptured rocks. Another ditch lined with flat rocks slopes gently away.

Clouds have been moving in and growing darker, and a sudden burst of cold rain now sends us scurrying for the bus. We're driven to a nearby facility and served a late lunch of hot, tasty potato soup and fried, coated white fish from Lake Titikaka. We end with coca tea that I think smells and tastes swampy. While we eat, the rain grows heavier, turns to hail, and the temperature is noticeably colder when we leave.

We take a different road back to La Paz, and small, low clouds race by a few hundred feet overhead, a sight I'd only seen before from an airplane. Overflowing streams have flooded many of the fields beside the road, and while some of the crops are unfamiliar, we recognize potatoes, beans, and a few grains.

When we arrive in La Paz, downtown streets are crowded with revelers, and as our driver inches the bus through, I catch sight of several brass bands and a few heavily-embroidered, richly-colored costumes. After dropping off everyone but a Dutch couple and ourselves, the driver tells us, "Your hotels are on the other side of the parade route, and I can't get across, so will drop you here."

That makes the Dutch lady very unhappy and she complains, "If we get off here, we'll be soaked!" She then asks, "Do you think we can get a taxi?"

Heaving a sigh, the driver presses on for another fifteen minutes and gets within three blocks of our hotel. We're able to see the square near the stadium, and the other couple's hotel is a block past ours. The four of us get out and walk, but part company when we cut through the square, as they won't go near it. While the celebrations may seem like small town high jinks, they can be daunting in a city with a million souls.

Once back at our hotel, I keep watch from the window. Everywhere I look, young people run about, popping out of side streets and climbing up onto roof tops. Snow is sprayed from aerosol cans but the weapon of choice is water, which is sprayed, thrown, and dropped. Music floats up from the square whenever a band arrives, and at 2000, a PA system is set up. For the next two hours, we're serenaded by singers and bands. A particularly heavy downpour brings festivities to an end, but partying in the hotel continues well into the night.

According to my guidebook, Bolivia's population is 95% Roman Catholic, but it's a form of the Christian faith that blends in ancient folk traditions and beliefs. Fiestas include lots of dancing, parades, food, alcohol, and generally unrestrained behavior. Loud noises that were meant to scare away demons and protect homes start next morning, with loud bursts of fireworks before 0600. People also wrap ribbons and flowers around tables, rooms, and even house exteriors to ensure good relationships.

We spend our last day in La Paz touring through a market area that we saw from the bus. It's early and only a few handicraft stalls are open, but I'm able to admire the attractive, colorful designs on sweaters and shawls at my leisure. More stalls are open in the Witches Market, where most items look mass produced. The many dried llama fetuses are an exception, as traditionally, they were sacrificed to Mother Earth after the harvest. I've read that they are still used in local remedies for all manner of ailments, including infertility. I also read that the people had dried potatoes by letting them freeze, then peeling them and setting them out in the sun.

The streets are now much quieter, although a few firecrackers and water bombs are thrown as we make our way back. Party noises come from a couple of small stores that we pass, and the staff at the hotel have streamers around their necks and dance in the lobby. Late in the afternoon, loud music again blares from the square.

As I pack up that night, I think about some of the unique aspects of the city. I'd been fascinated by the unmarked vans that made up the public transportation system. At busy times of the day, they'd been lined halfway up the block. When one approached an intersection, a man leaned out through the door and called out in a staccato monotone. It then stopped briefly to let passengers scurry off and on.

Shoeshine boys wearing ski masks had wandered about the plazas with their tool kits and Dave had been a favorite target. While trying to see their eyes through the holes in their woolen head coverings, he'd asked, "But how do you polish running shoes?"

The beggars presented a dilemma, as we did not want our presence to disrupt lives. After mulling over how best to deal with them, we concluded that the local community was best able to respond to their needs. Our contribution had to be to the economy of the city. (We found support for that decision in Nepal.)

Next morning, as we check out of the hotel, the desk clerk informs us, "There's no public transport today; all the drivers got drunk last night." But the travel agent from the airport prepared this part of our itinerary, and a van advertising Peru-Bolivia tours pulls in just after 0800. The driver confirms that he's there to take us to Copacabana on Lake Titicaca. We then wait fifteen minutes for our guide to arrive. While I'm soon satisfied that our driver is not hung over, the guide, Carlos, makes no effort to hide his suffering.

CHAPTER 25
LAKE TITICACA

The morning is cool and cloudy as we leave La Paz, but bits of blue sky peek through holes in the clouds as we drive north. Farmers tend to small gardens beside the road, usually with a cow or llama tethered close by, and small flocks of sheep are visible in the distance. Near the south end of Lake Titicaca, the road winds through the mud huts of a small village, and the bus slows to a crawl as people and animals wander across in front of us at will.

For the next half hour, the road crosses terraced ridges, providing scenic views down the lake. It comes to an end on the shore of a long, narrow reach, where a motor launch holding 20 passengers waits to take travelers across the channel. Within minutes, every seat is filled. The wind has pushed up high, rolling waves mid-channel, which toss the boat about pretty roughly, while the van tilts ominously on its small barge. Carlos now rouses himself long enough to admit, "In winter, we sometimes wait three or four hours before we can cross."

After we've reunited with the van, we cross more terraced hillsides, which now rise up in every direction. Areas currently cultivated show up as strips of green in an otherwise brown landscape. Around every bend, a solitary figure comes into view, either tending animals on a hillside, or holding a bouquet of vividly-colored gladiolas on the edge of the road. I'm astounded to see such flowers at this high altitude. We're now at 13,000 feet, 650 feet above the lake and 300 feet below the ridge tops.

Lake Titicaca is 230 km long and 97 km wide, and the Bolivia-Peru border cuts across it. It seems that Copacabana, which is in Bolivia, sits on a peninsula in the lake, and the road access runs through Peru. So, we again transfer to a motor launch and take an hour-long tour while the van is driven around the land route.

Carlos informs us, "We go to Isla del Sol (Island of the Sun), which was a sacred site of the ancient Incas. They believed that their first Emperor rose from the *Rock of the Puma* (*Titikaka*) on the island's northern tip." As we pass a large bay, he points to the shore and explains, "Visitors purified themselves there before crossing to the island. They brought gifts of gold and handfuls of dirt from their homes, and when they left, priests gave them three seeds to take home to plant."

The island is large, and countless narrow terraces climb the steep slope between rocky cliffs on the shoreline and the rounded summit. We don't see any villages, but Carlos points to power lines leading across the water and disapprovingly declares, "There are three villages on the island, each with 200 families, but the power isn't for them; it goes to a hotel and backpacker hostels."

After a twenty-minute ride, we pull into a dock at the base of a hill, then climb up 204 steep, stone steps. I climb slowly because of the altitude, so have plenty of time to admire my surroundings. Water cascades down a narrow ditch beside us, and the surrounding vegetation is lush and green. About ten feet on the other side are the ends of low rock walls that separate the narrow terraces.

Once on top, the ground is paved with flat stones that lead to another rock wall, where three columns of water gush out into a basin. I stoop, scooping water into my mouth with my hand, drinking thirstily; the water is sweet and cool, but I expected it to be colder. Carlos now boasts, "To drink from this spring is to remain forever young!"

The boat engine dies as we return down the lake, and the boat drifts for ten minutes while the men work on it. I spend the time drinking in the silence and admiring the crystal-clear water around us. All too soon, the engine roars back to life and we speed across the water to Copacabana, where the van awaits.

Several miracles reportedly occurred in Copacabana in the 16th century, and construction of a Moorish-style cathedral began in 1605. It took 200 years to complete, and the front plaza is said to be a replica of the one at St Peter's Basilica. The village is now a destination for pilgrims who walk from La Paz.

I'm most impressed with a small second-floor chapel, where tall vases of beautiful, freshly-cut gladiolas frame a wooden statue of the Virgin that was carved by an Indian artist. Carlos now clarifies, "Wherever the Catholic Church was greatly outnumbered by local people, as in South America, concessions were made to local customs. That's why our pre-Lent festivities appear more pagan than Catholic, people are actually paying homage to Mother Earth."

The van then bounces and sways down broad streets pitted with potholes and lined with square, faceless buildings. One of them proves to be our hotel. After checking in, we have a late lunch with the two men before they return to La Paz. As we eat chicken soup and king fish, Carlos tells us, "The lake has both wild and farmed fish, but trout and king fish, both introduced species, have replaced native fish."

We spend a couple of hours wandering about the lakefront before returning to our room, and when we do, Dave complains unhappily, "This place is just a big barn! There's no heat, and no TV!" But I'm enthralled with the view from our large picture window, as shadows of scurrying clouds play across the surface of the lake and the mountain ridge beyond. Storm clouds are building over the ridge at sunset and lightning later flashes in the night sky, revealing heavy clouds sitting down on the mountain tops.

We're to bed early, sleep eleven hours, and wake to the sound of rain drumming on the roof. After breakfast, we work on our journals, and by the time we check out at noon, the rain has stopped. We carry our bags down to the bus station, where we join a straggly line of passengers standing along a footpath. When our bus arrives, we watch to ensure our bags are loaded, then grab seats on the lake side.

The bus lurches slowly over a muddy, potholed trail to the border, giving us plenty of time to study the mud walls, mud houses, and small garden plots on either side. We then exit the bus, clear with Bolivian authorities, and walk 300 feet across to the Peruvian Immigration office. The room here is small and dark, and the printing on the arrival cards so tiny that people take them outside to read. An hour later, we board the bus for the 3.5-hour drive to Puno.

The sky is now bright and sunny, with a few wisps of white cirrus floating high above. Farmers work in large gardens between the road and the lake, and the ends of some rows are underwater. On the uphill side, irregular stone fences create a patchwork quilt of small garden plots. Cows and llamas graze near the road, and occasionally a large flock of sheep can be seen on a distant hillside.

Farther down, grain has been cut from a large field, leaving only yellow stubble, while potatoes are currently being dug up in another. Closer inspection of two moving haystacks reveals a burro under each. We pass a few small towns, and near the end of our journey see stooks of reeds drying near the shore, and fish farms of varying sizes along the edge of the lake.

In Puno, our driver maneuvers the bus through walled lanes that are just wide enough for it and a thin pedestrian on either side. We stop briefly while a gate is opened in a wall, and he then backs through it into a compound. After the gate closes, we offload, claim our luggage, and walk over to a narrow door where an attendant waits. When we show our Sky Tours coupon, he opens the door and calls out. A woman waiting in the crowd outside steps forward; she's holding a sign with our names on it. We're ushered into her care and don't even have time to look around before being whisked away.

Our hotel is located on a narrow, twisting, cobblestone lane, where every building looks the same. I never find out the name of our hotel, or even the street it's on. Our large, second-floor room is not overly warm and doesn't have a security safe, so we leave our valuables at the front desk when we go out. The lobby door is unlocked to let us out, then locked behind us.

The doorman gives us directions to a three-block-long pedestrian mall that is a ten-minute walk away. It's crowded with tourists and lined with restaurants, money changers, and souvenir shops. There's an obvious police presence, but I find their dark green fatigues more intimidating than reassuring. An attractive young senorita touting in front of a restaurant succeeds in luring us inside, where we wash down a meal with a *jarra* of pisco sour, a national drink made from white brandy, lemons, and egg whites.

We hear band music on and off all afternoon, and revelers can be heard on the street in front of our hotel long after we go to bed. The previous day was Ash Wednesday, so we thought Lent would have started, but apparently not. A loud explosion wakes us at 0600 next morning and more follow sporadically. Dave keeps count for a couple of hours, but loses interest at seventeen.

We make our way down to the lakefront about midmorning, where we board a motor launch for a tour of the islands built by the Uros people. The boat carries maybe 25 passengers, and during the short crossing, our guide explains, "The Uros built the islands using totora reeds that grow in the shallows of the lake. The reeds become water-logged quickly, and a new layer of up to six inches has to be added every two weeks. The houses, which are also built of reeds, are picked up and moved while the work is done. The bottom layers of the islands eventually rot away, but some of the older ones now extend to the bottom of the lake. The newer ones are free floating and have to be anchored."

"The people moved onto the islands centuries ago, trying to separate themselves from the Incas and Collas. They've since intermarried with Aymara-speaking Indians, and no pure-blooded Uros remain. The men spend their time fishing and the women do everything else, but because the islands are so small, women can lose the ability to walk any distance. About 300 people presently live here, but young people move ashore to attend school and don't want to return. In another generation, probably no one will live on the islands and they will just be maintained as a tourist attraction."

We approach the islands through a channel cut in the reeds, and as we draw nearer, the houses appear to float on the surface of the water. After the boat is secured to a narrow wooden dock, we step ashore rather gingerly, but find the surface firm beneath our feet. We walk about a central area, peeking into huts that are simply furnished and smell fresh and sweet. Dave then notices two small pigs foraging on a grassy hummock extending out into the water, and we walk toward them. That's when he starts to sink, and with water up around his ankles, we turn back. We visit two other islands, and on one of them, he sinks whenever he stops moving.

Bundles of reeds are fashioned into beautiful canoe-like boats that float lightly on the water; they're said to last about six months. We board one to cross to another island, and it sits a lot lower in the water with 18 passengers. A young Indian woman stands at the stern and uses her entire body to skull with a long oar. She works hard, as we're headed into a light breeze. Feeling the cool air on my face and watching wild ducks fly up from the reeds, I find myself admiring the hardiness of these people.

After returning to Puno, we stroll through the downtown. Outside the cathedral in the main plaza, we're approached by an older woman who shows off her knitted finger puppets. Dave responds with interest, and they start bargaining. Obviously enjoying the contact, he ends up with five puppets, a girl, llama, condor, parrot, and puma.

We now run into two young Americans who were also on the boat tour, and while we're chatting, a young woman comes over and sprinkles confetti in Dave's hair, then mine. "For luck," she says softly. A few minutes later she reappears with a spray can of snow and asks if it's okay to spray us. I duck away but the three men are ritually sprayed. We all laugh as do the watching locals, who are out enjoying the afternoon sun. I definitely feel more comfortable here than in La Paz, smaller crowds, I think. (The snow falls off on its own when it dries.)

Our wandering steps now take us to an outdoor market selling handicrafts, vegetables, fruits, and soda. I stop at a stall to examine a pile of colorful tote blankets, and the Indian woman looking after it shakes one out, drapes it over my back, and ties it around my shoulders. Pulling a package of buns out of our grocery bag, she places it in the folds of the blanket, then perches a felt bowler hat on top my head. I pose as Dave takes a picture and he then bargains for the blanket.

Shortly after returning to our hotel, I hear music and rush to the window of our room in time to see a dozen pairs of elegantly dressed dancers snake through the street below. The men wear black hats and beautifully colored shawls over white shirts; the women wear long-sleeved white blouses under their shawls and have on full skirts. The band includes an accordion, guitars, brass, and drums.

A younger-looking group appears a bit later, the band members playing local flutes and wearing Andes toques. The girls are dressed in traditional costumes, and a few clowns and demons tag along behind. While the sound of the flutes has become familiar, I sometimes find it discordant, as if everyone was playing a different melody.

CHAPTER 26
CUZCO AND MACHU PICCHU

Next day, we board a train for the ten-hour trip through the mountains to Cuzco. We're looking forward to an entire day of speaking English, as the two Americans we met, Todd and Russ, have adjacent seats. Seated nearby are two Swiss men on a three-month holiday; Raymond is an architect, Pascal an investment banker. It isn't long before the five men are playing a game using six dice, which keeps them entertained for hours.

The movements of the car are extraordinarily rough, and it bucks up and down while swaying from side to side. Trying to read is futile, navigating the aisle difficult, and it's almost impossible not to become airborne when sitting on the toilet in the closet at the end of the car. I stagger up and down the aisle numerous times, as I spend half my time standing on the rear platform outside, where I have an unrestricted view. Porters jumping from car to car while carrying trays earn my admiration, as they do so without mishap.

The railroad tracks follow the lakeshore leaving Puno and many fields are flooded, as are two small villages. The tracks then continue up a wide, gently-sloping valley dotted with a few small, mud-walled houses that have thatched roofs and high mud fences. At one point, I see a group of women laboring over wash buckets beside a small stream flowing from a culvert below the grade.

The valley then narrows, the ground grows steeper, and farms are replaced by meadows. Small herds of sheep and llamas graze beside a stream running near the tracks, and each has a herdsman with a dog that chases after the train. High up on steep mountain sides, terraced garden plots appear and I can't imagine how they're tended. Sheer, bare mountain walls close in around us as we near the 14,000-foot summit, and rain starts to fall as we cross through the pass.

When it clears, we're descending through a deep, narrow valley that appears more fertile than the previous one, as crops are greener and higher. Farms and villages are soon running into one another, and the train then slows as we enter a large town. Suddenly, a water bomb sails through an open window, hitting the far wall and showering Russ. A second one hits the edge of a window and splashes Dave.

Later, when the train slows while passing through a busy market in another town, I see a young boy reach into the front of his folded tee-shirt and throw something. Almost simultaneously, rocks rattle on the windows of the car, which are now closed. Mud is also thrown at the windows on the outskirts of Cuzco.

A van from Sky Tours meets us at the station and deliver us to a downtown hotel. We do not have a good night, as the sheets are too small for the bed and the bed too small for us. Then the toilet doesn't flush properly, leaks, and the seat falls off. First thing next morning, we arrange for a different room, then barely have time to eat before the van picks us up. That's not a problem, however, as breakfast includes only juice, white bread, jam, and coffee.

We're now off to Machu Picchu, but first drive 17 km to a train station on the other side of a landslide that blocks the tracks. The rail car looks very attractive when we enter, with glasses and silverware sparkling on white linen tablecloths. Two men already sit at our table, as seats were pre-assigned, and I give a cheery, "Buenos Dias," while sliding across the bench seat. Dave does the same, but we're ignored.

For the next two plus hours, the men speak only sporadically in Spanish. The older man has a sad, pained look in his eyes and doesn't eat much of the food he orders. The younger man doesn't look well but eats everything. His eyes bulge from a sunken face and he coughs every three minutes but never covers his mouth. I suspect he has AIDS.

From 11,000 feet at Cuzco, the tracks descend through a narrow gorge to 6.500 feet. At one point, the train comes to a full stop, backs uphill onto a siding, then continues. We see a switchman working a lever but nothing else, then read that the maneuver allows it to make a significant drop in elevation. We watch closely on the return trip and estimate the train gained maybe fifty feet in the process.

A tumbling mountain river, the Rio Urubamba, plunges down beside us, and as the peaks grow higher, the size of the river swells, with dirty, brown water crashing into huge rocks and spray flying high in the air. I feel a pang of envy at km 88, where a suspension bridge crosses the river. This is the trailhead for the 33-km-long Inca Trail, which starts at 6,500 feet and climbs through three mountain passes at 13,650, 13,000, and 12,000 feet. We considered hiking it but were put off when we found out that regulations required us to take a guide.

We're deep in the mountains when we exit the train at Aguas Calientes, and high peaks with steep sloping sides rise all around. We follow a dirt lane to a bridge over a roaring creek and see a row of buses waiting at the base of the mountain a block away. In between are handicraft stalls, a motley collection of buildings and plastic-covered kiosks that remind me of pictures I've seen of old mining towns.

The bus trip up the mountain takes about 25 minutes, and passengers sit quietly in their seats, listening to the screaming engine and trying to ignore the sheer drops that edge the narrow, zigzagging track. The road climbs 2,300 feet in 6 km. At the top, we split into two groups (Spanish and English) and are assigned guides. Our group climbs up rough, stone stairs for another 130 feet to the Watch House. We take it slowly, as even at 8,000 feet, most of us notice the altitude.

We're now looking down on the ruins, which sit in a small saddle between two mountain peaks, Machu Picchu and Huayna Picchu (Old and New Mountain). They look exactly as shown in photographs, except that on three sides, sheer walls fall 2,000 feet down to the tumultuous waters of the Rio Urubamba.

Our guide explains, "When the ruins were re-discovered in 1911, the site was thickly overgrown with vegetation and buildings were just piles of rubble. As it was cleared, several ceremonial sites were found, and the quality of the stonework indicated that it had been an important center.

"The top of the mountain was bare granite when the city was built during the 1400's, and an estimated 200 tonnes of soil was packed up the mountainside by donkeys, llamas, and humans. Soil in the terraces and packed surfaces of common areas comes from at least eight different sources, one of which is 200 km away. An estimated 700 people lived here for just over 100 years, and the small rock and mud-walled houses were homes for servants."

We now clamber down to the plaza area, where we examine walls built with large, precisely-cut blocks of granite. The main temple sits atop a low knoll and includes an area called *the Astronomical Platform*. The large, carved rock located here is referred to as a sundial, and its corners point in both true and magnetic directions.

A low wall along one side of the plaza overlooks the gorge and contains three large windows. According to our guide, "The sun rises opposite the center window during the equinox. That's Happy Mountain on the other side of the gorge." He then points to a corner where the wall is slumping and reports, "The site is actually sinking."

The reconstructed ruins provide a tantalizing glimpse into the past, but it's the physical attributes of the site that keep me spellbound. I've never been anywhere so isolated and desolate. As we wander about, low, grey cloud constantly forms and reforms around the peaks, and wisps of mist materialize in front of my eyes as air currents rise out of the depths. Views down the vertical, two-thousand-foot walls are extraordinary, and occasionally the river can be seen below.

I am so absorbed in my surroundings that I'm actually jolted when I see a double pipeline coming down a mountain slope to the southwest. Staring in disbelief, I can only wonder, *was it really necessary for modern technology to intrude on such an extraordinary place?*

As cloud slides across the face of Machu Picchu, our guide gathers us together and leads us to the northeast corner of the compound. Huayna Picchu now disappears behind a veil of rain, and we scurry from shelter to shelter, trying to stay dry. Suddenly, we round a corner and find ourselves at the most extraordinary sight of the day, the Temple of the Condor.

Two huge, black-streaked rocks lean out from the cliff face, soaring above us like the wings of a monstrous bird. In a sheltered space at their base, the body of a bird is outlined on a large, flat rock; with the head protruding from one corner. Holes and crevices nearby have been bricked over to strengthen the image. Before I have time to take in more, rain pelts down and we crowd in close to the base of the wings.

Our guide points to a narrow slit in the wall, and walking through in single file, we find ourselves in a sheltered crevice. This leads to a natural opening in the rock, where huge slabs of granite lean along one side, and large, finely-shaped stones fill in another. In the center of this clean, dry enclosure, three stone steps lead up to an altar.

He now explains, "The Incas made both animal and human sacrifices, and the large flat rock on the alter is a sacrificial table. This chamber is thought to have been a royal tomb. No bodies were found here, but numerous tombs were located beneath the crevice. The remains of 150 people were found on the site, which seems low, given the length of time and the number of people who lived here."

Subdued, we return through the ruins on a narrow, stone-paved path running between low stone walls with impressive arched gateways. Water floods down shallow gutters on intersecting pathways, creating fountains where one level plunges down to the next. The water supply comes from Machu Picchu, which is where the Inca Trail appears, traversing down slope from the Sun Gate, the spot at which the site can first be seen from the trail. Far below, a few llamas climb up and down steep steps between the terraces.

When clouds and rain completely obliterate the view, we make our way back to the buses and down the mountainside. We spend the hour until the train leaves at the handicraft stalls, where Dave haggles for tee shirts and a hat. He doesn't enjoy it, as there aren't many tourists, prices are high, and venders desperate.

We have only one day to spend in Cuzco and it's not enough. This former capital city of the Inca Empire sits at an elevation of 10,725 feet and has a current population of 300,000. Centuries before, its treasures of gold and silver were looted by Spanish conquistadors, but rock walls built by the Incas still line narrow, cobblestoned lanes downtown. On one corner, we marvel at huge sculptured rocks pieced together like a jigsaw puzzle.

We stop at an office of Sky Tours to review our ongoing travel arrangements and find that the door is kept locked. Our wandering footsteps then lead to a quiet square where we rest awhile on a sheltered bench. When the resident peddler and a shoeshine boy materialize beside us, we just smile, shake our heads, and repeatedly say no. It's actually very pleasant sitting in the sunshine, and soon we're hunting for words in Spanish with which to communicate. The woman sells decorated gourds and woven belts and now attaches several strands of wool to the armrest beside me, then weaves a shuttle through them. When the small baby she carries starts to fuss, she sits on the ground and breast feeds it.

An older brother of the shoeshine boy appears and both now badger us. When I remove my hat to better soak up the sunshine, the younger boy can't take his eyes off my hair and exclaims, "Blanco!" He wants to know how old I am. He tells me he has three white hairs, so I look, then shake my head and reply, "No, cinco (5)." Turning to the woman, I sorrowfully murmur, "Viejo (old)," and she laughs. Thirty minutes later, a third boy joins our circle, and feeling outnumbered, we move on.

CHAPTER 27
AREQUIPA, PERU

Sky Tours picks us up at 0540 next morning and delivers us to the airport for the short flight to Arequipa. Our driver not only escorts us to the airline counter, but stays with us until we've cleared through security. We're in cloud minutes after takeoff and emerge on top of the world, with barren, snow-streaked land below and a range of white mountain peaks to the west. After passing near two high, snow-clad volcanoes, we descend through another valley.

Arequipa is Peru's second largest city, with a population of a million people. The airport sits at 7,550 feet, and when we step onto the tarmac, three huge 20,000-foot mountains loom overhead, seeming to cover half the sky. While their snowy tops glisten in the sun, the lower flanks are hidden by haze and smog. Sky Tours meet us and deliver us to our hotel, where our room proves to be the nicest since Bangkok.

We're also a long way from the downtown and walk for an hour before finding the main plaza. We then sit on a sunny bench and watch the ebb and flow of people and vehicles around us. When the boom-booming of a drum drifts to our ears, we watch a group of about 50 protesters march into the square from a side street. They carry banners, and make two turns around the plaza before departing without incident.

We spend the afternoon with Mary, from Sky Tours, who drives us through narrow lanes to a small church in the old part of the city. She then takes us to Carmen Plain, where lush crops of alfalfa, peas, cabbage, corn, potatoes, and lettuce grow in wide terraces beside the Rio Chili. Cloud and smog totally obscure any sign of the mountains behind them.

She next drives downtown and drops us at the front gate of Monasterio de Santa Catalina, a sprawling facility surrounded by high walls that takes up three city blocks. The oldest structure inside was built in 1580, and others were added for 100 years. Nuns moved onto the property in 1598, and at one time it was home to 500 women (175 nuns and their servants). When the order became communal in the late 1800s, nuns had to give up their servants and start sharing in household duties. Thirty nuns still live a cloistered existence in a restricted area.

The monastery provides its own guides, and we're assigned to a large group that is just starting off. I'm soon frustrated, however, as I can't hear what's being said, or see what's being talked about. I complain, and after waiting a few minutes, we're provided with another guide, an attractive young woman who is a university student.

Alexandra keeps up a running commentary as she guides us down shadowy, tiled lanes and under archways into small plazas. She first explains, "Children from Catholic families were groomed for specific roles. The first son inherited the family assets and carried on the name. The first daughter looked after the parents, so never married. The second son could enter the army or the priesthood. If he chose the army, the second daughter became a nun; if he chose the church, she was free to marry. Every child understood that one of them would be given to the Church to pray for the rest of the family, ensuring their souls were saved."

She then confides, "I'm the second daughter in my family, and at another time, this could have been my life." The thought of this vibrant young woman living a cloistered life makes the tour even more poignant, and as we peer into small, bare, stone-walled rooms, I pay close attention to her words.

"Nuns stayed in cells of varying sizes, depending on the amount of dowry paid when a novice entered the order. Some had amenities, such as a kitchen or bathroom. If a young woman was able to work for her keep, the Mother Superior could reduce the amount of the dowry."

"Girls as young as twelve entered the monastery as novices and spent the next four years in solitude. They were allowed to leave their cells three times a day to pray, otherwise they prayed in their rooms. The only contact a novice had with her family was through a lattice-covered window in a wall that was two-feet thick. She couldn't be seen. Gifts were set on a turntable in the wall and checked by a listener, who monitored the conversation."

"Girls aged three to twelve were accepted into a boarding school run by the institution. Some of them became nuns and thus spent most of their lives here, but only if the family had money." She then explains, "A dowry of 2,400 pieces of silver (about $40,000 today) was paid to enter the convent, and the family had to continue to support their daughter and her servants in the style promised."

Alexandra now leads us into a small, dim room, where a statue of Jesus stands, bleeding from the face and in obvious pain. She points to a mirror hidden in the palette of his mouth and explains that a novice, kneeling in prayer before it, would have seen the reflection of the movement of her own lips. Young and impressionable, she would believe that he "spoke" to her.

We enter a large stone kitchen where the rocks are streaked with smoke from centuries of cooking fires and burning candles; it's still used to cater to events held in the courtyard. From a rooftop, we see the collapsed second floors of several buildings, the result of Arequipa's frequent earthquakes. By the time we return to the front gate, I have been so touched by this young woman that I can't find words to thank her.

Rejoining Mary, we now walk through a gentle rain to Basilica Catedral in the main square. I am pleasantly surprised when we step inside, as the space is open and bright, with great columns supporting a domed roof, and paintings and statues that are not of the dark, painful variety. It's obviously well used, a place for people, and most intriguing of all, the entire back wall is covered by a huge pipe organ.

Our last stop is *La Campania*, a church built with light-colored volcanic rock called *sillar* that is much used in the city. The structure was constructed by the Jesuits in 1738, and the main façade is extremely ornate. Adjacent to it stands *the Cloisters,* where members of the order stayed while in training. Columns in its courtyard are of the same stone and beautifully carved. Both structures have survived serious earthquakes, but the Order itself wasn't so lucky. It was expelled by the Spanish government in 1767, and its possessions turned over to the administration of the Fathers of the Oratory.

Sky Tours picks us up at 0620 next day and delivers us to a huge, chaotic bus depot, where hundreds of people are catching dozens of buses. Our driver stays with us as we check in at one counter, drop bags off at another, and pay the required tax at a third. He then sees us safely aboard the correct bus.

The five-hour drive to the coastal town of Tacna takes us through barren, rocky, brown hills, where the only contrast comes from a few green gardens growing down in ravines beside creek beds. When we step off the bus, we're surrounded by a mob of shouting touts, and I'm unable to see past them. Fortunately, Dave can and yells at a taxi driver he sees, "How much to go across the border to Chile?"

Beckoning him to follow, the man leads us through a second terminal before quoting a price of $4 US each. He then takes us to his car, seats us inside, and disappears for two hours. When he returns, he has three more passengers in tow, none of whom speak English. After a short drive to Immigration, he collects our passports and pushes his way through the crowd to a service window. He does the same thing on the Chilean side of the border, then nurses us through Customs. In a remarkably short time, we're driving into

Arica, where he drops us at the bus station. We find our own way to a hotel and next day catch a bus south to Iquique, where we're to meet my brother and his wife.

CHAPTER 28
MY BROTHER'S CHILE

Chile is a long, skinny country with an average width of only 180 km. A low mountain range runs down the Pacific coast for 3,000 km, and the Andes extend for 4,300 km along the inland border, so there's room for only a few long, narrow plains in between. In the northern part of the country, the Atacama Desert is officially the driest place on earth, with no measurable rainfall.

During the bus ride from Arica to Iquique, the highway winds down and up through several deep canyons that cut into the high desert from the coast. In one of them, our bus comes to a stop on a deserted stretch of asphalt. It's a lonely, isolated spot and I feel a bit uneasy when we're herded off by uniformed police. We line up at a table set up on the verge, where our papers are examined and hand luggage x-rayed, while dogs and their handlers search bus seats and baggage compartments.

After reboarding the bus, we continue on across the barren landscape and soon are passing through an area where the ground looks like it was plowed up. My guidebook describes it as "the leavings of an old nitrate mine". We then pass a military base, where tanks and armored personnel carriers are parked in long lines. Apparently, passions that date back to 1879 and the War of the Pacific are still strong. Chile is said to maintain an army in the belief that Bolivia, Peru, or even Argentina might be tempted to test its defenses.

As we near the end of our four-hour journey, I'm looking out the window at the stark landscape and comparing it to the green forests and tumbling streams of BC, where my brother and I grew up. We'd been two of eight siblings, and I was eleven years old when he was born. In the manner of large families, I'd been the *little mother,* and Ron had been very much my baby.

Nine years earlier, the mining company he'd worked for in Williams Lake had offered him a job in Chile. He'd accepted the challenge and relocated his family. This country was now his home, but his wife and two young sons had returned to Canada. He'd recently remarried and we're meeting him and his wife, Tamara, in a downtown mall in Iquique; they're flying in from Antofagasta, 500 km to the south.

Everything goes according to plan, and after a joyful reunion, we spend the weekend together at their holiday condo. The town was once a fishing village but is now a duty-free zone and tourist center. While visiting, we walk down a beautiful, sandy beach, where breaking waves wash up on a wide, sloping shore. I'm surprised at how pleasant the temperature is, I thought it would be hotter. We also tour through shops and a casino, then have dinner in a private dining room where all the furnishings come from Spain.

When Ron and Tamara return home on Sunday, I succumb to a bug that I've been fighting off for days. I suspect that I drank untreated water in Cuzco. At first, I ached all over, then came the sneezing and coughing, and now it's diarrhea. Dave confesses to having similar symptoms, and we're really sick for 48 hours. I finally buy some pills to control the diarrhea, although I'm sure I'll regret taking them. By Thursday, we've recovered enough to get back on a bus.

The highway now twists and turns down the mist-shrouded Pacific coast. We pass the dim outlines of several small, guano-covered islands that were once harvested by the Spanish and see large blocks of salt awaiting shipment beside the road at Puerto Patillos. After that, the land seems isolated in time, with a few buildings emerging from the mist in isolated coves, and a small fishing dory or two plying the waters. Toward the end of our journey, in another deep canyon, we cross the muddy waters of Rio Loa not far from its mouth. At 430 km, it's the longest river in Chile, and the only one to carry water across the desert.

Tamara waits for us at the bus depot in Antofagasta and takes us home to a roomy, two-story bungalow, where we meet her fourteen-year-old daughter, Nicole. They've invited friends for dinner, and it's after 2100 when the couple arrive, which is when we realize just how late Chileans eat. Ron spends hours translating for us, as the man speaks only a little English, and his wife and Tamara speak Spanish.

We're kept busy sightseeing for the next few days. At a viewpoint overlooking the ocean, we admire a rock formation called La Portada. The arched gateway stands just offshore, with the restless sea washing up on cliffs behind it and the city hazy in the background. A short drive up the coast, at Mejillones, we relax on a sunny, sandy beach and enjoy the picnic lunch that Tamara prepared. Another day, we climb through the rubble of an old silver smelter, a huge brick structure over 100 years old.

Tamara then drives us around the bay to Juan Lopez, a summer resort area that's closed for the season. We walk down the flat, sheltered beach, watching as a few fishermen unload catches from dory-like long boats pulled up on the sand. She disappears for a few minutes, then rejoins us carrying a small squid. When we return home, she beats it thoroughly against the cement floor of the patio, boils it for an hour and a half, scrapes off skin and tentacles, and cuts it into bite-sized pieces. At dinner, I chew on the same piece for ten minutes and still have trouble swallowing. (We had calamari in Australia once, and I found it much the same.)

We've soon discovered that the morning temperature on the back patio of their house is nearly perfect, so have our coffee there while reading or writing in our journals. In the afternoons, we go out with Tamara, visiting the market, and meet her mom and half-sister. We watch a bit of TV, particularly a Chilean series called Pampa Illusion, a local historical drama much like an American western. After a few days, I find myself recognizing an occasional Spanish word or phrase.

In the early mornings, I climb the dry, barren hills behind the house, which are part of the Coastal Range making up this section of the Atacama Desert. Ron shows me the way the first day and often the dog Osita joins me. Far below, ocean swells roll tirelessly up on shore, spreading a lacey white veil over the rocks, and a cool breeze sometimes carries the booming of the surf.

A low mist sitting out to sea marks the area where the cold water of the Humboldt current meets the warm air of a high-pressure center. Dropping upper air in the middle of the center traps the mist in the lower atmosphere, and high coastal mountains then prevent it from moving onshore. In the southern hemisphere, all west coasts between latitudes 10 and 25 degrees experience similar conditions and are deserts.

One morning, Ron takes us out to the mine, which is located inland at just under 10,000 feet. The road is good and the 180-km drive takes less than two hours. While he attends to his work, a young mining engineer takes us on a tour of the site, including the control office at the edge of the deep pit, where the supervisor maintains visual and radio contact with all operations.

Ron then drives us around the leach pile, which is 2 km long, over half a km wide, and maybe 50 feet high. After the ore goes through the tertiary crusher, it is spread across the pile by a network of conveyor belts. The pile is sprayed with a weak solution of sulfuric acid, which leaches out the copper as it seeps down to a catchment basin. (The bottom of the pile is lined with plastic to prevent loss.)

He explains, "The leaching process involves bacteria, something like the process used to treat sewage, and the hotter the pile, the better. It takes over a year to leach 75% of the copper from the ore, which is the time required to work down the length of the pile, removing waste ore and adding new. We then re-leach the waste ore and recover another 8%."

From the catchment basin, the bright, green liquid is piped to the processing plant and ends up in vats in which anodes have been placed. Cathodes attached to a moveable carriage are then immersed in them. Seven days later the mineral has solidified between the plates, and sheets of high-quality copper are removed. The process, known as electrolytic refining, would do justice to a wizard's cave.

That night, we attend a charity fashion show sponsored by area mines to raise money for a local hospital. As I have nothing appropriate to wear, Tamara generously searches through her closet and finds a pant suit for me to wear, as well as sandals with three-inch heels. I can't walk, but do I ever look smart!

We now have the opportunity to meet a few of the ex-pats working with Ron, as they're here attending a conference. They all seem as confident and enthusiastic about their work as my brother. We meet a few of their wives, too, and I gain an appreciation for the complications created for the women who follow their men to Chile. They've left behind friends and family, need to learn a new language and new customs, and the men are busy. It must be difficult.

After Ron finishes work on a Friday, we drive 200 km to Calama, where Tamara's dad lives. While crossing a desolate, flat plain, we see a large, rock-outlined drawing called a geoglyph on the slope of a hill. It's thought to be 1,000 years old. According to Ron, "It's always visible; the wind never covers it with sand."

We're still on the road as night falls, and the darkness now grows blacker as heavy rain pours down. Rain typically falls only two or three times in like eight years in the Atacama Desert, but this is the seventh recent rainfall, proving again that averages seldom make sense when applied to specific situations. Unlike Australia, the soil here is sterile and the desert doesn't bloom afterward.

We spend the night with Tamara's dad, who is also a miner, and Jorge makes us feel very much at home in his small, two-bedroom bungalow. The next day, we continue driving east across the plain, and the ghostly images of snow-clad peaks now rise high in a hazy sky. Soon, we're passing through the Cordillera de la Sal, weirdly shaped hills that were once layers of sediment on the bottom of a large lake.

Ron stops at a viewpoint on the far side, and we look down on a flat, arid plain, where splashes of green mark a river and irrigation canals near San Pedro de Atacama. Across from us, to the east, the ghostly peaks of the Andes now form a high, formidable barrier. To the south is the Salar de Atacama, a 3,000 sq km salt basin that traps the flow of several small rivers.

The Bolivian border is about 50 km to the east, and roughly 100 km beyond and just to the south is Mount Poquis, on the border with Argentina. From there, the distance to the coast near Mejillones is 380 km, making this the widest part of Chile.

Ron now takes us down the east side of the salt flat to a steep, narrow gorge where a stream tumbles out of the mountains. The water runs fast and deep, and the soft greens of grapes, figs, fruit trees, and pampas grass provide a cool, shady contrast to the brown of rocks and sand. Small garden plots line the sides of the gorge and cultivated fields extend down into the flat.

We spend that night in the small village of San Pedro de Atacama, which is located at the mouth of the largest river flowing into the salt basin. The Atacamiño people flourished here for 15,000 years, building irrigation canals and farming the land. Their culture came to an end in 1450, when the Inca Empire conquered the area.

A local museum is rich in their history and features a burial site with mummy, pottery, and other archeological treasures. Remarkably, they have several 800-year-old mummies. Preserved by the dry desert air, a young woman known as Miss Chile has thick black hair, all her teeth, and parchment skin that covers even her eye sockets. She sits in a fetal position, knees drawn up to her chest, and wears skin clothing.

We visit the town square, which is paved with stones and shaded by large pepper trees. Someone recently tried to burn down the church, which dates back to 1745, and the smell of smoke lingers as we examine the damage done to roof and wall. We then drive through narrow streets lined with mud-brick buildings and walls to a small motel where we spend the night.

The sun has set and the air is noticeably cooler when we walk to a nearby restaurant for dinner. Here, we meet friends of Ron, also ex-pats, and being able to speak freely in English makes the occasion even more enjoyable. When the lights go out halfway through the meal, we finish by candlelight. The cook is not fazed at all, just pulls a headlamp onto his forehead and continues preparing meals. The sky is clear and studded with stars as we walk back to the motel.

Next morning, we drive to a fortification called Pukara Quitor that was built by the Atacamiño people in the 12th century. The reconstructed stone walls cling to a steep slope, with the backside protected by a sheer cliff that drops down to the river. In 1540, the Incas who defended it were easily routed by 30 Spanish conquistadors on horseback. We then climb a nearby hill for a 360-degree view of the surrounding mountains and canyons, particularly the perfect cone shape of Licancabur Volcano.

On our way back to Antofagasta, we make a slight detour and stop in the Valley of the Moon. Sediment from the bottom of an ancient lake has been thrust up vertically here also, and subsequent erosion has created many strange-looking formations. They look even odder now, as recent rain has brought out the salt and the ground is white. The sky is clear and bright all day, until we reach the coast, then the sun sinks into thick haze and turns a deep red.

A few days later, the four of us again climb into a vehicle, and Ron drives south across the desert, then down the coast to Copiapo (540 km). The next day, we go on to La Serena (350 km), and for the first time, scattered clumps of low bush and cactus appear on the desert floor. A tall variety of cactus is in bloom, with a few plants bearing large red flowers.

At La Serena, Ron turns east into a narrow canyon and follows a sparkling stream into the mountains. Soon, green vineyards provide a welcome contrast to the monotonous brown of canyon walls. In a wide spot, grapes are strewn across large sheets of plastic spread on the ground. Two weeks in sun and wind turn them into raisins, and some are now being bagged. An hour later, we check into a two-bedroom cabana (cabin) near the small village of Vicuña.

We're just in time to tour the pisco distillery (Chile's national drink), and when we arrive, pickup trucks loaded with grapes and vines are lined up in the yard. The loads are forked into a pit, then pulled into a crusher by an auger, where the juice is sucked out and pumped into fermentation tanks. The product is then distilled, (the alcohol evaporated off and condensed), and stored in different types of wooden kegs for up to three years, depending on the flavor and quality desired.

Ron now drives us into the village and parks on a narrow, walled street near a small tourist shop offering internet services. Here we meet Tamara's half-brother and his girlfriend. Marco is a good looking, curly-haired man of 29 and seems a likeable sort. Nina speaks some English, but is very shy about it. We share a meal of empanadas with them, and Marco wants to know about our sailing, so Ron translates.

We spend the next day doing touristy things, including driving farther up the canyon, where rows of trees between vineyards provide protection from strong afternoon winds that blow up the valley. That night, we celebrate Tamara's birthday at dinner and eat too much. When we return to the cabana, I sit out by the pool a while to let my dinner digest. With stars sparkling in the clear air and a half-moon etched above the hills, it's a very pretty night.

Next day, we visit a vineyard owned by Nina's parents and her dad shows us around the property. The farmhouse and gardens sit on four hectares, and rows and rows of wine grapes grow on another eight. In the clear, calm morning air, the location is unbelievably beautiful, with green vines framed against sandy-colored mountains and blue sky. He tells us that he's retired and his son is the grape expert, then proudly explains, "The vines are eighteen months old and need three years to reach full production. We harvested 5,000 kg this year, expect 50,000 next year, and 100,00 the year after. They should produce for 20-25 years."

Seeing our interest, he goes on, "A small pond of water feeds the irrigation system, nutrients are mixed into it, and each vine is drip-fed. We normally feed them for an hour a day, but during very hot weather, they require two hours. Weeds are kept down chemically except during the first year, when vines are too vulnerable."

He then admits, "We almost have to patrol our feeder canal with a rifle when it's time to fill the pond. Adjacent farmers have been known to open their gates and drain off water that we're paying for."

Dave now drops behind, slowing his steps to accommodate a young boy walking in front of him. We all look back just in time to see a dog following behind come up and lick his leg. He does get teased, as he seems to attract small boys and dogs.

Before we leave, Tamara takes me over to a corner of the yard where the family have dedicated a small shrine to the Virgin Mary. It was built in memory of a son who died in a car accident less than a year before. I stand quietly in front of it, studying the barren hills in the background, and feel a calmness settle over me, a sense of peace.

Returning to La Serena, we check into a cabana near the ocean. The sky is bright and sunny, but there's a definite chill in the air as we stroll down the broad, sandy beach, which is pretty much deserted. Dave and I hike farther on our own and come across the half-eaten remains of two small penguins. Despite wind and blowing sand, a fisherman also brushes a bright, red coat of paint onto a small boat. We walk down the beach again after dinner, and it's even more beautiful under the light of a half-moon. Ghostly lights flicker above the surf line and it takes us a few minutes to recognize that lights on the promenade are reflecting off the feathers of a flock of seabirds.

Next morning, Ron tells us that it's the ninth anniversary of the day he arrived in Chile. It's also time to say goodbye, as they now fly back to Antofagasta. Words fail me when I try to thank him for making our visit so enjoyable. Not only did he and Tamara put in time and effort, but he'd spent many hours translating, which we much appreciated.

Having seen many adults struggle to find words in a second language during the past few weeks (both English and Spanish), I'd been impressed by his fluency. That feeling grows when my own efforts to speak the language prove futile. While I can put words together that say what I mean, I don't understand the responses. Months later, a fellow traveler on the other side of the world suggests, "You might not have an ear for language. I've heard that can be a problem for people who grew up in small, unilingual communities."

CHAPTER 29
CHILE ON OUR OWN

D ave and I now tour the south of Chile by bus. We first travel 450 km to Valparaiso, spending half of a very long day looking at the monotonous, shrub-covered desert, and the other half peering at a coastline shrouded in low cloud and haze. Darkness has fallen when we arrive in the city of Vina del Mar, which shares an ocean bay with Valparaiso. The two cities have a combined population of 600,000, and it takes two hours to drive the last 60 km, but as we drive around the bay, the views of lights sparkling across steep hillsides ahead and behind are spectacular.

It's past midnight when a cabbie drops us off in front of a hostel that Dave found in the *Lonely Planet*. It's a bit shabby, with worn carpets and walls that need paint, and I suspiciously check the room for vermin, but it's clean. We plan to stay two nights, as I'm hoping to get some exercise. The bus seats had been very uncomfortable and I ache all over, but even more, the diarrhea pills have blocked up my insides. The local food with its emphasis on meat and white bread hasn't helped.

Next morning, we make our way down to the waterfront. Valparaiso is Chile's main seaport, and several naval vessels are moored in the harbor, and a large ship is undergoing maintenance in a floating dry dock. We watch three freighters being loaded at the docks, then stroll down a long plaza, studying the well-maintained old buildings and monuments. I'm reminded that ships stopped here to resupply when making the arduous passage around Cape Horn early in the 19th century.

We climb the steep hillside overlooking the bay, finding our way through a maze of alleys, winding streets, and connecting stairs. The day is warm and sunny, and we've soon worked up a sweat, but the harbor view remains obscured by low cloud and haze. The top street proves to be just wide enough to push a wheelbarrow down, and numerous dogs lie along it, stretched out flat on their sides as they soak up the sun. We step carefully, as the cobblestones are dotted with piles of dog poop.

Next day, we travel 360 km to Talca. Our route takes us inland, across drab desert and barren hills to a smoggy central valley, where we stop briefly in the capital city, Santiago. We then continue south through dusty, tired-looking countryside. Fields are bare after the harvest, Lombardi poplars have dropped their leaves, and delays due to road construction are frequent.

It's late in the afternoon when we arrive in Talca, and unbeknownst to us, we're dropped at a new bus terminal, not the one shown on our map. I think the clerk at the counter tries to explain, but we don't understand. Picking up our bags, we walk in the wrong direction until we finally come to an intersection with street signs. Realizing our error, we reverse course and eventually come to the main square, where we locate a hotel and café.

Next day, there's not much to see on the 450-km drive to Temuco, so we amuse ourselves by reading road signs and looking up words in a Spanish-English dictionary. We then play bingo when the cobrador (assistant) hands out cards, putting our knowledge of Spanish numbers to the test, which is interesting!

At the bus terminal in Temuco, Dave picks up a brochure for a homestay. We've seen them advertised before and he'd like to try one. He talks to a man behind a counter, who happily makes a phone call, and we're soon picked up by an attractive older woman who seems friendly enough but doesn't speak much English. She drives us through back streets to a small *botelleria* and drops us off on the sidewalk. We carry our bags through a garage into a small salon, and she drives the car in behind us. There's just room on one side for her to squeeze out the car door.

We're shown upstairs to a small, sun-filled bedroom, with bathroom next door, and now learn that the price is higher than that advertised in the brochure. Looking at each other, we just shrug our shoulders; at that point, it's easier to stay. We're then told that two couples in other bedrooms will be sharing the bathroom.

The downtown (el centro) is supposed to be within walking distance, but when we ask for directions, our hostess insists on driving us. When she drops us off fifteen minutes later, we have no idea where we are. We walk for an hour through shabby-looking streets before finding the main square and a café. We take a taxi back.

The temperature drops overnight, and come morning, it's as cold inside the house as outside. After competing with other guests for the bathroom, we find white bread, butter, and hot water in a thermos in the downstairs salon. We now see that the car is gone and realize we didn't make arrangements to return to the depot for our 1000 departure. The daughter of the house tells us that her *madre* is having her hair done and doesn't know when she'll return. I ask her to call us a taxi, but that doesn't happen.

Instead, we stand on the edge of the curb, shivering, while any number of taxis go by in the wrong direction. When one finally stops across from us, I dash over and ask, "Terminal de bus?" The driver shakes his head and points back to the other side of the street. We wait some more, and again a cab stops across the street from us. I show him our bus tickets, pointing to the departure time, and he nods his head, takes them, and motions for us to get in.

A few minutes later, he picks up another passenger, who sits on the front seat beside him. He shows her our tickets and she then says, *"el centro,"* and we continue toward the downtown. We have no idea what's going on.

After dropping her at a market, he drives another block, then pulls over and removes the sign from the car roof. Only then does it dawn on us that we're in a *collectivo*, a form of transit that operates more like a bus than a taxi. He gets us to the terminal before our bus leaves, and we're so relieved that we just pay the fare, which is double what we expected.

From Temuco, the bus heads east to Puçon, a beautiful, two-hour drive through forested lands with incredible views of Villarica Volcano. Framed against a brilliant blue sky, the black, ash-covered cone rises some 5,000 feet above the surrounding terrain. Ash stains the snow on the lower slopes, and according to my guidebook, puffs of smoke often appear above the mountain and hikers report hearing it rumble.

We rent a cabana at a motel near the bus depot on the edge of town. For little more than half of what we paid the previous night, we have kitchen, bedroom, and bathroom. Our host provides a map of Lake Villarica, which is some twenty km long, and we spend the afternoon walking under the trees near the shore, while admiring the towering volcano, now eight km away. With clear air and green spaces, we enjoy ourselves immensely, then pick up empanadas and beer to eat at the motel.

Next morning, the wind howls through the trees, and when I open the curtains, the Lombardi poplars are showing the backs of their leaves and leaning to the west. Although it looks cold, the temperature is warmer than the day before. We climb a low hill to the Monastery of Santa Clara, which overlooks the town, then return to the lakeshore. Access to a long peninsula is restricted to residents of the condominiums that line the shore, but we see two sailboats at anchor and six kayakers are out enjoying themselves, going nowhere fast. Farther on, cabin windows are boarded up and decking has been removed from docks; closed for the season, we assume.

After returning to the motel, we sit outside in the shade, soothed by the drone of large honey bees feeding on masses of flowers that cover the bleeding-heart bushes beside us. At sunset, we go inside and again make a meal of empanadas and beer. We're acquiring a taste for the pastry, some of which are *carne* (meat), others are *jamon y queso* (ham and cheese).

The wind eases that evening and by morning the temperature is much cooler. We take a last walk along the lake and tour the downtown, where the many hotels and adventure tourism shops testify to its reputation as a jumping off point to two national parks. We then say goodbye to our host, who doesn't speak a lot of English, but communicates well with the help of hand gestures. From him, we learn that the day before was unusually warm, even for summer. The warm wind comes from Argentina, and after two days usually brings rain. The town also gets a bit of snow in winter that stays for a couple of hours, and some mornings bring frost with ice at the water's edge, but nothing too serious.

Next morning, we're back on a bus for the 400-km trip south to Puerto Montt. Within half an hour, we're in thick fog, and cloud and haze limit visibility for the rest of the day. Farms, orchards, and tree plantations line the road, many fields have recently been burnt, and road construction constantly slows us down. About halfway, near Valdivia, I notice that small streams and ponds alongside the road somehow look messy, as if they'd been disturbed. I then read in my guidebook that a powerful earthquake shook the area in 1960 and the city had to be completely rebuilt.

We've now realized that we can take a bus to Castro, on Isla Chiloe, 165 km south of Puerto Montt, so stay at a hotel near the depot and continue on next morning. The bus is loaded onto a barge holding twelve vehicles for the twenty-minute crossing of the channel joining the Gulf of Ancun to the Pacific Ocean. Thanks to tectonic plate movements and the last Ice Age, this part of Chile looks very different from the north. The hilltops of the Coastal

Range are now islands in the Chiloe archipelago, the sea has flooded the central valley, and fiords run up into the Andes.

Once on the island, we drive past fenced, cultivated fields that remind me of New Zealand. Hedges between fields on rolling hills near Castro give them the appearance of a patchwork quilt, and despite dark, threatening clouds, it's a very pretty spot. We check into a hotel overlooking the inlet, then spend hours wandering about the main plaza and the short, steep streets downtown. Stilt houses line the waterfront and we curiously study the various designs of their shingle-covered roofs and walls. (The shingles look much like cedar shakes.) We then stop at a tourist market and inspect the handicrafts on display. But the weather is cold and wet and our clothing not adequate, so we catch a bus back to Puerto Montt next morning.

Mud flats are exposed in large areas of the inlet as we leave, but the tide has turned and water races in under a bridge. We see birds and seals during the ferry crossing, then the road on the far side takes us through scruffy, abandoned fields and small, shabby villages. We share it with numerous horse-drawn carts and wagons, as well as one wagon with a team of bullocks. When the bus slows to a crawl through a roadside market, I catch glimpses of beautiful displays of leatherwork and woodwork.

We return to the same hotel in Puerto Montt, and the clerk now wants 2,000 pesos more for a room but Dave pays 1,000 less. Next morning, the sky is clear and sunny, and the temperature a nippy 3 degrees C. We set off for the fishing port of Angelmo, where the market offers a huge variety of fresh fish and shellfish. It's the cleanest we've ever seen, no smell and no flies! As we walk around the harbor, sacks and sacks of oysters are being unloaded from small fishing boats that sit high and dry on the rocks.

We spend the afternoon and most of the next day exploring the streets of Puerto Montt, which are bright, clean, and bustling. The sky stays clear and sunny, but the wind has a bite and people hurry about their activities. Vegetables and fruits are wheeled through the street in one area and the displays are a joy to behold, particularly luscious-looking tomatoes and grapes. We later tour through a tourist market, where stalls are filled with knitted sweaters, wall hangings, and wood carvings. As usual, our limited baggage keeps me from buying much of anything.

We take an overnight bus back to Santiago and are on the road fourteen hours, so pay extra for *salon cama*, which has fully reclining seats. We do sleep, but I wake every hour or so when the bus stops or slows in construction areas. At dawn, the rising sun shimmers through fog on the horizon, revealing orchards and corn fields on flat, irrigated land beside the road. When blue sky eventually appears overhead, a high mountain range to the east remains a shadow in haze.

A young Canadian couple are on the bus, and we talk to them briefly after we arrive in Santiago. They spent the summer operating a fly-fishing camp out of Puerto Montt and are on their way back to BC to run a similar camp in an area that we know well. They tell us that they're going directly to the airport because of reports of student rioting in the downtown.

We see nothing untoward on the taxi ride to our hotel, and after settling into our room, we set off to find an airline office. We need to confirm our onward flight. According to my map, it's not far away, but it doesn't show all the streets and we walk for an hour. Sidewalks are crowded and traffic is heavy, but the broad avenue is very pleasant, with tall, shady trees lining both sides, and open spaces marked by large, graceful churches and green parks.

On the way back, we're approached by two female students looking for donations. One explains, "We're protesting because we need student cards to ride the transit at discounted rates, and the government won't issue them.

They don't provide us with any funding either, though most of us come from middle-to-poor-income homes and have no spare cash."

Next day, to our surprise, streets are empty and shops closed; it's Good Friday. We spend the morning at Santa Lucia Hill, a downtown park that is quite busy despite the grey, overcast sky. After searching out hidden nooks and crannies in a large castle, we climb a stairway up the hill's rocky core but see only haze from the top. When we then walk into the downtown, heavy rain sends us scurrying back to the hotel.

The sky is clear next morning but it's cold, so we wait a bit before going out. As downtown stores are still closed, we find our way to a large open-air market near the Rio Mapacho. The place is packed with shoppers, and stalls are piled high with fish, meat, fruit, vegetables, pots, clothes, and handicrafts.

We now walk down another wide avenue, passing more green spaces and monuments, until we come to the Church of San Francisco. It was built in the 1600s and is the only structure from that era to have survived the city's many earthquakes. We pause in a plaza where an eternal flame burns at the base of the equestrian statue of Libertador O'Higgens, a hero of the war with Spain.

At the presidential palace, La Moneda, we wander about an inner courtyard until a uniformed guard tells us we have to walk straight through (in one gate and out the other). Taking a last look at the upper floors, I think of President Allende, who was killed here in a violent military coup d'état in September of 1973.

As we enter the Plaza de Armas, a crowd of people flood in from the far end. We're watchful, but no police are present and everyone seems relaxed. When hundreds stop in front of the cathedral, we stay awhile and mingle. A clown with painted face ties balloons for children, another amuses onlookers by following behind people or playing with cars in the street. Artists sit and paint ocean scenes on small pieces of glass, using their fingers to smear on colors, and one sprays paint on LP records. This is my last memory of Chile, as we leave for Canada the next day.

But later, at the hotel, I pick up an English-language newspaper and notice a reference to the country's democratically-elected government. I'm immediately curious and wonder, *when did this happen?* I'd only heard about the violent overthrow of the government by the military in 1973, followed by years of oppressive rule.

When I am able to research it, I learn that a national plebiscite was held in October, 1988. Chileans were asked if they wanted another eight years of military rule, and 56% voted *NO*. Preparations were then made to return the country to civilian rule, and a general election was held in December, 1989. Interestingly, subsequent civilian governments kept many of the structures and policies introduced by the military regime, which are credited with bringing years of economic and social development.

But I'm now even more curious and ask myself, *what kind of military dictator accepts the results of a referendum?* When I look further, I find reports on the internet indicating that, in 1973, the country had been in turmoil and on the verge of civil war. An overwhelming majority of Chileans are said to have supported the coup, and subsequent investigations stated that Allende took his own life.

Both Dave and I follow the news and like to think we're well informed, but the only news we recall hearing about Chile involved the military coup. We never heard anything about conditions in the country at the time, or anything about a referendum or democratic elections. We'd been similarly surprised when we were in Fiji in 1997 and learned that the prime minister and his cabinet had been kidnapped in a coup ten years earlier. As Fiji had the same form of government as Canada, we found that strange. I now wonder, *what else don't we know?*

CHAPTER 30
CHINA AND THE SILK ROAD

By the time we start flying from KLIA to Asian destinations, we've grown pretty comfortable traveling in Malaysia and Thailand. Our first such flight is in June of 2005, when we join a ten-day guided tour to China that includes a portion of the Silk Road we've long wanted to see. It's a new tour tailored for Chinese Malaysians, but we're allowed to come along as we make up the required minimum of twelve.

The 3,500-km flight takes us almost straight north to Xian in central China. We're above cloud for most of the five-hour flight, but as we descend, I see dark green, wooded hills rising in a series of ridges, and an occasional road running down through a river valley. We then drop down into a thick soup that blankets the city of Xian and its surroundings. I see only vague, hazy shapes as we land and not much more during the bus ride into town. I start to wonder, *are we really in China? How do you tell?*

My questions are answered minutes later, when a massive wall and wide, deep moat appear in the gloom beside the road. The bus soon turns and crosses the moat, passes through huge wooden gates, and stops at a central plaza. We're told we have an hour to walk around before going to our hotel.

As we stroll about, the adjacent street is chock-a-block with vehicles, and thick haze covers the sky. Nearby are two large, square 600-year-old wooden buildings with multi-tiered roofs known as the Bell Tower and the Drum Tower. In Buddhist tradition, the bell was rung in the morning, and the drum beaten at night. In fact, Xian is the capital of Shaanxi province and has a population of ten million people. It is also one of China's oldest cities and was the country's capital for 1,000 years.

Our tour officially starts next morning, with a visit to the brick and rammed-earth wall that stretches for 12 km around the old city. We climb up a steep staircase near the main gate, then stroll down the road on top, but can't see much due to haze. The wall is 40 feet high, 60 feet wide at the base, and 50 feet wide on top.

A large building overlooks the gate and we're led into a room where a young man is speaking in Chinese. When he's finished, our guide explains, "He was talking about Feng Shui, and how the positioning of doors, windows, and even buildings are important in Chinese custom." Pointing to a nearby jade carving, she adds, "That's a pixue (peeshoo), a mythical animal that protects the home. A pair of the statues are placed facing the main doorway or window, where their large mouths can draw in good fortune or eat any bad spirits that enter."

Simon, a member of our group, gleefully clarifies, "Pixue are all mouth and no ass, so can eat but can't expel." He and a few others provide us with more information at the next stop, which is a government-run store selling jade statues, terracotta figures, and handicrafts. (We will visit similar stores daily, as well as gem and carpet factories.)

Boarding the bus again, we're driven to the outskirts of the city, where three huge, hangar-like buildings house the excavation pits of the Terracotta Army Museum. Although I've seen many pictures of the soldiers, I am stunned at the sight of thousands of full-sized figures lined up in columns in the pits. The original bright colors are long gone, but each of the 6,000 figures is unique, with a different uniform, hair style, facial features, or footwear. They carried real weapons made of bronze, and interspersed amongst them are pottery horses and wooden chariots. Broken bodies are still being restored by archeologists.

The buildings sit on a 56-hectare site that is part of the cemetery of Emperor Qin Shi Huang. An estimated 700,000 conscripts worked on the project for 37 years; most were farmers and their families suffered as a result. The emperor died at age fifty in 210 BC, and a year later, his son was overthrown in *the Farmer's Rebellion*. They took their revenge by entering the pits and smashing every soldier, then set fire to timbers that supported the ceilings. The site was buried for 2,200 years and re-discovered in 1974, when farmers found pieces of pottery while digging a well.

Late in the afternoon, we squeeze in a visit to a 3,000-year-old palace and spa at hot springs in nearby hills, then it's off to an airport to catch a plane to Wulumuqi (Urumqi), 2,100 km to the northwest. The flight takes 3.5 hours and we cross three times zones, so arrive at 2100 (midnight by our time).

We tour a local market before checking into our hotel, and by then, Dave and I are parched and looking for water to drink. There is none in our room and we can't get any, so take beer from the fridge, which isn't very satisfying. After a few hours on a bed that feels like cement, we're on the bus again at 0800.

We now drive north across barren desert for an hour, then follow a turbulent stream up a deep ravine into the hills. Hundreds of goats graze on the steep slopes beside the road, with herdsmen on small ponies keeping watch. We soon pass a dozen colorful yurts set up on a flat beside the river; each with a stovepipe sticking out the top.

We transfer to a smaller bus to navigate the 53 hairpin turns up the steep 1,300-foot face of a mountain, then walk the last kilometer to the summit at 6,500 feet. In front of us is Tian Chi (Heaven Lake), with turquoise waters sparkling in crisp, clear air, and an arc of snowcapped mountains rising high in a blue sky on the far side. I'm reminded of Lake Louise without the crowds.

We're free to wander amongst the rocks and pine trees along the shore for an hour, then board a crowded boat for a half-hour cruise.

After returning to Wulumuqi late that afternoon, we spend an hour at the International Market, where the shops are crammed with an astonishing array of exotic goods. I'm soon admiring beautifully-colored Kazak dresses, fur hats, Kashmir and silk scarves, Russian stacking dolls, jewelry, knives, statues, carpets, and ivory tusks. I notice that the people around us appear more European than Chinese, with rounder eyes and paler skin (most of the city's population of 2.2 million are Islamic Uyghur).

Wulumuqi is the capital of China's largest province, Xinjiang Uygur Autonomous Region, and is 400 km from Kazakhstan and 300 km from Mongolia. It has a long history on the caravan routes that stretched from eastern China to India, Persia, Egypt, Greece, and Rome. The long pack trains brought not only exotic goods such as silk, porcelain, jewelry, and perfume, but also horses, camels, and grain. They enriched the cities they passed through, which then became centers for artists, artisans, and scholars, as well as officials and businessmen.

Our 2,000-km journey along the Silk Road begins in the cool air that evening, and as we start east across the Gobi Desert, small herds of cows and goats, plus two camels, graze peacefully on the flat desert floor. High, snowy mountains stand on the horizon to the northeast, while the ground slopes down into the Turpan Pendi to the south. This depression contains the lowest point in China, 500 feet below sea level.

The Gobi Desert is hot, dry, and windy, but two hours down the road, at Turpan, farms are intensely managed and produce cotton, silk, wheat, nuts, melons, and grapes. We spend the night here and next morning visit a family-run farm, where we sample a dozen varieties of raisins, plums, and prunes. Water for irrigation comes from natural springs and from the Karez Underground Irrigation Channels.

The channels were designed 2,200 years before and are considered one of the three greatest achievements in ancient Chinese engineering (along with the Great Wall and Grand Canal). Wells dug at the edge of the Bogda Mountains to the north capture snowmelt that previously ran out into the desert and evaporated. Underground tunnels then transport the water up to forty km. There are now 163,000 wells and 1,400 horizontal shafts.

We're escorted down into an irrigation tunnel and follow the running water upstream to where it emerges from a smaller tunnel. Climbing down two steps to the edge of the narrow ditch, I put my fingers in the water and find it pleasantly cold and elbow deep; there's a ripple of current on the surface and it's said to be pure enough to drink.

Peering at the hand dug walls of the smaller tunnel, I try to picture a man undertaking the work but my imagination fails. We're now 30 feet underground but the other end is said to be 1,400 feet below ground level. Apparently, crosses were aligned at the top and bottom of a well to establish the direction of a tunnel, and a lit candle behind a worker kept him digging in a straight line.

After leaving Turpan, we cross a desert that is flat as a tabletop and barren of plant life. The remains of the ancient city of Gaochang lie 40 km to the east, and we arrive there at midday. The temperature is 42° C, and there is no sign of the oasis that once existed. We ride through on a cart pulled by a mule that our guide refers to as a donkey. When Dave corrects him, he indignantly insists, "No, it's a donkey! Mules are only used in the fields."

I slowly realize that the tall, lumpy-looking mounds around us are the remains of clay-brick buildings that have been disintegrating for 600 years. The top of the city wall actually looks like it has melted. We then walk through a gateway into a courtyard where the walls of a temple and lecture hall are still recognizable. Our guide tells us, "Gaochang was a Uyghur city-state that flourished for 1,400 years. It was a center of Buddhism, with Sanskrit texts from India in its library. Muslim invaders killed or chased away the 2,500 people living here and desecrated the temple."

Climbing back on the bus, we travel for another eight hours before stopping for the night. The two-lane road is paved and traffic is light, mostly trucks that tend to wander all over the place. Our driver honks at almost every vehicle he sees, making sure the other driver's awake, I think. In the days to come, we always find a lunch stop and hotel to spend the night, but put up with *5-star pit stops* on occasion. The bus pulls off to the side of the road and we hurry down into a ravine or behind a hillock for privacy. I'm surprised at how pleasant the temperature is, I thought it would be hotter.

China's empty spaces fascinate me right from the start. The terrain varies from sandy flats with a sparse covering of sagebrush to low, rocky hills. Colors are mostly in shades of black and brown, but now and again, in the distance, I see splashes of red, pink, grey, tan, blue, or green. Even more intriguing are the small conical piles of earth scattered across the lonely reaches of the desert. Only when our companions mime sleeping, do we understand that they are graves.

We stay that night and the next in the town of Hami, and the following day tour the grasslands of the Kazakhs. Driving north across the rising desert floor, we follow a deep, rocky ravine into the hills and emerge in a shallow valley at 7,000 feet. A wide sweep of grassland stretches before us, with low, snowcapped mountains on either side and two flocks of sheep grazing in the distance.

While the sky is bright and sunny, the wind is cold and I zip up my jacket as we walk about. Several yurts are set up under the pine trees at the edge of the meadow, and I'm surprised to see dandelions growing in the short, green grasses nearby. We're invited into one of the yurts, and I stoop to enter the low doorway, then step onto a small circle of tiles. On the inner edge of the tiles sits a low stove with a very long stovepipe. The yurt is maybe twenty feet in diameter, and the surrounding floor is raised three inches and covered with thick felt pads and colorful blankets. The walls and ceiling are draped with rugs, and at the top, the edge of a plastic barrier is visible beneath the tarp covering the outside.

We're served yoghurt and milk tea while our guide explains, "The Kazakhs were nomads, but now graze their sheep in the high meadows during the summer, sell them in the fall, and spend the winter in the city." They also rent out yurts and sell rides on their small ponies to tourists like me. The handlers prove to be greedy for money and I'm almost run over in the stampede for customers, then the horses have so little life they could have been drugged.

Not long after leaving Hami next day, a dust cloud driven by brisk southerly winds rolls across the highway in front of us. When the bus slows, I see the dim outline of camels, then the puffs of dust rising from beneath their feet. There are maybe fifty animals, apparently wild, and they stalk off into the desert. A few minutes later, sand has drifted across part of the road. We later drive through the middle of an oil field with dozens of slow-moving pumps, then pass two wind farms, the large blades of the turbines turning ever so slowly.

After crossing the border into Gansu province, we enter the Hexi (Hushi) Corridor. With high mountains to the north and south, this natural corridor narrows to a 25-km-wide gateway through which all transportation, communication, and pipeline routes are funneled. Oddly shaped low mounds near the road turn out to be remnants of the western end of the Great Wall.

We spend the afternoon at Mogao Grottoes (Thousand Buddha Caves), which is near Dunhuang, one of the cities that flourished along the Silk Road. Buddhism and the practice of transforming caves into temples arrived here from India about the 4th century. Close to 500 temple-caves were dug into sandstone cliffs here, which extend for over a kilometer along a dry riverbed. In them were found 50,000 sq feet of murals and more than 2,000 painted statues.

I'm absolutely stunned when we enter the first cave and see the brightly painted murals covering the walls and ceiling. The restored 1,500-year-old artwork depicts followers of the Buddha, Hindu figures, animals, landscapes, and patterns. We tour through eight such caves, and one has beautifully carved wooden statues of the Buddha and his disciples. Behind a tall wooden façade, a giant Buddha several stories high is also carved into the cliff face.

Over time, the front walls of some caves collapsed, exposing their contents to wind and sun. Caves were also damaged by an earthquake, by Mao's followers during the Cultural Revolution, and by fires lit by soldiers during the Russian revolution in 1917. Now, the caves are fronted by a wall of cement and only some have been restored. I'm told no additional work is planned.

With the sun sinking low in the sky, we board the bus for a short drive to the edge of a sand desert that's roughly 40 km long and 20 km wide. We're going to see the 700-foot-high Mingsha Sand Dune. According to our guide, "Although the wind blows constantly and the sand drifts, the sand mountain never moves."

We're dropped off near a herd of kneeling camels and as we walk toward them the stench is overpowering. We're then assigned animals for the short ride out to the dune. The saddle is placed between the camel's two humps, and I have to swing my leg really high to clear the rear hump, then hang on for dear life when the camel stands up. They are tied in strings of three and ours is guided by two sharp-tongued, flashing-eyed women. They do a lot of yelling at their work mates during the half-hour ride, and at me when I don't hang on with both hands. The dune turns out to be a playground, with tourists climbing wooden ladders up the side, then skiing or sliding down.

The following day, we bump and grind for two hours through road construction. A huge dust cloud hangs overhead, and the wind whips up more wherever the ground is disturbed. When vehicles meet, visibility drops to zero. The project extends for 100 km and is in varying stages of completion, but we see little in the way of equipment.

A long line of laborers, including women, shovel and sweep at the road's edge, most have their faces covered. We also see two men, manually turning a windlass, bring up a bucket of dirt at a culvert excavation. Administration tents and those providing living quarters are dug into the ground or half hidden by high dirt berms.

In the narrow gateway of the Hexi Corridor, sections of the Great Wall have been rebuilt and lead to a restored fort named Jiayuguan (*Strategic Pass Under Heaven),* which was originally built in 1372. We approach it as did travelers of old, walking up to the high, thick walls and entering a narrow lane between two of them that takes us down one side and across the back. After passing through an enclosed gate, we enter the land of barbarian hordes.

When we return inside, we enter an inner courtyard surrounded by a high parapet. If enemy forces had managed to get in, they would have been trapped here, with archers above raining down arrows. We climb the steep ramp to the parapet, where Dave picks up a bow and lets fly an arrow that almost hits the target. We then follow the parapet around the perimeter of the fort, and I stop occasionally to look out over the desert and feel the silence. To the south, the high, snow-capped peaks of the Qilian Mountains stand on the horizon, with Tibet just beyond.

We visit several more sites that day and the next. Grasslands around an ancient spring were once used to raise the horses that carried the emperors' armies. The spring now bubbles slowly into a square basin at Quanhu Park, feeding a manmade lake with a landscaped island in the middle. It's a cool, green spot, shady and pleasant.

A large clay figure of the Buddha lies on its right side at the 700-year-old Giant Buddha Temple. Painted murals cover the walls and ceiling, and the library contains 6,000 Buddhist texts written on long paper that is folded accordion fashion, not rolled. We also tour a Confucian Temple established in 1439, which our guide describes as a center of learning, a university. It is now a museum.

The most interesting stop is Leitai Han Tomb, a large, brick-chambered tomb built for General Zhang about 200 AD. We enter through a doorway set into a cement wall that fronts the side of a small knoll. A long passageway lined with artifacts leads to three rooms, two of them have small storage rooms. All are empty. Miniature bronze figures of soldiers and horses were found in one of the storage rooms, as were ancient coins and objects made of gold, silver, copper, jade, and pottery.

A second doorway in the cement wall leads into a smaller tomb, and the long entrance tunnel takes us to a living room; through it is a middle room, and beyond it a bedroom. The rooms aren't very big and the doorway to each is lower than the one before; I double over to enter the bedroom and Dave doesn't even try. It's very cool inside and I'm filled with questions, never imagining that I'd see anything like this.

A large garden and tiled plaza lead down to the site and rows of full-sized replicas of the miniature figures found in the tomb are arranged in one section. Another figure, *galloping horse on a dove's back*, is the symbol for Tourism China and sits high on a pillar at the entrance. The figure is considered unique because the entire mass of the horse is supported on one small hoof. It is now that I understand China is not poor. The country might have poor people, but their history is rich and the cities and historical sites we've visited have been remarkable.

After dinner in Wuwei that night, we have a free hour before dark and set off to explore the area around our hotel. We stumble across a busy pedestrian mall, and as we stroll through, people turn and stare after us. One woman is so startled that she almost falls off her shoes. Feeling uncomfortable, as we obviously look strange, I try to meet eyes and smile; most people smile back, some with obvious delight.

Two blocks farther on, we enter a large square where dozens of women lined up in rows dance to taped music. Wearing everyday clothes, they move in unison and maybe half have white scarves draped across shoulders and arms. A large number of people sit about the square, watching, and we also pause to watch. Dave points to a small girl who stands behind a woman, attempting to copy her movements, while at the far end, twelve dancers beat on small drums as they perform.

Soon, I feel a tap on my shoulder and turn to see a woman waving me to a low wall where she'd obviously been sitting. Smiling, I shake my head and do my best to mime a response. Bending my knees as if sitting, I wave my arm to indicate the passage of time, then stand erect, stretch, and move my feet to show I need exercise. A second woman now waves me to the bench, so I repeat my movements. I don't know if they understand but everybody smiles all around.

With the light fading from the sky, we start back to the hotel and a young boy now comes up behind me and says, "Hello." When I smile and ask, "How are you?" he runs shyly ahead. A young woman walking nearby hears the exchange and says, "How are you?" Now it's my turn to respond delightedly and she smiles, nods, and is gone.

Shortly after leaving Wuwei next day, I notice a few workers standing near a mud-walled, flat-roofed compound in a field and wonder if that is where they live. We've seen only high rises in cities, nothing that resembles housing for workers. Our driver now turns onto a rough secondary road, and soon we are mystified by dozens of parallel trails climbing up the sides of high, steep hills on either side. They turn out to be narrow, irrigated terraces that are part of a tree-planting project initiated fifteen years earlier. I can't imagine the man hours involved, as they run on for endless miles.

Many high towers rise above a narrow river valley as we approach Lanzhou (lan-jo), the capital of Gansu province. The city has a population of 3.2 million people and stretches for 40 km along the Yellow River. We spend the afternoon walking through parks beside the river and pause at a larger-than-life sculpture of a reclining woman and her child that represent the river and the country. Our guide explains, "This river is called the Mother River of China because the water is the same color as the skin of the Chinese people."

The river is wide and high, with a strong current, and a young man tests out the buoyancy of a goatskin raft, once commonly seen on the river. Each skin forms a watertight bladder and twelve are needed to support the raft. A huge paddlewheel sits in a side channel and lifts water into a flume that turns a second wheel, which powers a large grinding wheel. At one time, the wheel ground all the province's wheat. In another park, we're the attraction, and I'm approached by a young couple who want to take my picture.

Next morning, we board a plane for the 500-km flight back to Xian. We're met by a new tour guide who doesn't speak English, and that pretty much ends the tour for us. After long days on the bus, and nights spent on rock-hard beds, we simply don't have the energy to figure out what's going on.

Instead, we spend the final morning exploring the area around the hotel on our own.

We find a very pleasant pedestrian mall a few blocks away, with shady trees and wide, tiled sidewalks. The shops are not yet open and employee groups stand in front of their workplaces, having a motivational start to the day. Six women dance in front of a Kodak shop, creating beautiful designs as they sweep floppy fans up and down. At least a dozen kitchen staff dressed in white and wearing chef's hats make up another group; administrative staff are lined up beside them.

We return to the hotel in time to rejoin our tour group for the bus ride to the airport at noon. As we pass through the city wall, I recall climbing up to the ramparts that first day and learning about pixues. Dave then honed his bartering skills in the government stores we'd visited, buying a pair of jade pixues, a small version of the flying horse, and a set of four pictures embroidered in silk.

The pictures had caught my eye, and I'd quietly brought him back for a second look, but a hawkeyed salesgirl was instantly beside us. She reduced the tag price by 30%, then knocked 100 RMB off, bringing the price down to 1,000 RMB. A manager got involved and reduced it to 800, then badgered Dave into offering 400 and laughed it off. As we walked out the door, the girl wanted 700, halfway across the yard it was 500, and as I climbed on the bus, she grabbed Dave's arm and said, "Okay, 400."

But not all transactions went his way. One day, he called me over to a pair of jade dragons that he was considering and explained that the salesgirl wanted 500 RMB. She overheard his remark and exclaimed, "Sold, we have a deal!" I protested, saying that he was talking to me, not her. Never mind! She wrapped up the articles while harshly muttering, "A deal's a deal!"

Every night, we'd dined on food from different regions, including bony fish, skewered lamb pieces, chicken, bite-sized dumplings, and noodles. Bowls and platters were always placed on a revolving central platform, and everyone stretched out with chopsticks to pick up a morsel to bring back to their plates. To my embarrassment, I never acquired the ability to do so elegantly.

We learned about the Xian Incident in December of 1936, when two of Chiang Kai Shek's generals mutinied. By forcing him to join with the Communists to fight the Japanese, they perhaps changed the course of history. We'd also been told that pictures of Chairman Mao were hung in buildings to keep them and their contents safe during the Cultural Revolution (1966 to 1976). Nothing was said, however, about the millions of Chinese who starved to death as a result of his policies.

CHAPTER 31
CAMBODIA

In January of 2006, Air Asia is promoting a new route to Cambodia and plane tickets are dirt cheap. Dave plans a ten-day trip, arriving in Siem Reap and leaving from Phnom Penh. I think seats are added in the cabin to offset the discount, however, because I've never been so crowded. I'm squeezed in on both sides by my seat mates, while my knees are jammed into the seat in front of me. Dave only survives the ninety-minute flight because he has an aisle seat.

We hire a taxi to take us into town, and the road is absolutely straight for seven km. It is also chockablock with buses, cars, motorcycles, and bicycles. Ornamental facades decorate the entrances to several large hotels on the way, and our driver confides, "In 1994, there were 4 hotels; now there are over 200, with more under construction." (In 2021, there were 980.)

For a bit extra, the driver finds us an acceptable hotel, and after checking in, we grab hats and water bottles and set off to explore. It's midday and steamy hot as we walk down dusty, narrow streets that buzz with activity. All are lined with small shops and stalls, and the first several blocks look much the same to me. We then cross a shallow stream, where the banks are littered with plastic bags. The Old Market is a few blocks farther on and is dark and humid inside. I'm disappointed to find that handicraft stalls carry the same items we'd already bought in Thailand.

When we emerge from the market, we're intercepted by three young girls, who want to sell us postcards. They're bright, outgoing youngsters, maybe ten years old, and we spend half an hour talking to them. In confident English, they explain that they go to school in the mornings and prove it by counting and naming countries and capital cities. I'm impressed to learn that they also speak French, Chinese, and Khmer. I come away thinking that Cambodia's children have to be their gift to the world.

We walk down a narrow lane on the way back to the hotel and see heavy, ornate wooden furniture displayed in a small shop. It doesn't fit with my notion of Cambodia, so I spend the evening reading my guidebook. I learn that between the 1st and 9th centuries, SE Asia was occupied by small, independent town-states that were frequently in conflict. The people grew rice and traded with China and India, and through that contact had been introduced to Hinduism and Buddhism.

The Khmer Empire in Cambodia flourished from the 9th to 13th centuries, and at one time controlled much of Indochina. Their religious beliefs, art, and architecture came directly from India, and the prosperity of the period was marked by the construction of many temples near Siem Reap.

Next morning, we ask the front-desk clerk about tuk-tuk services. He introduces us to Mr Seng, who we hire for the day. We're soon on our way to the walled city of Angkor Thom, and within ten minutes have left the chaotic city traffic behind and are driving through cool, fresh air in the countryside. We stop at a checkpoint, fill in forms, provide pictures, pay $40 US each, and receive 3-day park permits. When we leave, Mr Seng has on an ID badge and wears a vest with a large number written on the back.

We now put-put down the edge of a long, straight boulevard lined with palm trees. A steady stream of cars and the occasional tour bus race past on one side, while a few elephants lumber along in the shade of the trees on the other, their passengers swaying on bench seats on their backs.

Mr Seng parks the tuk-tuk near the south entrance to Angkor Thom, and we join a line of tourists walking out onto a stone bridge lined with large, stone images of gods and asuras (demons). The bridge crosses a 300-foot-wide moat that protects the earthen wall around the city. Built in the 12th century, the wall is 25 feet high and runs for 7.5 miles. A face tower overlooks a narrow entrance gate on the far side, where vehicles queue up to enter. When we join the line in the tuk-tuk, two large elephants loom high overhead as they squeeze in behind us.

Mr Seng drops us at the edge of a broad, dilapidated rock terrace in front of *the Bayan*, the state temple of Jayavarman VII. As we carefully pick our way across the crumbling rocks, I study the weathered structure in front of us, which includes many face towers. The Khmer temple was the palace of a god, and in the Buddhist religion, the gods sat on Mount Meru, the center of the world. This temple sits in the exact center of Angkor Thom, and the moat and towers represent oceans and mountains.

Walking down a narrow corridor along one side, we admire the arched ceiling overhead, and the bas relief sculptures (similar to raised images on coins) that decorate pillars and walls. We skirt piles of rocks in the mazelike interior, where sections of wall have collapsed, then climb to an upper level for a view of some of the 181 giant, smiling faces carved into 37 towers.

The foundation and inner core of the temple were built using laterite, an iron-rich clay that was relatively soft and easy to dress into blocks; it hardened after exposure to sun and air. Sandstone brought by water from the Kulen Mountains was used to finish the structure. Inscriptions were carved in bas relief on stone slabs and door jambs of sanctuaries, and lathe-turned balusters were inserted into stone window frames.

We now follow the flow of tourists across a long causeway to *the Bapuon*, a massive five-tiered pyramid built in the 11th century, which is currently under renovation by the French. Next, we come to a 10th-century temple that looks pretty crumbly, but shady trees on the terrace provide some relief from the sun. Walking eastward, we arrive at the Leper King Terrace, its walls carved in deep relief with mythological scenes. Adjacent to it is the Elephant Terrace, with hunting scenes of elephants and mahouts carved into its ten-foot-high, 1,000-foot-long wall. Three-headed elephants flank a staircase in the wall, their trunks pulling lotus plants from the ground.

Children, some very small, wander about selling postcards, and in a crowded lane, we run a gauntlet of young people selling flutes, Jew's harps, bells, and small brass ornaments. Hearing the clunk of a wooden bell, I turn my head toward the sound and a young girl, maybe 8 years old, sees the movement and scurries over. She's selling bamboo bells and I'm so impressed with her that I pay what she asks.

After four hours in the hot sun, we join Mr Seng at a row of concession stalls, and he directs us to a table where we order cold drinks. We're soon surrounded by four little girls, about seven years old, selling small, woven-paper fish. They are very competitive and the last one to arrive informs me, "To be fair, you should buy one from each of us." I buy from the one who arrived first, but want more than she has, so all contribute. A younger girl, maybe four, now appears and tries to sell us a wooden stork.

Now feeling somewhat revived, we listen to Mr Seng's pitch for a three-day tour, and when we agree, he takes us to two more temples. An effort has been made to keep the first much as it was when seen by Europeans in the 19th century. Some vegetation has been cleared away and significant work has been done to prevent further collapse, but trees still grow out of walls, their roots snaking down between stone blocks, sections of wall lean noticeably, and piles of rubble block a few paths. The second temple sits across the road from a large stone platform overlooking the King's Bath, a manmade lake built in the 10th century that is over 2,000 feet long and 1,000 feet wide.

I feel exhausted when we return to the hotel, more from the terrible neediness of the people than from the heat. After years of war, half the population is under fifteen years of age, and all of them, parents, children, and landmine victims, need to make a living off tourists, most of whom visit during a two-to-three-month period each year.

We spend half the next day at Angkor Wat, said to be the largest religious monument in the world, and the best example of classical Khmer construction. Its moat is 600 feet wide, and we stop to watch as workers using traditional methods replace a large block of stone in the bridge deck. We then follow a causeway over a grassy, treed space in front of the temple, where several sets of stairs lead down to the faint outlines of streets.

Angkor Wat is a pyramid with three levels and on top are five towers representing the peaks of Mount Meru. We enter the lower level at the southwest entrance and are immediately drawn to the bas relief sculptures of apsaras, the celestial dancers who entertained the Gods and were the sensual rewards of kings and heroes who died bravely.

We walk down corridors that extend for 2,000 feet around the base, marveling at the six-foot-high bas relief sculptures that decorate the inside walls. Some scenes come from Hindu mythology, others show the army of the builder, King Suryavarman II. From the second level, we view the central towers rising from the courtyard, then climb another 35 feet on ladder-like stairs to the top level, where we look out over the grounds.

Mr Seng takes us 20 km south that afternoon, to the Floating Village on Tonle Sap, a large freshwater lake that drains into the Mekong River. The road deteriorates quickly, and I'm jolted about until I think my teeth are going to fall out. Only later do I realize that the road is underwater for part of the year. When the Mekong is in flood, water flows back up to the lake, which can swell from 3,000 to 13,000 sq km. This phenomenon makes it one of the richest sources of freshwater fish in the world.

Small stilt shacks soon crowd both sides of the road, and women and children go about their chores while ignoring vehicles passing only a few feet away. Large hand-woven mats cover most roofs and walls, as well as the bamboo poles on the floors. Back walls rise up above reeds and bushes that grow along the edge of a canal behind. When the roadway broadens to expose the canal, dozens of boats sit bow-in to shore, large, canopied vessels about forty feet long.

Mr Seng drops us off in front of a boat, and a scruffy looking individual sells us tickets and escorts us aboard. While we make ourselves comfortable in armchairs with thick blue cushions, the helmsman backs the boat out of its slot and maneuvers down the canal. We soon pass several large barges unloading goods and see passengers climbing up the bank off the Phnom Penh ferry. The waterway then widens and we pass a busy fish market, where many small sampan-like boats are tied up.

House boats now appear amongst the reeds and bushes, their dark, cramped spaces looking even less appealing than the stilt shacks. Several small boats loaded with vegetables and other goods for sale are making their rounds, and we pass a church, school, and restaurant that operate out of buildings erected on barges. In the water beside the restaurant, two young children perform for tourists by spinning about in aluminum basins.

We make a quick turn out into the lake, where water is visible as far as the eye can see to the south and west. We watch two fishermen in a small boat pull in a net, one of them squatting on the flat prow. Mr Seng informs us, "The water will continue to drop for three more months, by which time the boats will have moved down to the lake front." I'm left wondering what people do for drinking water and sanitation.

Next day, Mr Seng drives us 37 km north of Siam Reap to a child-sized temple named Banteay Srei near the Kulen Mountains. The small, pink sandstone temple was built in the 10th century and walls and lintels are exquisitely carved. We also tour East Mebon, a 10th-century island temple surrounded by jungle. It's no longer an island, but the surrounding wall is extraordinarily high and we conclude that it sat in a reservoir built earlier in that century. The reservoir was contained by dikes (no excavation) and held 55 million cubic feet of water.

We tour three more temples before returning to Siem Reap, walking down long paths through the jungle to approach them. Rising up from a pool of water in front of one is the statue of a flying horse with men clinging to its flanks and tail. The horse, Balaha, is helping sea-faring merchants escape from an ogress.

While driving through the countryside, we pass roadside stands selling baskets, fruits, sugar, and liter bottles of petrol. I see small circular wells at the edge of most villages, and now and again spot a water buffalo. Farmers cut rice with machetes, and a fisherman stands in a small pond beside the road, using a net to catch fish that have been trapped by receding lake waters. Small haystacks are piled on top of wooden frames or around poles, and twists of hay are laid out, drying in the sun. There also seems to be a lot of garbage everywhere.

Dave asks Mr Seng about the charred wood sticking out of white bags piled beside the road, so he stops near one and talks to a farmer at a roadside stand. The man's wife and half a dozen kids then lead us into the jungle to a clay-covered pile about six feet high. As the woman speaks, Mr Seng translates, "When a tree is cut down, the wood is cut, piled, covered with clay, and lit on fire. It's left to smolder for three days, then the charcoal is put into sacks and delivered to the city."

As we walk back to the road, the woman points to a stalk of bamboo leaning up against a sugar palm. It appears to be a ladder of sorts, with branch stubs on either side. The farmer shows us a sprout from the top of a tree and gestures with a machete, showing how they cut it, then squeeze it and catch the palm juice in bamboo containers. Palm juice simmers in a wok nearby and is skimmed now and then. The process continues until only sugar granules are left, which are wrapped in leaves and sold at the stand.

As we drive through the city, bicycles, motorcycles, cars, and buses share the same space, and nobody walks. One morning, near a large market, I see a sign at a Children's Hospital, "Severe Hemorrhagic Dengue Fever Epidemic". Another day, we're driving down a narrow stretch of road under construction and pass women carrying gravel in flat wicker scoops. They dump the gravel onto the roadbed where men squat and spread it out using short narrow planks. Another woman sweeps off the shoulder of the road with what looks to be a banister brush.

When it comes time to say goodbye to Mr Seng, I tell him how impressed we've been with the children we've met. He responds soberly, "They're lucky; they go to school and learn English. You have to speak English to get a job, and outside the city, kids don't learn it."

Next day, we board a bus for the 314-km, six-hour journey to Phnom Penh. The road winds across flat terrain dotted with ponds, canals, and small lakes, and we pass through several small villages and two large towns. Our hotel in Siem Reap called ahead and we're met at the depot by a man from a hotel; he holds a sign with Dave's name on it. After we've checked in, the desk clerk writes his phone number on a business card and gives it to me, saying, "In case you need help."

Our hotel is located on a narrow, neglected side street a block off the Mekong River. It's old, but comfortable enough, and the high ceilings and decorative moldings reveal a French influence. We're soon walking down the street beside the river, looking for a place to eat. In the steamy heat of mid-afternoon, the far bank is barely visible through the haze, and the wide expanse of water in between is dotted with fish boats, barges, and ferries.

Menus are posted outside restaurants and prices are very expensive. When we finally choose one, we sit at a sidewalk table, which is a mistake, as we're approached by every street vendor and beggar for blocks. A young man hobbles up on crutches, one leg missing below the knee; another has no arms; and a boy pushes a wheelchair containing a person with no arms or legs. They all want money and linger nearby. Other youngsters sell books or small brass figures. We don't always say no.

When we later walk down the street, we're approached by a personable young man who has a tuk-tuk and offers to take us touring next day. Mr Ya is 28 years old and tells us, "I'm getting married in November and need to save $2,000 to pay to the bride's family for the celebration." After a bit more discussion, Dave agrees to pay the $15 US fee he requests.

Mr Ya picks us up at 0900 next day, then drives through busy streets that remind me of Siem Reap, with bicycles, motorcycles, cars, and buses all crowded together. They don't stop at intersections, just slow down and slip around each other. Outside the city, rows of lush green, leafy vegetables grow in low-lying, watery fields, and we meet several vehicles loaded with fresh produce. As we continue through small villages and treed grasslands, I recall that this was the route taken by thousands of Cambodians on their way to the killing fields. The country's violent history is so recent that I start to feel uncomfortable. I don't understand how it came to pass.

Before we left, Mr Ya asked Dave, "Do you want to go play first? Maybe fire an AK 47 or a grenade launcher? Get dressed up in army clothes?" Dave had been non-committal, and now, after passing the entrance to an army camp, he turns right onto a narrow dirt lane and stops 300 feet down it, in front of a battered, corrugated iron gate. After a man in sloppy, civilian clothes appears and opens the gate, he drives into a compound, then stops before an open-sided shed where a second man waits. Several guns are displayed on a wall at one end, and doors to two dressing rooms stand ajar at the other end.

Dave looks about with interest, noting the prices on a sign: $30 US to fire an AK 47, $60 for the grenade launcher. About the time he decides he's not interested and shakes his head, another vehicle pulls into the yard and an army officer gets out. Dave now raises his camera, and the officer quickly waves a hand and orders, "No pictures! Only after shooting!" Watched by the three men, we climb back into the tuk-tuk and I feel very uncomfortable as we drive away.

A couple of minutes later, Mr Ya drops us off in front of the Genocide Center, and we wait in a grassy, treed area for the tour group ahead of us to move on. We can't help but overhear their guide, and the words spoken in English by this attractive young woman bring a sick feeling to my stomach.

"Children dressed in black were amongst the soldiers who forcibly evacuated the city of Phnom Penh in April of 1975. These youngsters, aged 10-16 years, tortured and killed, even turned on members of their own families. Victims of the Khmer Rouge were mostly well-to-do, educated, and included men, women, and children. They were tortured at S-21 and brought here to die. As bullets cost money, many were bludgeoned and their throats cut; babies were bashed against trees."

While she speaks, I look at the nearby memorial stupa, where the stark, empty-eyed skulls of 8,000 victims are piled up before the windows on three floors. The bottom floor is heaped with clothing. When the group moves into the stupa, Dave follows but I stay outside. I am conflicted, thinking that the memorial for the victims of the Khmer Rouge is also a gruesome tribute to Pol Pot.

We now walk past several mass graves, and I'm struck by how small the pits are, given the number of bodies they contained. The site was once a Chinese cemetery, and in the shade of a plumeria tree is a small pile of human bones. The tour guide speaks again, telling stories of some of the 17,000 people who died here. The stories are gruesome, all ending with the brutal death of innocent people at the hands of their own government. Almost 9,000 bodies have been disinterred, and one-third of the graves are still not excavated.

As we drive back to the city, I study the traffic on the busy road, searching for normalcy, but cannot replace the images that fill my mind. I'm still struggling to process what I've seen when Mr Ya drops us off at Tuol Sleng, Security Prison 21 (S-21). The building was a high school before being turned into the largest center of detention and torture in Cambodia. Almost all the people held here were taken to Choeung Ek, the killing field we visited that morning. Thousands of such killing fields had existed across the country.

Although repulsed, I'm riveted by what we see as we tour the building. On the ground floor, enlarged, faded, framed pictures reveal what was found in each room, the bloody, battered bodies and iron bedsteads to which they were chained. The conditions in which people existed were inhuman, the methods of torture barbaric. An artist has created pictures of scenes he witnessed and some described to him, while hundreds of photos show the faces of Cambodians who passed through.

Climbing stained stairs to the third floor, we join a hundred others and watch a documentary film. When the Khmer Rouge occupied Phnom Penh on April 17, 1975, all the residents of the city were forced to leave their homes and travel into the countryside. They were told that Americans were going to bomb the city and to take only food, as they would be allowed to return in three days. The city stayed empty for 45 months. The rural population was forced to move in two later migrations, one at the end of 1975 and one in 1977.

Children were made to leave their parents, husbands to leave their wives. Few people had any idea where their families were. There was no religion, no education, no communication, no loving. People were killed for worshipping their Gods and for speaking a language other than Khmer. Hundreds of thousands slowly starved to death because rice crops were delivered to China in payment for armaments.

After Vietnam invaded the country on January 7, 1979, people were finally free to return to their home villages and look for family. The entire population did so, leaving rice crops unattended, and hundreds of thousands more starved to death.

That night, we try another restaurant beside the river, and although we sit inside, we're again beseeched by scrawny, sad-eyed creatures. I make an effort to respond with a smile and a shake of the head, and sometimes it works. Turning to Dave, I sadly confess, "It's a good thing we didn't come here when we first started traveling. I doubt that I'd have left the hotel after the first day."

The following morning, we seek relief from these tales of horror, which somehow seem worse because they occurred during our lifetime. We visit the National Museum, where we study the many bronze and sandstone carvings depicting Hindu and Buddhist deities. We walk around the Royal Palace, look in a few shops, and visit Wat Ounalom, a Buddhist education center founded in 1443 that is near our hotel. We've seen two large funeral wagons with dragons painted on the sides parked outside its walls, and a few young monks in the street. The buildings were heavily damaged under the Khmer Rouge and its extensive library was destroyed.

The next day, we track down and watch two more documentary films. The first is about Pol Pot, who was an educated man from a well-to-do family. The second is about the land mines hidden in fields and waterways. They do not kill, but cause horrific injuries, with up to 700 victims a year. Some of the mines were planted by the Khmer Rouge, who hid near Siem Reap after the Vietnamese invaded. Others, especially along the border with Vietnam, are unexploded ordinance dropped by Americans.

At breakfast on our last morning, Dave reads a local newspaper that looks more like a newsletter. He tells me, "Two sisters in their early forties were beaten to death for stealing bananas from a plantation. Apparently, the security guard on duty would have been held responsible for the loss and has disappeared." The story makes me think about the 15-year-olds who were in Pol Pot's army in 1975. Those who survived had returned to farming and would now be 42 years old.

When we leave the café, we're followed by a teenage boy for over a block. He's tall, dirty, and very aggressive in his demands for money. Dave finally stops and tells him to go. I repeat the word and point down the street, hoping to make people around us aware of the problem. He just stares at Dave, then me, and finally swaggers off. It's very disturbing.

We now walk through a street market that is full of shoppers inspecting piles of fresh vegetables, baskets of rice noodles and tofu, and stalls of fresh fruit. Meat hangs from stall roofs, fish wriggle in baskets, and I even see a pile of skinned water snakes. Men on motorcycles push their way through, stopping here and there to make a purchase, and people look at us curiously as we pass. Turning to Dave as we leave, I glumly comment, "It's incomprehensible that people could have starved to death in a country that can produce this amount and variety of food."

That night at dinner, I ask a young boy if he has a book entitled *The Pol Pot Regime* amongst the ones he is selling. He doesn't, but before long, another boy arrives with a copy. I read it after we return to Malaysia and learn in scrupulous detail how as many as two million people died during Pol Pot's four-year rule (25% of the population).

I then search a bookstore in KL for books on SE Asia and find a carefully researched biography of Mao Tse-tung that answers the questions I have about China. By some estimates, up to seventy million people died in peacetime because of his policies. Mao had had an intimate relationship with Stalin that dated back to the 1920s. Stalin became leader of the USSR when Lenin died in 1924, and his policies caused the deaths of perhaps twenty million people. I cannot fathom what drove these madmen, but have to conclude that they were abetted by a cadre of willing accomplices.

CHAPTER 32
VIETNAM

We plan another bus tour at the end of 2006, this time venturing into Vietnam. The terminal at KLIA is incredibly busy when we check in, with long lines at airline counters and dozens of people wandering about in the long white robes of Hajj pilgrims. As we leave the counter after checking our bags, a middle-aged Asian man stops Dave and asks, "Are you flying to Hanoi?"

When Dave nods his head, he waves to his two companions and says, "My friends are too and have their boarding passes, but don't know how to get to the gate. Can you help them? They don't speak English."

I check the boarding passes proffered by the man and woman, ensuring we're on the same flight, and Dave responds, "Sure, no problem!"

A young Asian woman overhears this exchange and comes up to me, extending her boarding pass. Dave talked to her earlier and didn't think she knew much English, but learned that she was Vietnamese and going to Hanoi. Assuming she wants to join us, I check the gate number, and nod my head. The five of us now make our way across the terminal and downstairs to Immigration, then pass the duty-free shops to a light rail platform. The train takes us across to the departure terminal, where we proceed down another long concourse, passing more duty-free shops, to our gate.

During our long wait there, the young woman reveals that she does know English, but speaks very softly and we have to listen closely. With excitement lighting up her face and voice, she divulges, "I stay in Malaysia three years and this my first trip home. I work for computer company, but there problems and not much money, so I not come back." Later, she explains, "My mother and three sisters live in village seventy km from Hanoi. My sisters all married. I number three daughter and have boy's name, "Bung". My father wanted boy; he died when I two years old."

When we ask her questions about her childhood, she doesn't respond. Dave then asks, "What are you going to do now?"

Shrugging her shoulders, she answers, "I don't know."

"Maybe you'll get married, too?"

Ruefully shaking her head, she replies, "No, I too old; I twenty-seven."

After a ninety-minute flight, we clear through Vietnamese Immigration in Ho Chi Minh City (Saigon), then are routed through three security checkpoints while walking down to our connecting flight to Hanoi. We're in the air two hours on this leg and arrive after dark. There is no glow of lights in the sky as we approach, and only as we descend do scattered pinpricks of light reveal the existence of the four million people below. A few dimly lit buildings then appear alongside a shadowy road as we land.

After we've all claimed our luggage, we say goodbye to our traveling companions. With eyes shining and a catch in her voice, Bung explains, "My mother and sister come to get me; they arrange car." She then waves wildly to someone in the lounge outside the secure area and says, "That my sister!" We wish her good luck as she sets off with two suitcases that presumably hold all her belongings.

Our tour guide, Sam, waits in the lounge and gathers together the thirty-two members of our group and escorts us to a bus. As we drive through the darkness, he points out bridges that we can't see and talks about reunification of the country. We then drive down a street where dim light spills from buildings; it looks to be about the same intensity as the glow off a TV screen.

We eventually turn onto a street where dim street lights reveal the shadowy outlines of four-story-high buildings that abut each other. They're long and narrow, and some are barely fifteen feet wide. According to Sam, "Land fronting the road is very valuable, and people living over shops just added floors as their families grew."

The bus comes to a stop in front of a building that's wider than most, and we're escorted up to a second-floor dining room, which is decorated for Christmas and includes a tree. We're seated at two long tables and enjoy a meal of rice, noodles, fish, chicken, and vegetables. Meanwhile, we're entertained with Vietnamese folk music by performers wearing traditional costumes.

After reboarding the bus, we drive through dimly-lit streets that are filled with people. Some sit on low stools on the sidewalk and appear to be eating or visiting in small family groups. Motorcycles are parked everywhere. Many more are on the road, most have passengers, and no one wears a helmet. Their drivers flit back and forth through traffic, looking only straight ahead, so our bus driver keeps one hand on the horn, giving constant warning that he's coming up behind.

We're dropped off at the Thang Long Water Puppet Theater, where the performance has already started. A group of musicians and actors sit off to one side, while four brightly colored dragons play on the surface of a pool of water. The puppets enter and exit the pool through grass mats that cover the base of a high-roofed building behind. For the next forty minutes, six puppeteers manipulate characters that plant rice, catch fish and frogs, or just play. Sam explains, "This type of entertainment originated in North Vietnam, and the puppets tell stories about village life and local legends."

Our hotel is not far away, and before we leave the bus, San warns, "We're going to Ho Chi Minh's mausoleum tomorrow, and they don't allow shorts or sleeveless shirts, so please dress appropriately." The hotel is very comfortable, provides an excellent breakfast next morning, and everyone is suitably dressed when we board the bus.

As we near the mausoleum, a queue of darkly-dressed figures stretches around the block, but we're dropped off at the main gate. Sam instructs us to leave our tote bags on the bus, then has us line up in pairs and takes our cameras. We're ushered through a metal detector before joining a queue that leads past tables where uniformed officers sit and examine wallets and ID's.

Half a block farther on, still lined up in pairs, we enter a large parade ground and soldiers in dress-uniform now maintain an orderly line. After we make a sharp left turn toward a building, they become more numerous and watch us closely. Putting a finger to lips for quiet, they tell people to remove hats, take hands out of pockets, and stay within two painted lines.

Inside the building, we're funneled left then right to a flight of stairs leading up to the room where Ho Chi Minh's body lies in a glass sarcophagus. A soldier stands stiffly at each corner of the dais and light shines on the bearded face of the leader, making it clearly visible in the dimly lit room. As I look, my footsteps slow and a guard touches my arm, motioning me to catch up to the couple ahead. When Dave wanders over a painted line, a guard is there to wave him back. We're in the room maybe a minute, entering from behind Ho's head and walking past his left side, feet, and right side, then exiting. (Apparently, the body goes back to Moscow annually for upkeep.)

With Sam speaking reverently about the dead leader whenever he mentions his name, I feel like we've just visited the shrine of a new state religion. But he later tells us, "I'm not a communist and most people aren't, but those who control the police, the army, and the government are. There's now a two-child policy, and a government worker can expect to be demoted with loss of pay if he/she has a third."

The day is pleasantly warm as we stroll about the parade ground, and Sam now gently steers us towards the Presidential Palace on the far side. This very ornate building was constructed by the French in 1906 as home for the Governor General of Indochina. Following a path through the trees, we come to a house that Ho lived in from 1954 to 1958, and a stilt house where he lived until his death in 1969. We obediently peer through garage windows at two cars, one given to him by the French, the other by the Russians. The buildings sit on the edge of a small lake stocked with goldfish and surrounded by flowering bushes.

A short bus ride then takes us to a 900-year-old temple that was dedicated to Confucius in 1070. Named the Temple of Literature, it is described as the country's first university and 82 stone stelae recognize the graduates of triennial examinations dating back to 1442. It's easy to picture teachers and students sitting beneath the columns, space now occupied by drink and souvenir stands.

We tour the old city that afternoon in pedicabs, a vehicle that is little more than a bicycle with the front wheel replaced by a chair with two wheels. I feel a little vulnerable in the hectic traffic, especially when a bus screeches to a stop barely a foot from my elbow. This part of the city is said to be 1,000 years old, and the narrow streets remind me of Katmandu. Small shops are crammed with goods that spill out onto sidewalks and range from silk and jewelry to sleeping bags. I see someone getting a haircut on the sidewalk, someone else having a perm, and conclude that people do much of their living on the street.

We end the day with a three-hour-long bus ride (145 km) to Ha Long Bay. When we claim the front seat, Sam is dubious and warns, "It's very dangerous, you could go through the front window!" He makes us promise not to sleep. Posted speeds are twenty km lower for the bus than for smaller vehicles, and police monitor the traffic with radar. We see only the buildings lining the highway when we cross the Red River delta.

Bicycles become more numerous after we leave Hanoi and make up nearly half the traffic on the coast. As the light fades, we see strange cargo being transported on motorcycles. Two large hogs lie trussed up on a platform balanced behind one driver, and a load of live chickens is carried by another. We then stare in disbelief as we make out a water buffalo balanced behind a third. It is lying on its side, feet tied together on one side and head twisted around and secured a few inches above the ground on the other. Although it's almost dark, Dave gets a picture, otherwise I expect that even we would come to doubt what we saw.

Our hotel is located on Ha Long Bay, and next morning the misty outlines of several tall, dark islets are visible from our window. We're to spend the day cruising on the Gulf of Tonkin, and the bus is soon dropping us off at a dock. Sam shepherds us through a crowd of milling tourists to the far end of the beach, where our vessel pushes up against other boats, as the crew tries to keep it within stepping distance of shore.

Once aboard the vessel, we make our way to an open observation deck. The morning is pleasantly warm, with just a ripple on the surface of the water, and visibility is about a km in mist, which Sam says is normal in winter. We watch as boats leave, falling into line bow to stern, and then it's our turn to join them. After motoring for twenty minutes, we enter a sheltered cove on a larger island. Each boat in turn now pushes up to a landing dock to disgorge passengers, then backs off to wait near a loading dock.

We climb narrow stone steps up the hillside, again in pairs, pushed on by tourists behind us. With no place to step aside, I begin to wonder if Mr Ho is here. Only the guards are missing. Actually, many of the 3,000-plus islands scattered across the northern part of the Gulf of Tonkin have unusual limestone formations, and this one has a huge grotto.

We enter the cave through a narrow slit in the hillside. About ten feet below, the cavern floor has been cleared of rubble, and paved stairs and walkways lead past limestone formations, where discreetly-placed colored lights accent the natural beauty. Although there are too many people standing about, it's an interesting stop.

After reboarding our vessel, we motor around the island to a floating village sheltered by the tall peaks of several small islands. We tie up to a barge with small, submerged cages in the deck that contain fish, and passengers are now able to buy their lunch. Visibility has improved by the time we depart, and boats now go their separate ways. Other than going below for lunch, Dave and I stay on deck for the next three hours, undisturbed as we watch misty islands emerge from the haze.

The bus is waiting when we return to shore and takes us directly to Hanoi airport. We don't see much on the way because visibility is poor, but do see four accidents involving motorcycles. After landing in Saigon, we have dinner on the way downtown, then are introduced to the city's horrendous traffic as we wait to reboard the bus.

A family of four stands at a crosswalk on the busy street, wanting to cross several lanes of traffic. None of the buses, cars, or motorcycles even slow down. The four people then form a flying wedge and slowly and deliberately step out into the street. Traffic still doesn't slow down, but alters course just enough to flow around them and continues to do so while they cross.

We spend next day touring in the Mekong River delta, and our new guide, Steve, won't allow us to sit in the front seat. According to him, "Saigon traffic is too heavy and the risk too great!" When we drive through a light-controlled intersection, he points to a traffic officer and explains, "Drivers ignore the signal unless a policeman is present."

Thousands of motorcycles roar through the streets, and at red lights push to the front, forming mobs half-a-block long. When our bus is forced to stop behind a turning vehicle, they flow around us like water around a rock in a riverbed. Steve now sighs and mutters, "Saigon! Eight million people and four million motorcycles."

The 75-km drive to My Tho takes two hours and we then board a boat for a four-hour cruise. The Mekong is three km wide at the mouth, has several large islands mid-stream, and commercial boats of all sizes come and go. Pointing to the bow of a local boat, Steve explains, "The eye painted there is meant to scare off crocodiles; fishing boats don't have them as they would scare off the fish."

We go ashore on Thai Son Islet and soon are sitting at a small table under a thatched roof, drinking tea with honey. As we study a piece of honeycomb from nearby hives, a woman with a large python wrapped around her torso approaches. She invites us to hold it and have a picture taken, but no one is interested. We follow large paving stones through scattered fruit trees to a small shop where women make coconut-candy, and are served fresh fruits in another compound, while listening to a small troupe of young women singing folk songs. We then walk past fish ponds and patchy gardens to the edge of a narrow canal, where small boats wait to take us back to the tour boat.

A man holding a long pole stands at the stern of his boat as five of us climb in and warns, "Make sure to keep your hands inside." A woman crouching on the flat prow then digs deeply with her paddle and the boat slides forward, rocking roughly. She propels us past several boats before meeting one, and now the gunnels scrape harshly against each other. The ride could have been very pleasant, as the canal is lined with water palms and shaded from the sun, but is much too rushed. We're back at the tour boat within ten minutes.

After recrossing the Mekong, we have lunch at a restaurant specializing in fish from the river. We're served a flat fish identified as elephant-ear, and the waitress gains our admiration by filleting it with chopsticks. She then makes spring rolls with rice paper, fish, and small slices of vegetables, which we dip in tamarind sauce. Later, we visit Thien Hau Pagoda, a temple dedicated to the Chinese Goddess of the Sea. The temple roofline is decorated with the usual small figures, but new to us are the large spiral coils of incense hanging from the ceiling that burn for two days.

At 0800 next morning, we board the bus for a two-hour drive through mostly urban streets to Cuchi tunnels, 60 km northwest of the city. We're dropped off in front of a building and directed into a large, bare room, where we sit on plastic chairs in front of a small TV set and watch a twenty-minute propaganda film about the Vietnam War. Filled with references to "glorious, revolutionary fighters", the film includes sketches of the 200-km-long tunnel network that had sleeping rooms, kitchens, and a well.

Although the sun is now high in the sky, the air is still cool when we start down a shady path through open forest. Within minutes, we're passing deep depressions marked as B-52 bomb craters, then come to a burnt-out American tank. I take in the scene soberly, recognizing that the Vietnam War cost many men their lives, so am bewildered when a group of Asian tourists excitedly crowd around the tank, laughing and calling to have their pictures taken.

Farther down the trail, we stop near a small hole in the ground that provides access to a tunnel. Beside it is a soldier wearing fatigues. Although the hole looks much too small, the soldier drops down into it, chest deep, then lifts an adjacent wooden lid over his head, straightens his arms, and disappears into the ground. The lid is covered with dirt and leaves and is invisible once in place.

We pass two more tunnel entrances, black holes in the ground that reveal a few steep stairs rising to the surface. A third is marked by a big, well-lit entrance and is obviously designed for tourists. When the tour group ahead follows their guide inside, I find myself drawn along. Eight steps down is a large underground room, and across it, another eight steps lead down to the tunnel entrance. Then, a few steps into the tunnel, the line stops moving and half dozen people bunch up in front of me.

I'm not much over five feet tall, but stand bent over, with my hands resting on my knees. The tunnel is lit, and I have ample time to study the narrow dirt walls and low ceiling that burrow through the dirt with no structural support. Then suddenly, the knowledge that *men fought and died down here* surfaces in my mind, and I want out. I'm able to back up, then push my way past the long line of tourists on the steps and in the room until I'm again above ground.

My mind in turmoil, I look for Dave and find him waiting at the tunnel exit maybe 150 feet away. We stand and watch as people emerge from underground, babbling excitedly, and suddenly I realize that I am offended by everything around me. *This was a battlefield, men fought and died here! It shouldn't be a playground for tourists.* I feel like we're disrespecting all the men who served here.

I walk around in shocked silence for the next few hours, following the flow of tourists past half-buried rooms depicting scenes of tunnel life. One room shows shells from American bombs being cut up to make deadly traps. In the forest nearby, two soldiers trigger the same trap with a stick, revealing sharpened stakes ready to pierce vulnerable flesh. We then hear automatic weapons fire as visitors eagerly line up to shoot AK 47s at a rifle range.

At first, I'm puzzled by my reaction, as Canadians didn't fight in this war. I then recall that I'd spent several months in Hawaii in 1968 and 1969, when traveling to and from Australia. I'd met many young Americans who were on their way to and from the war. While I'd been too inexperienced to recognize the sacrifice in their service then, I saw it all too clearly now.

I also suspect that I'd grown accustomed to hearing that the US lost the war because the public grew tired of it, so wasn't prepared for the in-your-face victory that the North Vietnamese celebrate. The communists exuberantly gloat over the fact that they defeated the mighty American military machine; they kicked ass and want everyone to know.

The front plaza at the War Remnant Museum is crowded with captured American military planes, tanks, and a helicopter. Inside, rooms are filled with pictures of the fighting, the wounded, and the destruction. Three million Vietnamese are said to have died during the war, two million of them civilians, while two million hectares of forest and agricultural land were destroyed by toxic chemicals.

We end the day on the grounds of the US Embassy and our guide explains, "After our government returned the property to the Americans, they razed the old building and erected a new one at a different location on the site." I suspect that the infamous images of US helicopters lifting fleeing personnel from the rooftop are ones that American leaders would prefer to forget, but the communists of SE Asia never will.

We fly back to Malaysia next day and the bus picks us up early to take us to the airport. Hundreds of motorcycles fill block after block during the drive out to the terminal. We queue up behind a young Brit at the check-in counter, who tells us he's spending a year at the university in Saigon. He explains, "I'm going to Bangkok for a week to get away from the noise and chaos; I haven't had a decent night's sleep in three months."

When I ask him whether he rides a motorcycle, he shakes his head emphatically and replies, "Thirty people die every day in Saigon as a result of motorcycle accidents. I take a taxi."

CHAPTER 33
CHENNAI, INDIA

When we return from Vietnam, Dave's hip is really bothering him. He'd had tests the previous summer at a private medical clinic in Vancouver and been told that he needed hip replacement surgery. He hadn't been ready to commit then, although the waiting list was a year long. In April of 2007, he makes another appointment.

During a pre-op checkup, he is diagnosed with heart arrhythmia and high blood pressure. He is prescribed medication and a month later has a stroke. He spends five days in Vancouver General Hospital, and what he hears there convinces him that the medication was a contributing factor. He suffers no permanent physical damage, but complains of numbness in one hand and foot for years. The experience is devastating, and he's angry with everyone. Life is very difficult for a while.

Because of the stroke, his name is removed from the surgery waiting list for three months. At the end of that time, he phones the surgeon's office to see if he's been put back on. No one answers. He leaves voice messages but never hears back. (Apparently, the doctor has staffing problems.) His frustration building, he sends an email or two. The surgeon responds by email, telling him to go find another doctor.

Dave immediately gets on the Internet, searches websites, and sends off an email. Within three hours, the phone rings and a man in New York asks, "Where do you want to have the surgery?" He not only has a choice of cities at a time of his choosing, but also the option of hip resurfacing instead of replacement.

He submits his medical information over the internet, including digital x-rays, then researches the two procedures. Deciding on resurfacing, he opts for November 12 in Chennai, India, as we can travel there from Malaysia. He'll be in hospital eight days, and I'll have a bed in his room. Because of the stroke, he'll be put on a temporary pacemaker during the operation.

Of course, Dave worries about having surgery, but not about having it overseas. We'd been out of the country long enough to know that Canada's health care system was no better than many others. India's bureaucratic red tape is daunting, but we have help dealing with that. Any concerns that he still has are put to rest when he meets with Dr Bose after being admitted to Apollo Hospital.

From my perspective, he has better care here than he did a few months earlier at Vancouver General. Nurses there hadn't been able to take his blood pressure, never had the supplies they needed when tending to him, his bedding was never straightened, and he was constantly disturbed by the flow of people in and out of the room.

In Chennai, there are no such problems. The nursing staff are caring, efficient, and focused solely on his comfort and recovery. He has a large private room with bathroom and both are cleaned twice a day. When we first arrive, we're interviewed by a dietician to determine the kinds of food we each prefer.

Dave faithfully exercises on his own after leaving hospital and has a follow-up visit with the surgeon a week after being discharged. He spends about six weeks on crutches and within a few months has fully recovered. The hip never bothers him again.

That's not to say that I'm not pretty worried for a while. Mostly, I think, because I'm not familiar with hospital procedures. On the day of the surgery, Dave is sedated and taken from the room at 0600; his operation is scheduled for noon. I expect him back in the room that evening. Then, after waiting all day, a nurse comes into the room at 1630 and tells me I'm wanted in post-op.

Dr Bose's overseas patients are isolated on an upper floor in a wing of the cancer hospital, so I'm provided with directions to a lower floor. Apprehensively, I find my way through crowded hallways lined with patients in beds. Dave is surrounded by a crowd of people when I enter the room, and I am shocked when I see him. His face is grey, the sweat streams off him, and a fan set on high blows on his face. Dr Bose tells me that everything went well, and I'm sent away a few minutes later. But I can't believe that such a visit is normal and now really worry.

After a long night with no news, a nurse enters the room at noon next day and tells me I'm wanted in recovery. I again make my way through the hospital's unfamiliar corridors until I come to a room filled with dozens of beds. A nurse escorts me to Dave, complaining, "He won't eat or drink and can't go back to his room until he does. Will you talk to him?"

I now see that he's moving his arms, but before I can say a word, a physiotherapist starts putting him through exercises. He's not very cooperative and sullenly does what he's told. When they're finished, he asks a nurse for some water and I'm able to ask, "Have you had anything to eat?" He grumpily responds, "I don't want to eat until after surgery!"

When I tell him the surgery is over, a look of astonishment sweeps across his face. After his 0600 shot the previous morning, he remembers being taken downstairs and hooked up to a temporary pacemaker, but nothing else. He now understands why his groin hurts, why the therapist was manipulating his leg, and why the nurses are trying to get him to eat and drink. He's brought some lunch and shortly after is returned to our room.

We spend a month in Chennai, arriving a week before Dave goes into hospital, as he has to be weaned off a blood thinner that he is taking. A few days later, the city celebrates Deepavali (Diwali), the Hindu Festival of Lights, commemorating the triumph of good over evil. From our hotel room, we watch as a dozen young people on a rooftop across the back lane set off rockets, fountains, pinwheels, noisemakers, and chains of firecrackers. Giant sparkling arrays of color then lightt up the horizon for hours.

While there, we hire a tuk-tuk to take us about and always look for the same driver, as John Samuel is reliable and helpful. Then, out of the blue, Dave asks him, "Can we come to your home for a meal the night before I go into hospital?"

I'm appalled and try to discourage him because local people can carry bugs that don't affect them but can affect us, which is the last thing he needs before going into hospital. He responds belligerently, "It's my last night and that's how I want to spend it!" John's wife is reluctant too, but he talks her into it and Dave pays for everything.

At dusk the following day, John picks us up in his tuk-tuk. After a thirty-minute drive, he turns into a narrow lane between two long, low, narrow buildings. It's too dark to see much, but we pass numerous doorways before he stops. He then steps over a cement ledge, leads the way across an eight-foot-wide cement porch, and ushers us into a room that he shares with his wife Rosie and their three children. It measures eight feet by eight feet.

We're seated in plastic chairs behind a small table (similar to a card table) that is covered by a greyish-looking cloth and sits a few feet inside the doorway. Half a dozen children immediately crowd around, and they sparkle like newly minted pennies. They are clean and well-dressed and have spent the day visiting family, as it's Sunday and they are Christians. Rosie and another woman (her sister) come and go, and it's obvious the food is being prepared elsewhere. When I ask the children to show me where, Gracie, the oldest, takes me across the lane, down a doorway, and pops inside.

I start to follow her in, but stop when I see her uncle. We met earlier, when he brought two freshly-washed wine glasses over to John's house, and he now invites me inside. Everyone speaks English. The room is a copy of John's, but one-third of the floor space is covered with cooking pots; our dinner is obviously a joint effort.

Shortly before dinner is served, new plates and spoons are set in front of us. We know they're new because John picked them up at a store on the way over. He now turns on a mosquito zapper, and as we brought our own water bottle and no one is coughing, I'm able to relax and enjoy myself.

John and Rosie won't eat with us, but at Dave's insistence the children do. They sit on the floor with plates in front of them and use their hands. Dave tells me that he's sure they said grace after their mother filled their plates. We're served fried rice with vegetables, chicken masala in gravy, and grilled chicken pieces. The food is good, the chicken spicy, but there is far too much of it. When I struggle with a piece of bone, John tells me, "It's okay to use your hands." And when Dave asks Rosie which spices she used in the chicken, she shyly shows him an envelope for a commercial masala mix, and we all laugh.

We learn that the children attend a private school, as the government school teaches only the Tamil language. They will go to grade 12, and if their marks are good enough and the family can afford it, they will go to college. They have two basic uniforms, white and maroon, and mix the colors differently each day.

In one corner of the room is a small, two-burner gas stove, similar to what we'd see in a cabin. Along an adjacent wall, narrow open shelves are overflowing with pans and food storage containers. Bed clothes are kept in a closet in another corner. We passed a handpump at the corner of the lane, and John has a circular well inside his porch. He pulls up a bucket, revealing the water level is down only two or three feet, and explains, "This water is only for washing, we buy bottled water to drink."

We visit John Samuel's home again a few days before returning to Malaysia. The images I have from our first visit prove fairly accurate in daylight, with many families living in one-room units in low buildings on either side of the narrow lane. John tells us that the rent is 1000 rupees a month ($24). We have lunch of dhosa, dhal, prawn curry, and fish soup. It's all very tasty and we rip off pieces of dhosa, then wrap them around clumps of food to eat. We take lots of pictures of the children, but we are the oddity and someone new constantly appears in the doorway to stare at us.

Chennai is a chaotic city of thirteen million people. The sky is smoggy, the streets are grimy and dusty, and garbage is strewn everywhere. People defecate and urinate on the sidewalks, and occasionally a cow (a sacred animal) can be seen. When driving in from the airport, I noticed that old, worn-looking public buses contain mostly men. Women in colorful saris had walked along the edge of the road. When we leave in the gloomy evening twilight, thousands of men stand about on sidewalks and the front entrances of buildings along the route.

Sitting behind John in the tuk-tuk, our view of city traffic is up close and personal. Traffic lights at major intersections are ignored unless police are there to enforce them. When traffic does stop, motorcycles and tuk-tuks work their way to the head of the line, squeezing past larger vehicles. John takes advantage of every bit of space in front of him, but pauses to let a motorcycle slip past, with only a hair's breadth between them. Vehicles come within two or three inches of each other, but nobody gets excited.

I thought I'd seen everything when it comes to traffic, but I was wrong. Bicycles now join the flow of motorcycles, tuk-tuks, cars, and trucks winding down narrow streets and across busy intersections at major thoroughfares.

The sight of bare arms and legs in heavy traffic makes me shudder. I see a sign urging lane discipline in one street, but it seems to be ignored everywhere else. While Dave is in hospital, I have to report to the visa office and need to cross one of those busy streets. It's just like in Saigon. I wait until I see two men about to cross, then draft behind them while vehicles wind around us.

Housing units similar to John's, two long buildings separated by a ten-foot-wide lane, are all over the city. The lanes are often littered with garbage. While walking down a back street, we pass a store with a flour mill, and nearby see women sitting on the sidewalk threading flowers into garlands. Down the block, a man has set up an ironing board on the sidewalk. The iron is huge, and when Dave asks him how it is heated, he pulls up the top, revealing two pieces of burning charcoal.

When Dave is ready for his first excursion on crutches, John choses a quiet time to take us to the Indian Market. Dave then walks up the street and back down over a broken cement walkway in front of shops. But he's an easy target for the beggars, and a very persistent young women sets her sights on him. I hear John speaking to her and turn around to see him with a stick in his hand. He appears ready to use it. Another woman later attaches herself to me. Although the encounter is unpleasant, I realize that this is how these people survive and wave John away.

When Dave is able to struggle into a car, John arranges for a daytrip down the coast to the south. I take pictures of rock sculptures and temples, and we see lots of people on broad, sandy beaches. We also see rows of stark, mud-walled, thatch-roofed sheds that practically sit on top of one another, while dogs, goats, and children roam about and a ripe smell hangs overhead.

Farther down, rows of fishing boats are pulled up on shore and the smell of fish is strong. This area is flat, not much above sea level, and was hit by the Boxing Day Tsunami. Of the 10,000 people lost that day, 5,000 are still missing.

We return to Malaysia in early December, and I'm amazed when I look at my pictures. John Samuel's skin is so black that his features don't show up, neither do Dr Bose's. I then remember being surprised when I looked at a picture taken in the yurt on our China trip. Dave and I had stood out like two white beans in a bowl of brown ones, even our clothing had been different. I now wonder if that was what our companions saw when they looked at us.

Epilogue

D ave and I lived on *Windy Lady* for sixteen extraordinary years. An abiding curiosity about people and places kept us traveling, even though our plans didn't always work out. In 1999, while at sea, we changed course from Fiji to Tonga, which put us in the path of a storm with 50-kt winds. In 2001, our attempt to sail around the world was thwarted by the events of 9-11. We then traveled by plane, train, bus, and car. Over the years, we met many good people in the islands and on five continents, all just trying to take care of their families.

In 2010, we finally ran out of steam. Boat maintenance had become a never-ending chore, our beautiful marina had started to fall apart, and travel was just aggravating. When Dave first talked about selling the boat, I couldn't imagine living elsewhere, but the day came when I had to acknowledge that we couldn't go on. We sold *Windy Lady* in October and delivered her to Singapore. Packing what we could, we returned to Canada in late November.

Writing about our experiences helped me make the transition to life ashore, and also helped me understand events that I'd been too busy living to think about. Now, having seen how frantic the pace of change has become, I recognize how fortunate we are to have seen the world when we did.

The years spent on *Windy Lady* also forged a bond between Dave and me that continues to deepen. The fact that we grew up at a time when friends and family looked out for one other probably helps. That's what we do now; take care of each other.

GLOSSARY

Swimming pool at Admiral Marina

Admiral Marina and Windy Lady

Admiral Marina

Windy Lady and Dave

Terraced hillside in Nepal

At the summit of Thorong La

Mule train on suspension bridge

Crossing the broken bridge

Rubber mats drying in Thailand

Camel ride at sunset

City wall in Xian

Terracotta soldiers

aft, abaft: near or toward the stern

autopilot: self-steering mechanism used under power

boom: a horizontal spar that supports the foot of the mainsail

bow: forward part of a boat

coaming: the raised edge around the cockpit that keeps water out

cockpit: an opening in the deck from which a boat is steered

companionway: stairs between cockpit and cabin

course: the direction in which a boat is steered

dodger: a fiberglass structure protecting the cockpit

fender: a cushioning object placed between boat and dock

freeboard: distance from top of side to waterline

to flog: for a sail to flap or flutter when no longer supported by the wind

foredeck: deck area between mast and bow

HF radio: high-frequency radio used for long distances

halyard: a rope used to raise or lower a sail

hatch: an opening in the deck that can be sealed off

heading: the direction in which the bow points at any given time

headsail: sail attached to the headstay

headstay, forestay: supporting cable running from upper mast to bow

helm: the wheel controlling the rudder

hull: the body of a boat, much of which is underwater

keel: an extension of the hull that goes deeper into the water

km: kilometer, equals .54 nautical mile

kt: knot, equals one nautical mile/hour, or 1.852 km/hour

mainsail: principal sail on the main mast

mast: a pole on a boat that supports the sails

nm: equal to one minute of latitude, or 1.852 kilometers

port: the left side of the boat when facing the bow

rigging: the system of ropes and cables used to support the mast and sails

rudder: an underwater vertical surface that steers the boat *sheet:* a rope attached to the lower corner of a sail that allows it to be moved

sole: cabin or cockpit floor

spreader: a horizontal strut approximately halfway up a mast
that holds supporting side cables apart

starboard: the right side of a boat when facing the bow

stern: back end of a boat

squall: a sudden violent windstorm that is brief and usually brings rain

thru-hull: a fitting that provides a secure hole through
the hull below the waterline

toe rail, rail: the outer edge of the deck, usually raised

VHF radio: very high frequency radio used for local communication